Luther, Martin; Lenker, John Nicholas

Luther´s Epistle Sermons

Inktank publishing

Luther, Martin; Lenker, John Nicholas

Luther´s Epistle Sermons

Inktank publishing, 2018

www.inktank-publishing.com

ISBN/EAN: 9783747737323

LUTHER'S

EPISTLE SERMONS

ADVENT AND CHRISTMAS SEASON

TRANSLATED WITH THE HELP OF OTHERS

BY

PROF. JOHN NICHOLAS LENKER, D. D.

AUTHOR OF "LUTHERANS IN ALL LANDS," TRANSLATOR OF
LUTHER'S WORKS INTO ENGLISH, AND PRESIDENT OF
THE NATIONAL LUTHERAN LIBRARY ASSOCIATION

VOL. I

(Volume VII of Luther's Complete Works)

THIRD THOUSAND

The Luther Press
MINNEAPOLIS, MINN., U. S. A.
1908

Dedication.

To the Memory of "The Luther Readers" in the days of Luther and Spener in Germany, of Rosenius in Sweden, of Hauge in Norway, of Grundtvig in Denmark, of Calvin in France, of Bunyan and the Wesleys in England, and of their spiritual children in all lands, this volume of Christmas Epistle sermons of the English Luther is gratefully and prayerfully dedicated.

Foreword.

It is now a year since The Luther Press issued its last volume, "Luther on Christian Education," containing his best catechetical writings. We are happy in assuring the growing list of advance subscribers, however, that the enterprise has received no backset. On the contrary, it has grown in every respect, especially in the efficiency of our co-laborers and in the favor it has received from our institutions of learning. The problem of the young people is the burning question at present; and as Catechetics is about the only branch of theology teaching future pastors their duties to the young, the last volume met a long-felt want, both as a text-book and as a help for side reading on many subjects. For example, the president of one institution ordered one hundred copies and turned his whole school into a Luther-class for one period every Thursday afternoon to study it. The experiment was a success. It is better to study the classics Luther wrote than what others have written about him. "He is, in the best sense, modern, up-to-date, the prophet of our times." Read him, and judge for yourself.

State schools also support chapel services, a Y. M. C. A. and occasional Christian sermons and lectures. But church schools are expected to do more. It is indeed a sad sight to see a foundation going to ruin because the building is not erected. Supporters of Christian schools are now beginning to realize that the only reason for their existence is that they are Christian. No church lays a better foundation in the hearts of the young for Christian culture than the Lutheran and no worse advertisement of a Lutheran school is conceivable than for its students to return home without any growth or development in harmony with their catechism foundation. It has been overlooked that Luther furnishes the best material for the building as well as for the foundation. He is the great evangelist in the evangelization of the Gentiles.

This volume of practical sermons on the epistle texts furnishes the best material for the building, because it exhorts to practice the Christian lessons taught by parent and pastor. In teaching Luther's catechism the aim should be to prepare and interest the pupil to read also his best sermons and commentaries on the Word of God, for God's Word is the chief glory and hope of all Protestants. This was the natural, continued development of our German and Scandinavian parents, whose stable Christian characters their children admire so much, but fail to learn the simple way to imitate. Alas, how many never read a book written by Luther except his Small Catechism!

The connection between this volume of "Christmas Sermons" and the last volume on "Christian Education" is very intimate. It will, we believe, bring Christmas joy to the widening circle of "Luther Readers." In its opening paragraph Luther says: "Paul, in Romans 12, 7-8, devotes the office of the ministry to two things, doctrine and exhortation. The doctrinal part consists in preaching truths not generally known; in instructing and enlightening the people. Exhortation is inciting and urging to duties already well understood." By example as well as precept Luther did both. He repeatedly warns against neglecting either. Christian knowledge and zeal, teaching and exhorting, go together and develop a balanced Christianity. Recently at a large young people's convention one asked, "What would be the state of things if all Lutherans lived the simple lessons of the five parts of their catechism?" The answer came, "They would be in paradise." The "Epistle Postil" contains sermons of exhortation and admonition, and are timely both for the individual life and for the work of the Church in evangelization at home and abroad.

Pastors who preach in two languages generally use English in the evening and as they preach on the Gospel texts in the morning these epistle sermons will be especially helpful in the evening services to all pastors who strive not for new truths, but to put old, familiar truths in the plainest and strongest English. Luther wrote these sermons as models for the preachers of his day, models they are now, and models they ought to be until God raises up a greater preacher. They will aid in making English Lutheran preaching and teaching easy for pastors overburdened not only by large pastorates, but by two languages in their large fields.

It is a cherished hope that these practical spiritual writings, teaching true faith in God and right love to our neighbor, may, like "Lutherans In All Lands," contribute to the literature of inner missions. Men like Spener, Wichern, Fliedner and Von Bodelschwingh, developed inner missions on the foundation laid by Luther's writings in the hearts of the German people. The last branch or division of inner missions is literature. This, like all Lutheran literature, must be based on the Luther literature.

For the history of the writing of these sermons the reader is refered to volumes 10, 11, 12 and 13 of the Gospel sermons of the English Luther.

The German text will be readily found in the 12th volume of the Walch and the St. Louis Walch editions, and in the 7th volume of the Erlangen edition.

Due acknowledgement is hereby made of aid received from the translation of Pastor Ambrose Henkel and published in 1869 at New Market, Virginia.

With profound gratitude to the God of all grace for his rich blessings upon this undertaking since its beginning and with the prayer that the same may continue and finally crown the work in every way with success, this volume is now sent forth on its mission of service for the glory of the triune God and the uplifting of fallen man.

J. N. LENKER.

Lutheran Home for Young Women,
Minneapolis, Minn., November 28, 1908.

Contents.

Page.

First Sunday in Advent.—An Exhortation to Good Works. The Day of Grace. Romans 13, 11-14...... 9

Second Sunday in Advent.—Exhortation to Bear with the Weak. The Word of Hope. Missions to the Heathen. Romans 15, 4-13.................... 28

Third Sunday in Advent.—Stewards of God's Mysteries. Faithfulness in Stewards. Man's Judgment and God's. 1 Corinthians 4, 1-5................. 64

Fourth Sunday in Advent.—A Christian's Conduct toward God and Man. Prayer. The Peace of God. Philippians 4, 4-7 93

First Christmas Sermon.—The Appearing of the Grace of God. Ungodliness. Worldly Lusts. The Christian Life. Titus 2, 11-15 113

Second Christmas Sermon.—God's Grace Received and Good Works to Our Neighbor. Titus 3, 4-8........ 142

Third Christmas Sermon.—The Divinity of Christ. Hebrews 1, 1-12 166

St. Stephen's Day.—Stephen an Example of Christian Faith, Zeal and Love. Building Churches. Authority of Laymen to Preach. Acts 6, 8-14............ 194

St. John's Day.—Exhortation to Piety and Righteousness. Ecclesiasticus 15, 1-8...................... 212

Sunday After Christmas.—The People of Law and of Grace. Galatians 4, 1-7 224

New Year's Day.—The Law and Its Works. Faith. Unity in Christ. Galatians 3, 23-29................ 267

Epiphany.—The Conversion of the Heathen. The True Light. Isaiah 60, 1-6 311

First Sunday in Advent

Epistle Text: Romans 13, 11-14.

11 And this, knowing the season, that already it is time for you to awake out of sleep: for now is salvation nearer to us than when we first believed. 12 The night is far spent, and the day is at hand: let us therefore cast off the works of darkness, and let us put on the armor of light. 13 Let us walk becomingly, as in the day; not in revelling and drunkenness, not in chambering and wantonness, not in strife and jealousy. 14 But put ye on the Lord Jesus Christ, and make not provision for the flesh, to fulfil the lusts thereof.

AN EXHORTATION TO GOOD WORKS.

1. This epistle lesson treats not of faith, but of its fruits, or works. It teaches how a Christian should conduct himself outwardly in his relations to other men upon earth. But how we should walk in the spirit before God, comes under the head of faith. Of faith Paul treats comprehensively and in apostolic manner in the chapters preceding this text. A close consideration of our passage shows it to be not didactic; rather it is meant to incite, to exhort, urge and arouse souls already aware of their duty. Paul in Romans 12, 7-8 devotes the office of the ministry to two things, doctrine and exhortation. The doctrinal part consists in preaching truths not generally known; in instructing and enlightening the people. Exhortation is inciting and urging to duties already well understood. Necessarily both obligations claim the attention of the minister, and hence Paul takes up both.

2. For the sake of effect and emphasis the apostle in his

admonition employs pleasing figures and makes an eloquent appeal. He introduces certain words—"Armor," "work," "sleep," "awake," "darkness," "light," "day," "night"—which are purely figurative, intended to convey other than a literal and native meaning. He has no reference here to the things they ordinarily stand for. The words are employed as similes, to help us grasp the spiritual thought. The meaning is: Since for sake of temporal gain men rise from sleep, put aside the things of darkness and take up the day's work when night has given place to morning, how much greater the necessity for us to awake from our spiritual sleep, to cast off the things of darkness and enter upon the works of light, since our night has passed and our day breaks.

3. "Sleep" here stands for the works of wickedness and unbelief. For sleep is properly incident to the night time; and then, too, the explanation is given in the added words: "Let us cast off the works of darkness." Similarly in the thought of awakening and rising are suggested the works of faith and piety. Rising from sleep is naturally an event of the morning. Relative to the same conception are Paul's words in First Thessalonians 5, 4-10: "But ye, brethren, are not in darkness . . . ye are all sons of light, and sons of the day: we are not of the night, nor of darkness; so then let us not sleep, as do the rest, but let us watch and be sober. For they that sleep sleep in the night; and they that are drunken are drunken in the night. But let us, since we are of the day, be sober, putting on the breastplate of faith and love; and for a helmet, the hope of salvation. For God appointed us not unto wrath, but unto the obtaining of salvation through our Lord Jesus Christ, who died for us, that, whether we wake or sleep, we should live together with him."

4. Paul, of course, is here not enjoining against physical sleep. His contrasting figures of sleep and wakefulness are used as illustrations of spiritual lethargy and activity—the godly and the ungodly life. In short, his conception here of rising out of sleep is the same as that expressed in his declaration (Tit 2, 11-13): "For the grace of God hath ap-

peared, bringing salvation to all men, instructing us, to the intent that, denying ungodliness and worldly lusts, we should live soberly and righteously and godly in this present world; looking for the blessed hope and appearing of the glory of the great God and our Saviour Jesus Christ." That which in the passage just quoted is called "denying ungodliness and worldly lusts," is here in our text described as a rising from sleep; and the "sober, righteous, godly life" is the waking and the putting on the armor of light; while the appearing of grace is the day and the light, as we shall hear.

5. Now, note the analogy between natural and spiritual sleep. The sleeper sees nothing about him; he is not sensitive to any of earth's realities. In the midst of them he lies as one dead, useless; as without power or purpose. Though having life in himself he is practically dead to all outside. Moreover, his mind is occupied, not with realities, but with dreams, wherein he beholds mere images, vain forms, of the real; and he is foolish enough to think them true. But when he wakes, these illusions or dreams vanish. Then he begins to occupy himself with realities; phantoms are discarded.

6. So it is in the spiritual life. The ungodly individual sleeps. He is in a sense dead in the sight of God. He does not recognize—is not sensitive to—the real spiritual blessings extended him through the Gospel; he regards them as valueless. For these blessings are only to be recognized by the believing heart; they are concealed from the natural man. The ungodly individual is occupied with temporal, transitory things, such as luxury and honor, which are to eternal life and joy as dream images are to flesh-and-blood creatures.

When the unbeliever awakes to faith, the transitory things of earth will pass from his contemplation, and their futility will appear. In relation to this subject Psalm 76, 5, reads: "The stouthearted are made a spoil, they have slept their sleep; and none of the men of might have found their hands." And Psalm 73, 20: "As a dream when one awaketh, so, O Lord, when thou awakest, thou wilt despise their image." Also Isaiah 29, 8: "And it shall be as when a hungry man dreameth, and, behold, he eateth; but he awaketh, and his soul is empty: or as when a thirsty man dreameth, and, behold, he drinketh; but he awaketh, and, behold, he is faint, and his soul hath appetite: so shall the multitude of all the nations be, that fight against mount Zion."

But is it not showing altogether too much contempt for worldly power, wealth, pleasure and honor to compare them to dreams—to dream images? Who has courage to declare kings and princes, wealth, pleasure and power but creations of a dream, in the face of the mad rage of earth after such things? The reason for such conduct is failure to rise from sleep and by faith behold the light.

"For now is salvation nearer to us than when we first believed."

7. What do these words imply? Did we believe before, or have we now ceased to believe? Right here we must know that, as Paul in Romans 1, 2-3 says, God through his prophets promised in the holy Scriptures the Gospel of his Son Jesus Christ our Lord, through whom all the world was to be saved. The word to Abraham reads: "In thy seed shall all the nations of the earth be blessed." Gen. 22, 18. The blessing here promised to the patriarch, in his seed, is simply that grace and salvation in Christ which the Gospel presents to the whole world, as Paul declares in the fourth chapter of Romans and the fourth of Galatians. For Christ is the seed of Abraham, his own flesh and blood, and in Christ all believing inquirers will be blessed.

8. This promise to the patriarch was later more minutely set forth and more widely circulated by the prophets. All of them wrote of the advent of Christ, and his grace and Gospel, as Peter in Acts 3, 18-24 says: The divine promise was believed by the saints prior to the birth of Christ; thus, through the coming Messiah they were preserved and saved by faith. Christ himself (Lk 16, 22) pictures the promise under the figure of Abraham's bosom, into which all saints from the time of Abraham to Christ's time, were gathered.

Thus is explained Paul's declaration, "Now is salvation nearer to us than when we first believed." He means practically: "The promise of God to Abraham is not a thing for future fulfilment; it is already fulfilled. Christ is come. The Gospel has been revealed and the blessing distributed throughout the world. All that we waited for in the promise, believing, is here." The sentence has reference to the spiritual day Paul later speaks of—the rising light of the Gospel; as we shall hear.

9. But faith is not abolished in the fulfilment of the promise; rather it is established. As they of former time believed in the future fulfilment, we believe now in the completed fulfilment. Faith, in the two instances, is essentially the same, but one belief succeeds the other as fulfilment succeeds promise. For in both cases faith is based on the seed of Abraham; that is, on Christ. In one instance it precedes his advent and in the other follows. He who would now, like the Jews, believe in a Christ yet to come, as if the promise were still unfulfilled, would be condemned. For he would make God a liar in holding that his word is unredeemed, contrary to fact. Were the promise not fulfilled, our salvation would still be far off; we would have to wait its future accomplishment.

10. Having in mind faith under these two conditions, Paul asserts in Romans 1, 17: "In the Gospel is revealed a righteousness of God from faith unto faith." What is meant by the phrase "from faith unto faith"? Simply that we must now believe not only in the promise but in its past fulfilment. For though the faith of the fathers is one with our faith, they trusting in a Christ to come and we in a Christ revealed, yet the Gospel leads from the former faith to the latter. It is now necessary to believe not only the promise, but also its fulfilment. Abraham and the ancients were not called upon to believe in accomplished fulfilment, though they had the same Christ with us. There is one faith, one spirit, one Christ, one community of saints; but they preceded, while we come after, Christ.

11. Thus we—the fathers and ourselves—have had and

still have a common faith in the one Christ, but under different conditions. Because of this common faith in the Messiah, we speak of their act of faith as our own, notwithstanding we were not alive in their day. And similarly, when they make mention of hearing, seeing and believing Christ, the reference is to ourselves, in whose day they live not. David says (Ps 8, 3): "When I consider thy heavens, the work of thy fingers," that is, the apostles. Yet David did not live to see their day. And (Ps 9, 2): "I will be glad and exult in thee; I will sing praise to thy name, O Thou Most High." And there are many similar passages where one individual speaks in the person of another in consequence of a common faith whereby believers unite in Christ as one body.

12. Paul's statement "Now is salvation nearer to us than when we first believed" cannot be understood to refer to nearness of possession. For the fathers had the same faith and the same Christ with us, and Christ was equally near to them. Hebrews 13, 8 says, "Jesus Christ is the same yesterday and today, yea and for ever." That is, Christ exists from the beginning of the world to all time, and through him and in him all are preserved. To him of strongest faith Christ is nearest; and from him who least believes, is salvation farthest, so far as personal possession of it goes. Paul's reference here is to nearness of the revelation of salvation. When Christ came the promise was fulfilled. The Gospel was revealed to the world. Through Christ's coming it was publicly preached to all men. In recognition of these things, the apostle says: "Salvation is nearer to us" than when unrevealed and unfulfilled in the promise. In Titus 2, 11, it is said: "For the grace of God hath appeared, bringing salvation." In other words, God's grace is revealed and publicly proclaimed; though the saints who lived prior to its manifestation nevertheless possessed it.

13. So the Scriptures teach the coming of Christ, notwithstanding he was already present to the fathers. However, he was not publicly proclaimed to mankind until after his resurrection from the dead. It is of this coming in the

Gospel the Scriptures for the most part teach. Incident to this revelation he came in human form. The taking upon himself of humanity would have profited no one had it not meant the proclamation of the Gospel. The Gospel was to present him to the whole world, revealing the fact that he became man for the sake of imparting the blessing to all who, accepting the Gospel, should believe in him. Paul tells us (Rom 1, 2) the Gospel was promised of God; from which we may infer God placed more emphasis upon the Gospel, the public revelation of Christ through the Word, than upon his physical birth, his advent in human form. God's purpose was concerning the Gospel and our faith, and he permitted his Son to assume humanity for the sake of making possible the preaching of the Gospel of Christ; that through the revealed Word salvation in Christ might be brought near—might come—to all the world.

14. Some have presented four different forms of Christ's advent, adapted to the four Sundays in Advent. But the most vital form of his coming, that upon which all efficacy depends, the coming to which Paul here refers, they have failed to recognize. They know not what constitutes the Gospel, nor for what purpose it was given. Despite their much talk about the advent of Christ, they thrust him from us farther than heaven is from earth. How can Christ profit us unless he be embraced by faith? But how can he be embraced by faith where the Gospel is not preached?

THE DAY OF GRACE.

"The night is far spent, and the day is at hand."

15. This is equivalent to saying "salvation is near to us." By the word "day" Paul means the Gospel; the Gospel is like day in that it enlightens the heart or soul. Now, day having broken, salvation is near to us. In other words, Christ and his grace, promised to Abraham, are now revealed; they are preached in all the world, enlightening mankind, awakening us from sleep and making manifest the true, eternal blessings, that we may occupy ourselves with the Gospel of Christ and walk honorably in the day. By the word "night" we are to understand all doctrines

apart from the Gospel. For there is no other saving doctrine; all else is night and darkness.

16. Notice carefully Paul's words. He designates the most beautiful and vivifying time of the day—the delightful, joyous dawn, the hour of sunrise. Then the night has passed and the day broken. In response to the morning dawn, birds sing, beasts arouse themselves and all humanity arises. At daybreak, when the sky is red in the east, the world is apparently new and all things reanimated. In many places in the Scriptures, the comforting, vivifying preaching of the Gospel is compared to the morning dawn, to the rising of the sun; sometimes the figure is implied and sometimes plainly expressed, as here where Paul styles the Gospel the breaking day. Again, Psalm 110, 3: "Thy people offer themselves willingly in the day of thy power, in holy array: out of the womb of the morning thou hast the dew of thy youth." Here the Gospel is plainly denominated the womb of the morning, the day of Christ's power, wherein, as the dew is born of the morning, we are conceived and born children of Christ; and by no work of man, but from heaven and through the Holy Spirit's grace.

17. This Gospel day is produced by the glorious Sun Jesus Christ. Hence Malachi calls him the Sun of Righteousness, saying, "But unto you that fear my name shall the Sun of Righteousness arise with healing in its wings." Mal. 4, 2. All believers in Christ receive the light of his grace, and righteousness, and shall rejoice in the shelter of his wings. Again in Psalm 118, 24, we read: "This is the day which Jehovah hath made; we will rejoice and be glad in it." The meaning is: The natural sun makes the natural day, but the Lord himself is the author of the spiritual day. Christ is the Sun, the source of the Gospel day. From him the Gospel brightness shines throughout the world. John 9, 5 reads: "I am the light of the world."

18. Psalm 19, 1 beautifully describes Christ the Sun, and the Gospel day: "The heavens declare the glory of God." As the natural heavens bring the sun and the day, and the sun is in the heavens, so the apostles in their preaching

possess and bring to us the real Sun, Christ. The Psalm continues: "In them hath he set a tabernacle for the sun, which is as a bridegroom coming out of his chamber, and rejoiceth as a strong man to run his course. His going forth is from the end of the heavens, and his circuit unto the ends of it; and there is nothing hid from the heat thereof." It all refers to the beautiful daybreak of the Gospel. Scripture sublimely exalts the Gospel day, for it is the source of life, joy, pleasure and energy, and brings all good. Hence the name "Gospel"—joyful news.

19. Who can enumerate the things revealed to us by this day—by the Gospel? It teaches us everything—the nature of God, of ourselves, and what has been and is to be in regard to heaven, hell and earth, to angels and devils. It enables us to know how to conduct ourselves in relation to these—whence we are and whither we go. But, being deceived by the devil, we forsake the light of day and seek to find truth among philosophers and heathen totally ignorant of such matters. In permitting ourselves to be blinded by human doctrines, we return to the night. Whatsoever is not the Gospel day surely cannot be light. Otherwise Paul, and in fact all Scripture, would not urge that day upon us and pronounce everything else night.

20. Our disposition to run counter to the perfectly plain teachings of Scripture and seek inferior light, when the Lord declares himself the Light and Sun of the world, must result from our having incurred the displeasure of Providence. Had we no other evidence that the high schools of the Pope are the devil's abominable fostering-places of harlots and knaves, the fact is amply plain in the way they shamelessly introduce and extol Aristotle, the inferior light, exercising themselves in him more than in Christ; rather they exercise themselves wholly in Aristotle and not at all in Christ.

"Let us therefore cast off the works of darkness, and let us put on the armor of light."

21. As Christ is the Sun and the Gospel is the day, so faith is the light, or the seeing and watching on that day.

We are not profited by the shining of the sun, and the day it produces, if our eyes fail to perceive its light. Similarly, though the Gospel is revealed, and proclaims Christ to the world, it enlightens none but those who receive it, who have risen from sleep through the agency of the light of faith. They who sleep are not affected by the sun and the day; they receive no light therefrom, and see as little as if there were neither sun nor day. It is to our day Paul refers when he says: "Dear brethren, knowing the season, that already it is time for you to awake out of sleep, etc." Though the hour is one of spiritual opportunity, it has been revealed in secular time, and is daily being revealed. In the light of our spiritual knowledge we are to rise from sleep and lay aside the works of darkness. Thus it is plain Paul is not addressing unbelievers. As before said, he is not here teaching the doctrine of faith, but its works and fruits. He tells the Romans they know the time is at hand, that the night is past and the day has broken.

22. Do you ask, Why this passage to believers? As already stated, preaching is twofold in character: it may teach or it may incite and exhort. No one ever gets to the point of knowledge where it is not necessary to admonish him—continually to urge him—to new reflections upon what he already knows; for there is danger of his untiring enemies—the devil, the world and the flesh—wearying him and causing him to become negligent, and ultimately lulling him to sleep. Peter says (1 Pet 5, 8): "Your adversary the devil, as a roaring lion, walketh about, seeking whom he may devour." In consequence of this fact, he says: "Be sober, be watchful." Similarly Paul's thought here is that since the devil, the world and the flesh cease not to assail us, there should be continuous exhorting and impelling to vigilance and activity. Hence the Holy Spirit is called the Paraclete, the Comforter or Helper, who incites and urges to good.

23. Hence Paul's appropriate choice of words. Not the works of darkness but the works of light he terms "armor." And why "armor" rather than "works"? Doubtless to teach

that only at the cost of conflicts, pain, labor and danger will the truly watchful and godly life be maintained; for these three powerful enemies, the devil, the world and the flesh, unceasingly oppose us day and night. Hence Job (ch 7, 1) regards the life of man on earth as a life of trial and warfare.

Now, it is no easy thing to stand always in battle array during the whole of life. Good trumpets and bugles are necessary preaching and exhortation of the sort to enable us valiantly to maintain our position in battle. Good works are armor: evil works are not; unless, indeed, we submit and give them control over us. Then they likewise become armor. Paul says, "Neither present your members unto sin as instruments of unrighteousness" (Rom 6, 13), meaning: Let not the works of darkness get such control of you as to render your members weapons of unrighteousness.

24. Now, as already made plain, the word "light" here carries the thought of "faith." The light of faith, in the Gospel day, shines from Christ the Sun into our hearts. The armor of light, then, is simply the works of faith. On the other hand, "darkness" is unbelief; it reigns in the absence of the Gospel and of Christ, through the instrumentality of the doctrines of men—of human reason—instigated by the devil. The "works of darkness" are, therefore, the "works of unbelief." As Christ is Lord and Ruler in the realm of that illuminating faith, so, as Paul says (Eph 6, 12), the devil is ruler of this darkness; that is, over unbelievers. For he says again (2 Cor 4, 3-4): "And even if our gospel is veiled, it is veiled in them that perish: in whom the god of this world [that is, the devil] hath blinded the minds of the unbelieving, that the light of the gospel of the glory of Christ . . . should not dawn upon them." The character of the two kinds of works, however, will be discussed later.

"Let us walk, becomingly (honestly), as in the day."

25. Works of darkness are not wrought in the day. Fear of being shamed before men makes one conduct himself honorably. The proverbial expression "shameless night" is a true one. Works we are ashamed to perform in the day are

wrought in the night. The day, being shamefaced, constrains us to walk honorably. A Christian should so live that he need never be ashamed of the character of his works, though they be revealed to all the world. He whose life and conduct are such as to make him unwilling his deeds should be manifest to everyone, certainly does not live in a Christian manner. In this connection Christ says: "For everyone that doeth evil hateth the light, and cometh not to the light, lest his works should be reproved. But he that doeth the truth cometh to the light, that his works may be made manifest, that they have been wrought in God." Jn 3, 20-21.

26. So you see the urgent necessity for inciting and exhorting to be vigilant and to put on the armor of light. How many Christians now could endure the revelation of all their works to the light of day? What kind of Christian life do we hypocrites lead if we cannot endure the exposure of our conduct before men, when it is now exposed to God, his angels and creatures, and on the last day shall be revealed to all? A Christian ought to live as he would be found in the last day before all men. "Walk as children of light, for the fruit of the light is in all goodness and righteousness and truth." Eph 5, 9. "Take thought for things honorable," not only in the sight of God, but also "in the sight of all men." Rom 12, 17. "For our glorying is this, the testimony of our conscience, that in holiness and sincerity of God, not in fleshly wisdom . . . we behaved ourselves in the world." 2 Cor 1, 12.

27. But such a life certainly cannot be maintained in the absence of faith, when faith itself—vigilant, active, valiant faith—has enough to do to remain constant, sleepless and unwearied. Essential as it is that doctrine be preached to the illiterate, it is just as essential to exhort the learned not to fall from their incipient right living, under the assaults of raging flesh, subtle world and treacherous devil.

"Not in revelling and drunkenness, not in chambering and wantonness, not in strife and jealousy."

28. Here Paul enumerates certain works of darkness.

In the beginning of the discourse he alludes to one as "sleep." In First Thessalonians 5, 6, it is written: "Let us not sleep, as do the rest, but let us watch and be sober." Not that the apostle warns against physical sleep; he means spiritual sleep—unbelief, productive of the works of darkness. Yet physical sleep may likewise be an evil work when indulged in from lust and revelling, through indolence and excessive inebriety, to the obstruction of light and the weakening of the armor of light. These six works of darkness include all others, such as are enumerated in Galatians 5, 19-21, and Colossians 3, 5 and 8. We will divide them into two general classes, the right hand class and the left hand class. Upon the right are arrayed these four—revelling, drunkenness, chambering and wantonness; on the left, strife and jealousy. For scripturally, the left side signifies adversity and its attendant evils—wrath, jealousy, and so on. The right side stands for prosperity and its results—rioting, drunkenness, lust, indolence, and the like.

29. Plainly, then, Paul means to include under the two mentioned works of darkness—strife and jealousy—all of similar character. For instance, the things enumerated in Ephesians 4, 31, which says: "Let all bitterness, and wrath, and anger, and clamor, and railing, be put away from you, with all malice"; and again in Galatians 5, 19-21, reading: "Now the works of the flesh are . . . enmities, strife, jealousies, wraths, factions, divisions, parties, envyings, drunkenness, revellings and such like." In short, "strife and jealousy" here stand for innumerable evils resulting from wrath, be it in word or deed.

30. Likewise under the four vices—revelling, drunkenness, indolence and lewdness—the apostle includes all the vices of unchastity in word or deed, things none would wish to enumerate. The six works mentioned suffice to teach that he who lives in the darkness of unbelief does not keep himself pure in his neighbor's sight, but is immoderate in all his conduct, toward himself and toward his fellow-man. Further comment on these words is unnecesary. Everyone knows the meaning of "revelling and drunkenness"—excess-

ive eating and drinking, more for the gratification of appetite than for nourishment of the body. Again, it is not hard to understand the reference to idleness in bed-chambers, to lewdness and unchasity. The apostle's words stand for the indulgence of the lusts and appetites of the flesh: excessive sleeping and indolence; every form of unchastity and sensuality practiced by the satiated, indolent and stupid, in daytime or nighttime, in retirement or elsewhere, privately or publicly—vices that seek material darkness and secret places. These vices Paul terms "chambering and wantonness." And the meaning of "strife" and of "jealousy" is generally understood.

PUT ON CHRIST, THE ARMOR OF LIGHT.

"But put ye on the Lord Jesus Christ."

31. In this admonition to put on Christ, Paul briefly prescribes all the armor of light. Christ is "put on" in two ways. First, we may clothe ourselves with his virtues. This is effected through the faith that relies on the fact of Christ having in his death accomplished all for us. For not our righteousness, but the righteousness of Christ, reconciled us to God and redeemed us from sin. This manner of putting on Christ is treated of in the doctrine concerning faith; it gives Christ to us as a gift and a pledge. Relative to this topic more will be said in the epistle for New Year's day, Galatians 3, 27: "For as many of you as were baptized into Christ did put on Christ."

32. Secondly, Christ being our example and pattern, whom we are to follow and copy, clothing ourselves in the virtuous garment of his walk, Paul fittingly says we should "put on" Christ. As expressed in First Corinthians 15, 49: "As we have borne the image of the earthy, we shall also bear the image of the heavenly." And again (Eph 4, 22-24): "That ye put away, as concerning your former manner of life, the old man, that waxeth corrupt after the lusts of deceit; and that ye be renewed in the spirit of your mind, and put on the new man, that after God hath been created in righteousness and holiness of truth."

33. Now, in Christ we behold only the true armor of

light. No gormandizing or drunkenness is here; nothing but fasting, moderation, and restraint of the flesh, incident to labor, exertion, preaching, praying and doing good to mankind. No indolence, apathy or unchastity exists, but true discipline, purity, vigilance, early rising. The fields are couch for him who has neither house, chamber nor bed. With him is no wrath, strife or envying; rather utter goodness, love, mercy, patience. Paul presents Christ the example in a few words where he says (Col 3, 12-15): "Put on therefore, as God's elect, holy and beloved, a heart of compassion, kindness, lowliness, meekness, longsuffering; forbearing one another, and forgiving each other, if any man have a complaint against any, even as the Lord forgave you, so also do ye: and above all these things put on love, which is the bond of perfectness, and let the peace of Christ rule in your hearts, to the which also ye were called in one body; and be ye thankful." Again, in Philippians 2, 5-8, after commanding his flock to love and serve one another, he presents as an example the same Christ who became servant unto us. He says: "Have this mind in you, which was also in Christ Jesus: who, existing in the form of God, counted not the being on an equality with God a thing to be grasped, but emptied himself, taking the form of a servant, being made in the likeness of men; and being found in fashion as a man."

34. Now, the armor of light is, briefly, the good works opposed to gluttony, drunkenness, licentiousness; to indolence, strife and envying: such as fasting, watchfulness, prayer, labor, chastity, modesty, temperance, goodness, endurance of hunger and thirst, of cold and heat. Not to employ my own words, let us hear Paul's enumeration of good works in Galatians 5, 22-23: "The fruit of the Spirit is love, joy, peace, longsuffering, kindness, goodness, faithfulness, meekness, self-control." But he makes a still more comprehensive count in Second Corinthians 6, 1-10: "We entreat also that ye receive not the grace of God in vain (for he saith, At an acceptable time I hearkened unto thee, and in a day of salvation did I succor thee: behold, now is the ac-

ceptable time; behold, now is the day of salvation) [in other words, For now is salvation nearer to us than when we first believed, and now is the time to awake out of sleep]: giving no occasion of stumbling in anything, that our ministration be not blamed; but in everything commending ourselves, as ministers of God, in much patience, in afflictions, in necessities, in distresses, in stripes, in imprisonments, in tumults, in labors, in watchings, in fastings; in pureness, in knowledge, in longsuffering, in kindness, in the Holy Spirit, in love unfeigned, in the word of truth, in the power of God; by the armor of righteousness on the right hand and on the left, by glory and dishonor, by evil report and good report; as deceivers, and yet true; as unknown, and yet well known; as dying, and behold, we live; as chastened, and not killed; as sorrowful, yet always rejoicing; as poor, yet making many rich; as having nothing, and yet possessing all things." What a rich stream of eloquence flows from Paul's lips! He makes plain enough in what consists the armor of light on the left hand and on the right. To practice these good works is truly putting on Jesus Christ.

35. It is a very beautiful feature in this passage that it presents the very highest example, the Lord himself, when it says, "Put ye on the Lord." Here is a strong incentive. For the individual who can see his master fasting, laboring, watching, enduring hunger and fatigue, while he himself feasts, idles, sleeps, and lives in luxury, must be a scoundrel. What master could tolerate such conduct in a servant? Or what servant would dare attempt such things? We can but blush with shame when we behold our unlikeness to Christ.

36. Who can influence to action him who refuses to be warmed and aroused by the example of Christ himself? What is to be accomplished by the rustling of leaves and the sound of words when the thunder-clap of Christ's example fails to move us? Paul was particular to add the word "Lord," saying, "Put ye on the Lord Jesus Christ." As if to say: "Ye servants, think not yourselves great and exalted. Look upon your Lord, who, though under no obligation, denied himself."

"And make not provision for the flesh, to fulfil the lusts thereof."

37. Paul here briefly notices two different provisions for the flesh. One is supplying its natural wants—furnishing the body with food and raiment necessary to sustain life and vigor; guarding against enfeebling it and unfitting it for labor by too much restraint.

38. The other provision is a sinful one, the gratification of the lusts and inordinate appetites. This Paul here forbids. It is conducive to works of darkness. The flesh must be restrained and made subservient to the spirit. It must not dismount its master, but carry him if necessary. Sirach (ch 33, 24) says: "Fodder, a wand, and burdens are for the ass; and bread, correction, and work for a servant." He does not say the animal is to be mistreated or maimed; nor does he say the servant is to be abused or imprisoned. Thus to the body pertains subjection, labor and whatever is essential to its proper welfare. Paul says of himself: "I buffet my body, and bring it into bondage [subjection]." 1 Cor 9, 27. He does not say he brings his body to illness or death, but makes it serve in submission to the spirit.

39. Paul adds this last admonition for the sake of two classes of people. One class is represented by them who make natural necessity an excuse to indulge their lusts and gratify their desires. Because of humanity's proneness to such error, many saints, deploring the sin, have often in the attempt to resist it, unduly restrained their bodies. So subtle and deceptive is nature in the matter of its demands and its lusts, no man can wholly handle it; he must live this life in insecurity and concern.

The other class is represented by the blind saints who imagine the kingdom of God and his righteousness are dependent upon the particular meat and drink, clothing and couch, of their own choice. They look no farther than at their individual work in this respect, and fancy that in fasting until the brain is disordered, the stomach deranged or the body emaciated, they have done well. Upon this subject Paul says (1 Cor 8, 8): "Food will not commend us to

God; neither, if we eat not, are we the worse; nor, if we eat, are we the better." Again (Col 2, 18-23): "Let no man rob you of your prize by a voluntary humility and worshipping of the angels . . . which things have indeed a show of wisdom in will-worship, and humility, and severity to the body; but are not of any value against the indulgence of the flesh."

40. Gerson commended the Carthusians for not eating meat, even though debility made meat a necessity. He would deny it even at the cost of life. Thus was the great man deceived by this superstitious, angelic spirituality. What if God judges its votaries as murderers of themselves? Indeed, no orders, statutes or vows contrary to the command of God can rightfully be made; and if made they would profit no more than would a vow to break one's marriage contract. Certainly God has here in the words of Paul forbidden such destruction of our own bodies. It is our duty to allow the body all necessary food, whether wine, meat, eggs or anything else; whether the time be Friday, Sunday, in Lent or after the feast of Easter; regardless of all orders, traditions and vows, and of the Pope. No prohibition contrary to God's command can avail, though made by the angels even.

41. This wretched folly of vows has its rise in darkness and blindness; the looking upon mere works and trusting to be saved by the number and magnitude of them. Paul would make of works "armor of light," and employ them to overcome the works of darkness. Thus far, then, and no farther, should fasting, vigilance and exertion be practiced. Before God it matters not at all whether you eat fish or meat, drink water or wine, wear red or green, do this or that. All foods are good creations of God and to be used. Only take heed to be temperate in appropriating them and to abstain when it is necessary to the conquest of the works of darkness. It is impossible to lay down a common rule of abstinence, for all bodies are not constituted alike. One needs more, another less. Everyone must judge for himself, and must care for his body according to the advice of Paul:

"Make not provision for the flesh, to fulfil the lusts thereof." Had there been any other rule for us, Paul would not have omitted it here.

42. Hence, you see, the ecclesiastical traditions that flatly forbid the eating of meat are contrary to the Gospel. Paul predicts their appearance in First Timothy 4, 1-3, where he says: "But the Spirit saith expressly, that in later times some shall fall away from the faith, giving heed to seducing spirits and doctrines of demons, through the hypocrisy of men that speak lies, branded in their own conscience as with a hot iron; forbidding to marry, and commanding to abstain from meats, which God created to be received with thanksgiving." That these words have reference to ecclesiastical orders and those of the entire Papacy, no one can deny. They are plain. Hence the nature of papistical works is manifest.

43. Also you will note here Paul does not sanction the fanatical devotion of certain effeminate saints who set apart to themselves particular days for fasting, as a special service to God, one for this saint, another for that. These are all blind paths, leading us to base our blessings on works. Without distinction of days and meats, our lives should be temperate and sober throughout. If good works are to be our armor of light, and if the entire life is to be pure and chaste, we must never lay off the arms of defense, but always be found sober, temperate, vigilant, energetic. These fanatical saints, however, fast one day on bread and water and then eat and drink to excess every day for one-fourth of the year. Again, some fast from food in the evening but drink immoderately. And who can mention all the folly and works of darkness originating from regarding works for the sake of the efforts themselves and not for the purpose they serve. Men convert the armor of good works into a mirror, fasting without knowing the reason for abstinence. They are like those who bear a sword merely to look at, and when assailed do not use it. This is enough on today's epistle lesson.

Second Sunday in Advent

Epistle Text: Romans 15, 4-13.

4 For whatsoever things were written aforetime were
written for our learning, that through patience and
through comfort of the scriptures we might have hope.
5 Now the God of patience and of comfort grant you to
be of the same mind one with another according to
Christ Jesus: 6 that with one accord ye may with one
mouth glorify the God and Father of our Lord Jesus
Christ. 7 Wherefore receive ye one another, even as
Christ also received you, to the glory of God. 8 For I
say that Christ hath been made a minister of the circumcision for the truth of God, that he might confirm
the promises given unto the fathers, 9 and that the
Gentiles might glorify God for his mercy; as it is
written,

Therefore will I give praise unto thee among the
Gentiles,
And sing unto thy name.

10 And again he saith,

Rejoice, ye Gentiles, with his people.

11 And again,

Praise the Lord, all ye Gentiles;
And let all the peoples praise him.

12 And again, Isaiah saith,

There shall be the root of Jesse,
And he that ariseth to rule over the Gentiles;
On him shall the Gentiles hope.

13 Now the God of hope fill you with all joy and peace
in believing, that ye may abound in hope, in the power
of the Holy Spirit.

EXHORTATION TO BEAR WITH THE WEAK.

1. It is quite probable the individual who arranged this epistle text knew little about Paul. He includes in the

selection more than pertains to the theme. The beginning—"Whatsoever things were written," etc.—relates to what goes before. The text should have begun with the words, "Now the God of patience." It is necessary to a clear and methodical understanding of the passage that we remember this: the Romans to whom the apostle writes were converts to Christianity from both Jews and gentiles. At that time there were many Jews living in all countries, and especially were they found in Rome, as we learn from the seventeenth and eighteenth chapters of the Acts of the Apostles. Having properly inculcated the doctrines of faith and of good works all through the epistle, the apostle in conclusion introduces several exhortations to the Romans to preserve harmony in faith and in good works, removing what might be productive of discord and subversive to unity of the Spirit. There are two difficulties which today as in all times strongly militate against the unity of the Spirit, against faith and good works. They must here be carefully noted and described.

2. The first difficulty was this: Some Jewish converts feared that deviating from former customs would be committing sin. Notwithstanding they had been taught the New Testament freedom regarding meats, days, clothing, vessels, persons, conditions, customs; that only faith renders us righteous in God's sight; and that the restrictions of the Law concerning the eating of flesh and fish, concerning holidays, places, vessels, were entirely abolished; yet so completely fettered by old customs were their weak consciences and imperfect faith, they could not exercise such liberties. Again, both Jews and gentiles, in consequence of this same disordered idea, could not venture to eat of bread and meat offered to idols by unbelievers, though sold in the public market. They imagined that to eat thereof was to honor the idols and deny Christ, when in fact the act had no significance. For all kinds of food are clean, and good creatures of God, whether in the hands of heathen or Christians, whether offered to God or to the devil.

3. The second difficulty was this: They of better understanding and stronger faith had not sufficient regard for the

weak, but exercised their liberty indiscreetly, offending the weak by eating and drinking without discrimination whatever was set before them. Not that there was any wrong in the act so far as the food was concerned; the wrong consisted in their indiscretion in causing the weak to err through the act. For the latter, beholding, could neither agree with them nor dissent from them. Had they thought to consent, their weak consciences would have interposed, protesting, "It is sinful; do it not." Had they thought to dissent, conscience again would have interposed, objecting, "You are not Christians for you do not as other Christians do; your faith must be false." Thus they could neither do one thing nor the other without opposing conscience. Now, to violate conscience is equivalent to violating faith, and is a grievous sin.

4. Paul here teaches us to have patience and bear with the weak, and not to conduct ourselves carelessly before them; rather to agree with them—become weak with them—until they grow stronger in the faith and recognize their liberty. We are to guard against creating discord in faith over the subject of meats and drinks or any other temporal thing.

The apostle, however, discriminates upon this point, for in general his teaching recognizes two classes of individuals to be considered in the matter. One consists of those weak in the faith, of whom we have already spoken. It is to this class alone Paul here refers. They are good, pious, common people, willingly doing better when they have the knowledge or power. They are not tenacious of their opinions; the trouble lies altogether in weakness of conscience and lack of faith. They are unable to extricate themselves from prevailing doctrines and customs. The other class are obstinate. Not satisfied to enjoy liberty of conduct for themselves, they must enforce it upon others, constraining them to their own practices. They claim that because certain liberty is permissible, it must be enjoined. They will not listen to real truth in the matter of Christian liberty, but strive against it. They are to blame for the weakness of the first class. For their doctrine disregards the weak consciences and misleads them into the belief that certain conduct is essential. This domineering class delight in bringing simple consciences into subjection to their demands. Paul does not here refer to that manner of people; no, but he elsewhere teaches us to faithfully oppose them and always do the opposite. Titus 1.

5. The best rule to follow in such matters is the rule of love. You should hold the same attitude toward these two classes that you would toward a wolf and a sheep. Suppose a wolf were to wound almost fatally a sheep, and you were to proceed with rage against the sheep, declaring it to be wrong in being wounded, that it should be sound; and you were violently to compel it to follow the other sheep to the pasture and to the fold, giving it no special care; would not all men declare you inconsiderate? The sheep might well say: "Certainly it is wrong for me to be wounded, and unquestionably I ought to be sound; but direct your anger toward the inflicter of my wounds, and assist in my recovery." So should these Romans have done and have faithfully repelled the wolf-like teachers. At the same time, the consciences weakened and discouraged by false doctrines should have received consideration. The Church at Rome ought not to have denounced nor ignored them, but rather to have carefully healed their spiritual disorder and ultimately eradicated the wrong doctrines, in patience bearing with their weak brethren lest they should cause them to err.

6. Now, the circumstance Paul here speaks of has long since passed, and the law of Moses concerning meats, drinks, apparel, place, and so on, is no longer pertinent; yet another has been introduced in its stead, causing even greater trouble, and Paul's doctrine on this point is more necessary now than then. There is today established by the Pope and the clergy a world-wide system of human devices in regard to meats and drinks, apparel and place, days and seasons, persons and orders, customs and performances, so elaborate that one can scarce eat a morsel, drink a drop, or open his eyes even, but there is a law concerning the act. Thus is

our liberty usurped. Particularly is it true in convents and cloisters, where it is unanimously contended that we must be clothed and shorn in a certain way, must conduct ourselves by certain rules, and must not eat this meat, drink that drink, and so on, lest we sin by disobedience. There obedience to human doctrines has been exalted to the point of highest esteem. The monks and nuns regard it the foundation, the corner-stone, of their religion, and base upon it their souls' salvation.

7. No one will open his eyes to the fact that mere human devices and doctrines are ensnaring souls, weakening consciences, dissipating Christian liberty and faith, and replenishing hell. Wolves! wolves! How abominably, awfully, murderous, how harassing and destructive, are these things the world over! This matter of obedience to human doctrine has never been agitated sufficiently to discover weak consciences. No one has opposed in word or act the teachings harmful to them. Whosoever has deviated from the doctrines has been condemned, and denounced as an apostate, a roving monk, an abandoned Christian. Thus forcibly have the sheep not only been enfeebled, but driven into the jaws of the wolf. Oh, the wrath, the indignation, the displeasure, of the Divine Majesty!

8. If now, by the mercy of God, these papistical doctrines should be recognized as merely human, as false and assumed, things God has not commanded; and if some were to have courage enough to depart from custom in the matter of masses, prayers, garb, meats, and to maintain their Christian liberty according to the Gospel, the two classes referred to would take offense. The first, the Papists, would rant and rage, making loud outcry: "Our teachings must be observed! He who disregards them is a heretic, a heathen, a Jew, and disobedient to the Church." They would continue to cry "Obedience to the Church!" solely for the sake of retaining in fetters and spiritual death the consciences which, as they have been taught to do, regard their obedience as unto the Church, when in reality it is unto mere papistical knavery and satanic devices, things whereby many

saints, even, have been misled and deceived; St. Francis, for instance, and others.

The second class—the weak—in the face of the others' outcry and of their own established custom, would err, being puzzled as to whose doctrine to accept, though sincerely desirous to follow the right. But whatever course they might take, conscience would oppose them. Should they essay to accept our Christian liberty, their own established custom and the outcry of the Papists would deter them. Their consciences bound by these two restraints, they would not dare deviate from the old way lest they oppose God. On the other hand, should they not accept our Christian liberty, they would again fear they were opposing the God we proclaim. Whither, then, shall flee the poor, weak conscience over whom Christ and the devil contend?

9. To this situation Paul's teaching appropriately applies. The doctrine of the devil and his Papists is wholly destitute of compassion. In violent rage it compels immediate retraction from our doctrine of liberty. It excommunicates and curses the offender, casting him down four thousand miles below hell, if he does not recant in the twinkling of an eye and renounce every letter and tittle of his belief. From the fact of the rage manifested, as well as from the fruit of papistical doctrine, we perceive who is its author. The teaching of Christ, however, does not so. It calls not for summary rejection of the individual who fails to quickly retract and readily desist when found to err in faith; notwithstanding there is more reason it should than in the case of papal teaching. Recognizing the weak and wounded condition of the offender, Christ's doctrine comes in a friendly way, teaching the real truth about human laws—that of Christian liberty. It is patient, bearing with him who does not immediately abandon his erroneous ways, and giving him time to learn to forsake them. It allows him to do the best he can, according to what he has been used to, until he is made whole and clearly perceives the truth.

10. Therefore, the Christian must on this point discriminate between the two classes mentioned. The weak should

receive his kindly and patient instruction, but the roving, ranting kind are to meet with his earnest opposition. Let him teach and perform everything calculated to annoy and oppose the latter, and quietly omit whatever is pleasing to them, and let him honor their ban with a great easel-box. This is the consistent course of Christian love. It is the treatment every man desires for himself. Were any one of us misled by a weak conscience, he would desire a little time to retrieve instead of being precipitately cut off from the Church. He would like to be kindly instructed, to be borne with for a while and to be delivered from the wolves. Such is Christ's conduct toward us, and such does he desire our conduct toward one another to be.

11. The second cause of discord Paul also removes. There is, and always will be, among Christ's followers a class who are weak and sickly in good works, just as the first were defective in faith. We have, then, two kinds of invalid Christians—those affected inwardly, in faith and conscience; and those outwardly unsound, in works and deportment. Christ desires none of them to be rejected, but would have all received. He would give Christian love abundant opportunity to exercise itself, to heal its neighbors, to do them good and to bear with them, in matters inward and outward—in faith and conduct. The weak in conduct are they who sometimes fall into open sin; or again they who are called in German "wunderliche Koepfe und Seltsame," people easily irritated or with other shortcomings which make it difficult to get along with them. Especially have we instances among husbands and wives, masters and servants, rulers and subjects.

12. Now, where Paul's Christian doctrine does not obtain, naturally each individual forgets the beam in his own eye and perceives only the mote in his neighbor's. One will not bear with the faults of the other; each requires perfection of his fellow. Hence they reflect upon each other's conduct. One resorts to this subterfuge, the other to that, to evade the harassing censure and displeasure of his neighbor. He who can, cuts the other's acquaintance, drops

him, and then justifies himself with the excuse that his motive was love of righteousness; that he did not want to associate with wicked persons, but desired the company of only the good and godly like himself.

13. This evil holds sway chiefly in individuals ranking more or less high in the estimation of their fellows, who lead respectable lives and are particularly favored. These puff themselves up and put on airs. Whoever is not just like them is held in disgrace, in disparagement and contempt. Only themselves are worthy of admiration. But he who measures up to them, whose life is equally respectable—ah! he is righteous and a good friend; with him they can associate with perfect satisfaction to themselves as individuals who love only righteousness and the righteous, and hate nothing but wickedness and the wicked. They are not aware of the secret satanical pride in the inmost recesses of their hearts, which pride is the very reason they haughtily and meanly despise their neighbors for their imperfections.

14. Love of virtue and hatred of vice may spring from two different motives; one heathenish, the other Christian. Christ, too, is an enemy to sin and a friend to righteousness. Psalms 45, 7 says of him, "Thou hast loved righteousness, and hated wickedness." And this saying does not conflict with Moses' declaration concerning Christ, "Dilexit populos," Yea, he loveth the people." Deut 33, 3. But heathen love of virtue and hatred of vice, like the unreasoning swine, indiscriminately roots up and tosses together vices and virtues, regardless of the individual; truly a friend to no one but itself. This truth is evident from the fact that so long and so far as virtue adorns the individual, so long and so far heathenism loves him and is interested in him; but when virtue is lacking, the individual is rejected.

15. Now, the Christian hatred of sin discriminates between the vices and the individual. It endeavors to exterminate only the former and to preserve the latter. It does not flee from, evade, reject nor despise anyone; rather it receives every man, takes a warm interest in him and accords him treatment calculated to relieve him of his vices.

It admonishes, instructs and prays for him. It patiently bears with him. It does only as the doer would be done by in circumstances of like infirmities.

16. The Christian's whole purpose in life is to be useful to mankind; not to cast out the individual, but to exterminate his vices. This we cannot do if we refuse to tolerate the faulty person. It would be a very inconsistent case of charity in which you should desire to feed the hungry, satisfy the thirsty, clothe the naked, visit the sick, but at the same time should not permit the hungering, the thirsting, the naked and the sick to approach you. But just so your unwillingness to tolerate a wicked or faulty person is inconsistent with your willingness to help him, or to aid him to godly living.

17. Let us learn from this that the life of Christian love does not consist in seeking godly, upright, holy individuals, but in making them godly, upright and holy. Let this be the Christian's earthly labor, whether it calls for admonition, prayer, patience or other exercise. For the Christian does not live to seek after the wealthy and strong in virtue, but to make such virtuous ones from the poor, weak and infirm.

18. So, then, the text admonishes to two thoughts—to Christian love and to good and noble works; not only to bearing with our neighbor's spiritual imperfections of faith and conduct, but also to receiving him into fellowship, to healing him and to restoring from infirmities. They who fail so to do, create seditions, sects and divisions; as in time past the heretics, Donatists and Novatians, and many others, separated from the Church because unwilling to tolerate sinners and the faulty. There must be heretics and sects where the doctrine of Christian love is ignored; it cannot be otherwise.

19. St. Augustine, commenting on the sixth chapter of Galatians, says: "In nothing is one's religious character so well shown as when, in dealing with the sinful individual, he insists on redemption of the sinner rather than on reproach; on his welfare rather than on reproof." Upon this subject of Christian love, Paul says (Gal 6, 1-2): "Brethren, even if

a man be overtaken in any trespass, ye who are spiritual, restore such a one in a spirit of gentleness; looking to thyself, lest thou also be tempted. Bear ye one another's burdens, and so fulfill the law of Christ." In other words: "Neglect not to take upon yourselves the burdens of your neighbor—whatever is hard for him to bear. Seek not to derive advantage from him, but bear his burdens." To use him for your own advantage is not bearing but being borne. Advantage belongs to the angels in yonder life. At the same time we are to make a distinction between the two classes before mentioned. We are to avoid as heathen those who obstinately attempt to justify their sins and are unwilling to forsake them. For so we are taught in Matthew 18, 17. The doctrine of Christian love is applicable only to them who, though perceiving the wrong, yet stumble through weakness or imperfection. Let us examine the text.

THE WORD OF HOPE.

> "For whatsoever things were written aforetime were written for our learning, that through patience and through comfort of the Scriptures we might have hope."

20. In the selection of this epistle passage it should not have been made to begin with these words. They pertain to the first part of the chapter. We shall therefore present the text in its proper order. The apostle with the fifteenth chapter begins to teach the aforesaid principle of love which is to have expression in our attitude toward our neighbor of erring conduct; even as in the fourteenth chapter he taught us to manifest love toward our neighbor of imperfect faith. He says, "We that are strong ought to bear the infirmities of the weak, and not to please ourselves. Let each one of us please his neighbor for that which is good, unto edifying. For Christ also pleased not himself; but, as it is written, The reproaches of them that reproached thee fell upon me. For whatsoever things were written aforetime were written for our learning, that through patience and through comfort of the scriptures we might have hope." In these truly forcible words Paul teaches the principle of love

that is to enable us to bear with the imperfect conduct of our neighbor.

21. First, he tells us we are under obligation to forbear. Whence arises this obligation? Doubtless from the Law and from love (Mt 7, 12): "All things whatsoever ye would that men should do unto you, even so do ye also unto them; for this is the law and the prophets." Now, there is no one of us who would not have others bear with him in his infirmities and help him to do better. In return, we are under obligation to conduct ourselves in a similar manner toward our fellows. The strong should bear with the feeble and help them to better things.

22. Secondly, Paul teaches we are not to take pleasure in ourselves; that is, not to consider ourselves good because of abilities superior to those of our neighbors. For that means but to delight in beholding others in sin and depravity, from unwillingness to see them our equals or our superiors; and to rejoice at the misfortunes which prevent their gaining ascendancy. Truly this spirit is diametrically and fundamentally opposed to love. The Pharisee in the Gospel (Lk 18, 11) thanks God he is not like other men. So good does he regard himself and so does he delight in himself, it would be painful indeed to him were there any other without sin.

23. Now, are not they detestable individuals who begrudge grace and salvation to others, and who rejoice to see them ruined in sin, but at the same time are ambitious to be regarded pious and holy, strong enemies to sin and friends to godliness? But what is Paul's teaching? Emphatically not this. He says no one should unduly approve himself—regard himself good. What then? Let him secure the approbation of others. Let everyone so conduct himself as to gain the approval of his neighbor. Each should bear his neighbor's infirmities with patience and gentleness, and by kindness win his love and confidence. Let him not treat his neighbor with a rashness and severity that shall warrant the latter's fear and shall drive him farther away, leading him to expect no favors ever and to become but more sinful.

24. But you will say, "If I proceed in the way that shall please my neighbor I must let him have his own way and allow him to continue as he is. But this is not Paul's thought, for he adds the modifier "for his good." His meaning is that each should so conduct himself as to please his neighbor in the things that make for that neighbor's betterment, and in those only. And, indeed, our conduct toward our fellow may be such as to deny him his will without incurring his displeasure. But if he be dissolute beyond our power to benefit him, let him go; we have made a reasonable effort to gratify him in so far as we could contribute to his improvement. We cannot force his approval of our efforts to please him. Paul requires no more of us than to please our neighbor in the way of ministering to his good. The world does not delight even in the fact that God gave his own Son to die for its happiness.

25. Therefore, when Paul tells us everyone should please his neighbor in that which is good, his intent is not for us merely to strive to please our fellows; that is not what is required of us. But he would have us, in obedience to the rule of love, conduct ourselves in a way we might reasonably expect pleasing to them; in a way that if we fail we are not at fault. Paul says in First Corinthians 10, 33: "Even as I also please all men in all things." So would he have us please everyone in all things. How did Paul please all men when Jews and gentiles were his deadly enemies? He did everything for their benefit, and what reasonably should have pleased them.

26. Now, in the third place, to more effectually impress this doctrine, the apostle cites the example of Christ, saying Christ did not please himself. And what does he mean? Simply that notwithstanding Christ's holiness and graciousness, he did not despise us. Nor did he have pride in himself as the Pharisee did because he possessed something we had not. He rejoiced not in the fact that we had nothing while he had all things and all power. On the contrary, because he was grieved over our destitute condition, he devised a plan to be with us whereby we may become like

him—possessing what he possesses and being liberated from our sins. There being no other way, he put forth his whole being and all his powers to accomplish our redemption. He assumed our sins and exterminated them. His purpose in it all was to please us and to win our affection. Thus is fulfilled Psalms 69, 9: "The reproaches of them that reproach thee are fallen upon me." Our sins reproach and dishonor God, as our good conduct contributes to his honor and praise. So the prophet speaks of God's reproach and dishonor. All our sins are fallen upon Christ so as to be removed from us. Had Christ treated us as the Pharisee treated the publican, and as haughty saints do poor, faulty sinners, who of us would have been redeemed? Paul again holds up the example of Christ in Philippians 2, 5-8: "Have this mind in you, which was also in Christ Jesus: who, existing in the form of God, counted not the being on an equality with God a thing to be grasped, but emptied himself, taking the form of a servant, being made in the likeness of men; and being found in fashion as a man, he humbled himself, becoming obedient even unto death, yea, the death of the cross."

27. Such should be our spirit in regard to the sins of our neighbor. We should not judge, backbite nor condemn him. We should keep an undesigning eye upon him, solely for the purpose of delivering him, even at the hazard of our own bodies, our lives, fortunes and honor. Let him who fails here, know he has lost Christ and is a heathen saint.

28. Now follows our text. It is because of the words cited from Psalm 69 concerning Christ that Paul says, "For whatsoever things were written aforetime," etc. By way of explaining the bearing of that passage here, and in what way it concerns us when it was spoken of Christ and is fulfilled in him, the apostle goes on to give us a general admonition from the Scriptures, saying that not only this passage but the entire Scriptures were written for our learning. True, the Bible contains much about Christ. But so it contains much about numerous saints—Adam, Abel, Noah, Abraham, Isaac, Jacob—which was not recorded for

their sakes. The Bible was written long after their time; they never saw it.

29. So, however much is written about Christ, it is not for his sake; he had no need for it. It is recorded for our instruction. The record of Christ's words and deeds is for our edification, the model for us to follow. It is with this same understanding Paul says in First Corinthians 9, 9: "For it is written in the law of Moses, Thou shalt not muzzle the ox when he treadeth out the corn." Do you suppose God's care is for the ox, or is not the verse written for our sakes? Surely for our sakes. As if the apostle had said: "God's care is not for the ox but for us." Not that God does not govern and provide for all creatures, but that he does not write and speak for them. What should he write and speak to oxen? Only to man does he speak. So here; although the words are about Christ, they are not directed to him but to us, for our learning: we, too, are to conduct ourselves as the Scriptures tell us Christ and his saints have done.

30. Mark the book the apostle here presents for the perusal and study of Christians—none other than the holy Scriptures. And he tells us it contains doctrine for us. Now if our doctrine is to be found in the Bible, we certainly should not seek it elsewhere; all Christians should make daily use of this book.

31. Observe, however, what the devil has accomplished through the Papists. It was not enough for them to throw the Bible under the table, to make it so rare that few doctors of the holy Scriptures possess a copy, much less read it; but lest it be brought to public notice they have branded it with infamy. For they blasphemously say it is obscure; we must follow the interpretations of men and not the pure Scriptures. What else is their proceeding but giving Paul the lie here where he says the Bible is our manual of instruction? They say it is obscure and calculated to mislead.

32. How was God to reward such blasphemers and criminal destroyers of the Scriptures? Had he consulted with me about the matter, I would have entreated him—since

they cast reproach upon his clear word, declaring it obscure and unsafe, and exclude it from the sight and knowledge of men, throwing it under the table—to give them in its stead Aristotle and Averrois, along with the endless statutes and fallacies of the Pope; to let them rave after these, studying Aristotle all the days of their lives and learning nothing; and yet to permit the dolts to be crowned masters of the liberal arts and doctors of the holy Scriptures.

Yet up to this time none of them have understood a single line in Aristotle, or at most have learned no more than a five-year-old child or the most depraved dolt knows. For Aristotle is a hundredfold more obscure than the holy Scriptures. If you would know what he teaches, I will tell you in few words: "A potter can make a pot from clay; a blacksmith cannot unless he learns how." If there is anything in Aristotle more exalted than this, believe not a word I have said. Demand of me to prove it and I will.

33. I say this to show how well Christ has rewarded the Papists for denouncing his Scriptures as obscure and unsafe, and for perverting their design; for he permits the Papists to read the writings of a dead heathen, who is not strong in real science, no, not in anything but darkness. What I have cited is the very best thing in Aristotle. I say nothing of his virulent and fatal positions. The universities deserve annihilation. Nothing more pernicious and satanic ever has been or ever will be on earth.

34. Now, let us return to Paul. He tells us here what we should read and where we should seek our doctrine. Were there any other book he would have designated it. Further, he shows the nature of the fruit resulting from perusal of the Bible; for he says, "That through patience and through comfort of the scriptures we might have hope." Now let all other doctrine present itself, let all other books be introduced, and see if they have any virtue or power to comfort a single soul in its least tribulation. Truly, no comfort but that of God's word is possible to the soul. But where will we find God's word except in the Scriptures? What do we accomplish by reading other books to the exclusion of the

Book? Other books may have power to slay us, indeed, but no book except the holy Scriptures has power to comfort us. No other bears the title here given by Paul—book of comfort—one that can support the soul in all tribulations, helping it not to despair but to maintain hope. For thereby the soul apprehends God's word and, learning his gracious will, cleaves to it, continuing steadfast in life and death. He who knows not God's will must doubt, for he is unaware what relation he sustains to God.

35. But how shall I express the situation? The calamity is beyond the power of words, even inconceivable. The evil spirit has accomplished his design; he has suppressed the Book and introduced in its stead so many books of human doctrine that we may well say we are deluged with them. Yet these contain only error, falsehood, darkness, venom, death, destruction, hell and the devil. This condition of things our abominable ingratitude has merited.

36. Observe the aptness of Paul's expression where he links patience with the comfort of the Scriptures. The Bible does not remove adversity, suffering and death. No, it simply reveals the holy cross—Paul calls it the Word of the Cross—therefore patience is necessary. In the midst of suffering, however, the Bible consoles and strengthens, that our patience may not fail but press on unto victory. Under the strong comfort of God's solacing assurance that he is present to direct, the soul bears up with courage and joy beneath its sufferings.

This life is simply a mortification of the old Adam, which must die. So patience is essential. Again, since the life to come is not evident to mortal sense, it is necessary for the soul to have something to which it may cleave in patience, something to help it to a partial comprehension of that future life, and upon which it can rest. That something is God's Word. To it the soul cleaves; therein it abides, and therein is conveyed from this earthly life to the life to come as in a safe ship. Thus does the hope of the soul continue steadfast.

37. Mark you, the real mission of the Scriptures is to

comfort the suffering, distressed and dying. Then he who has had no experience of suffering or death cannot at all understand the comfort of the Bible. Not words but experience must be the medium of tasting and finding this comfort. Paul mentions "patience" before "comfort of the Scriptures" to indicate that he who, unwilling to endure suffering, seeks consolation elsewhere cannot taste the comfort of the Word. It is the province of the Word alone to comfort. It must therefore meet with patience first. It is jealous and will not permit human relief on a level with itself, which would be to frustrate the purpose of patience and suffering.

38. Now, it is no small cross and calls for no little measure of patience to bear the imperfections and sins of our neighbors. In some instances these things are oppressive enough to evoke, on the part of the sufferers, desire for death, either for themselves or someone else. To maintain Christian patience under these trials, the afflicted must comfort themselves with those portions of Scripture that show Christ's example. They will be helped to steadfastness and submission in suffering by perceiving that for their sakes Christ has submitted to far greater suffering, and has taken upon himself the infinitely heavier burden of their sins in the effort to redeem them.

39. Note, the comfort accompanying this patience is productive of a firm hope in Christ that we shall be like him. By contemplation of his record we are assured that for our sakes he has submitted, and continues to submit, to suffering. But to him who forgets Christ's example and the Scriptures, there remains very little comfort and patience, even when reason and material things have done their best to comfort him. For their efforts must be ineffectual. They cannot reach the inmost life of the heart. All the patience and comfort they are capable of affording is merely visionary.

> "Now, the God of patience and consolation grant you to be like-minded one toward another according to Christ Jesus."

40. This epistle lesson should have commenced here. This verse has reference to the imperfections of both our faith and our conduct, but more especially to the frailties of faith, as we shall see. It is a prayer, with which Paul follows his preaching and teaching and concludes his letter to the Romans. Lest one might presume to exercise patience and to know the comfort of the Scriptures all by his own power, Paul in his prayer reminds us they are gifts of God, to be obtained through prayer. Particularly is it beyond our power to bear with the imperfections of others and to preserve the simple unity of faith.

41. Therefore, Paul says, "God of patience and of consolation;" that is, God is the Lord, and grants patience and consolation. Just as he is the God of heaven and earth, so is he the God of patience and consolation. All are his gifts and his creatures. Paul says God "grants" patience and comfort; we do not possess them of ourselves. If they are granted they are not of nature but of grace, and are gifts. If God does not direct his Word to the heart to fit the needs of the individual, the heart will never discover this patience and consolation. Indeed, where God does not grant them, the Scripture is neglected and human doctrine sought, as in the case of condemned popery. But where he grants grace to search the Scriptures first, he gives likewise patience and consolation. There is no more marked manifestation of God's wrath than the fact that he permits the decline of his spoken and written Word; so not undesignedly the apostle uses the particular language of this prayer. On the other hand, God gives no greater blessing than when he exalts his Word among us and permits it to be read. Truly, then, we should all repeat this prayer with the apostle.

42. "To be like-minded one towards another." What do these words imply? How can the weak be "minded" like the strong? The phrase means each to tolerate the prejudices of another, and think that may be good which appears proper to another. Prejudice is the cause of all parties, sects, discord and heresy. As the proverb says,

"Pleased with his own way is everyone,
Hence the land with fools is overrun."

Paul here would arrest self-pleasing and prejudice. Nothing is more intolerable and pernicious to the Christian faith and the Church than prejudice. The victim of it cannot rid himself of the fault. He must follow his own way, differing from the commonly-accepted one. He must establish a course pleasing to himself. This is the cause of the many parties and various customs in the different institutions and cloisters of the world, all mutually discordant. Each one is best pleased with his own choice and condemns the way of others.

43. But the apostle enjoins the Romans to be of one mind and tolerant of one another. The weak in conscience should accept as right what they of strong faith and sound conscience observe. The effort should be for a oneness of faith and conscience, and a sameness of opinion; and to avoid the wrangling occasioned by conflicting personal ideas of what is right. He would have them illustrate the psalmist's declarations (Ps 68, 6): "God setteth the solitary in families;" and (Ps 133, 1): "Behold, how good and how pleasant it is for brethren to dwell together in unity!" For instance, should one of weak faith observe one whose faith is strong eat meat or indulge in drink, or do what to him appears sinful, let him refrain from judging, even though he would not and could not do likewise. He should be of Paul's opinion on the subject: "Let each man be fully assured in his own mind." Rom 14, 5. Then malice, contention and condemning may be avoided, and unanimity of purpose and disposition maintained. On the other hand, if the weak in faith is unable to do as his stronger brethren, they should not force him to it or despise him, but be content to tolerate him in regard to his eating, drinking and doing until he is likewise strong. Paul says, "Him that is weak in faith receive ye, yet not for decision of scruples." Rom 14, 1. That is, ye shall not compel him saying, "This is right and that wrong," but treat him considerately and instruct him until he, too, shall become strong.

44. It is not necessary that we should all follow the same occupation. One may be a smith and another a tailor without impairing unity of faith and purpose, only let one tolerate the outward calling of the other. If some foolish individual were to interfere and teach that the occupation of a smith is an ungodly trade, he would be responsible for erring consciences and weakened faith. As privilege of occupation is right, so in the external things of meats, apparel and place, we are at liberty to follow our own pleasure. Then he who comes along and teaches it is wrong for you to use such and such things, as the Pope and the clergy teach, causes you to err. On the other hand, if another comes saying you must use certain things, he likewise causes you to err. But he who pursues a medium course, teaching liberty in the matter, not condemning you but permitting you to retain your own custom until you extricate yourself, and at the same time hard presses the wolves that would force you into that custom as a thing not optional but binding—this teacher gives you true instruction.

45. It is not wrong to fast in honor of the name of an apostle, or to confess during Lent. But neither does he who omits these things commit any evil by this omission. Let him who desires to fast and make confession, do so, but let not one censure, judge, condemn or quarrel with his fellow over the matter. One individual should be like-minded with another—tolerant of what the other does and regarding his action as right because in itself blameless.

46. He deserves censure who in these questions rashly presumes to judge according to the dictates of his own doctrine and destroys this unity saying, "Do so and you do right; do not so and you do wrong." He is an apostle of the devil, and his teaching is the doctrine of Satan. This is the manner of the Pope and the Papists. It pertains not to shepherds but to wolves to preach doctrine of this character. Under such a condition of things, Christian unity must be dissolved. Difference of opinion becomes manifest: "You are a heretic"; "you are disobedient to the Church"; "you do wrong," and so on—just what the devil desires.

47. Having destroyed unity, taken captive the conscience and deprived of liberty, the Pope proceeds to take your money. Then he gives you a bill of exchange permitting you to eat butter, eggs and meat, a privilege Christ gave you in the Gospel, a privilege whereof the Pope robbed you and which he as the pious shepherd sells to you again. But your indulgence in the privilege again, gives offense to your fellows. In short, the government of the Pope so abounds with grasping and re-grasping, with offense and repetition of offenses, with exchanges and re-exchanges, that it is plainly evident it simply belongs to the designing devil who effects confusion of conscience until no one is able to comprehend the right course.

48. But I refer to toleration only in the things wherein we are at liberty to be lenient. We should resist the Pope with his wicked and foolish laws as we would resist a wolf; and yet we are to permit the weak in faith to continue in their practices for a time, until we are able finally to extricate them from error. They must not be too hastily and rashly rejected, with disastrous results to their consciences.

49. But in things not optional with us, things prescribed or prohibited by Christ, there is little room for disputation, whether it be the weak in conscience or the strong who are concerned. In such case every individual, the least as well as the greatest, is under obligation to withstand the Pope; for instance, when he and all his followers teach that the mass is to be regarded as in the nature of a sacrifice and a good work. This is the most monstrous abomination that ever arose on earth. On it is founded the Pope's government with all its cloisters and other institutions. In this error no one is excusable, whether weak or strong; for Christ instituted the mass as a sacrament and testament. No one can sell or transfer it or give it away. As in the case of baptism, each must receive it for himself. There are in the Pope's canons many more abominations similar to this misuse of the mass. Indeed, considering the foundation, it is easy to perceive the character of the building. Everything existing in popedom is the wantonness of the

devil, from turret to foundation. He who does not believe it, will experience it.

50. The apostle enjoins us to be like-minded "according to Christ Jesus"; that is, from a Christian point of view. For unbelievers, too, are like-minded, but according to the flesh, the world and the devil, and not according to Christ. The Jews were of one mind against God and his Christ, as Psalm 2, 2 tells us. Christian unity resists sin and everything opposed to the religion of Christ without, however, committing or designing any sin. It works to the unifying of Christians generally, first with reference to faith and then to outward conduct.

51. When one is weak in faith and defective in conduct, the spirit of Christian unity, though deploring his condition, does not forsake him, much less disparage, reject or condemn him. His Christian fellow is interested in his welfare and conducts himself toward the weak one as he would himself be treated, and as Christ has indeed treated him in similar and more important matters. Thus is perpetuated that principle wherein the individual follows the way approved of others, conforming to their views and adhering to the same opinions. But the obstinate pursue a course quite the reverse, forsaking, rejecting and judging him who differs from them, and following their own ways, guided by their own opinions; as do the orders of popery, and other sects.

"That with one accord ye may with one mouth glorify the God and Father of our Lord Jesus Christ."

52. All the good we can do to God is to praise and to thank him. This is the only true service we can render him, according to his words in Psalm 50, 23: "Whoso offereth the sacrifice of thanksgiving glorifieth me; and to him that ordereth his way aright will I show the salvation of God." We receive all blessings from him, in return for which we should make the offering of praise. If anything else purporting to be service to God is presented for your consideration rest assured it is erroneous and delusive. For instance, the distracted world attempts to serve God by setting apart houses, churches, cloisters; vestures, gold-trimmed, silk and

every other kind; silver vessels and images; bells and organs, candles and lamps; the money for which expense should have been appropriated to the poor if the object was to make an offering to God. Further, it keeps up a muttering and wailing in the churches day and night. But true praise and honor of God, a service that cannot be confined to place or person, is quietly ignored the world over. The pretenses of priests and monks about their system of exercises being service to the Lord, are false and delusive.

53. Service to God is praise of him. It must be free and voluntary, at table, in the chamber, cellar, garret, in house or field, in all places, with all persons, at all times. Whosoever teaches otherwise is no less guilty of falsehood than the Pope and the devil himself.

But how shall there be with us honor and praise of God, true service to him, when we neither love him nor receive his blessings? And how shall we love him when we do not know him and his blessings? And how shall we know him and his blessings when no word is preached concerning them and when the Gospel is left to lie under the table? Where the Gospel is not in evidence, knowledge of God is an impossibility. Then to love and praise him is likewise impossible. As a further consequence it is necessarily impossible for divine service to exist. Even if all the choristers were one chorister, all the priests one priest, all the monks one monk, all the churches one church, all the bells one bell; in brief if all the foolish services offered to God in the institutions, churches and cloisters were a hundred thousand times greater and more numerous than they are, what does God care for such carnivals and juggling?

54. Therefore, God complains most of the Jews in the second chapter of Micah, because they silenced his praise, while at the same time, they piped, blared and moaned like we do. True divine service of praise cannot be established with revenues, nor be circumscribed by laws and statutes. High and low festivals have nothing to do with it. It emanates from the Gospel, and certainly is as often rendered by a poor, rustic servant as by a great bishop.

55. It is plainly evident who have abolished divine service and still daily suppress it. They are none but that hopeless rabble, the Pope and his blockheads the bishops and priests, monks and nuns, whose great boast is of their divine services; who delight to be called the spiritual class and, by their juggling, grasp the advantages and honors of the world and live in riotousness. Yet they pretend to help others to heaven with their foolish works and no mention of the Gospel. Indeed, they persecute and condemn the Gospel, giving Peter just occasion to term them children of condemnation.

56. Note, Paul says divine service must be rendered with "one mind" and with "one mouth." We render divine service when we are harmonious, and when we recognize our common equality and our common blessings in Christ; when none exalts himself above another nor assumes special advantages.

Do you ask how it is we are equal, I reply: All outside of Christ are equally condemned. One needs Christ as much as another. When converted, all receive the same baptism and sacrament, the same faith, the same Christ and Spirit, the same Gospel—in a word, the same God. Here in this wilderness the heavenly bread is impartially distributed. Then how can it possibly be right for one to exalt himself over his fellow spiritually, one priest above the other? What can he have that surpasses Christ? And each has the same Christ, and Christ receives each one unreservedly.

57. True, one may embrace Christ more fervently than another; he may love him more and be more steadfast in his faith. Nevertheless, he has not for that received of Christ more than another. Christ is one and the same Christ to all, and in the things of salvation alike to everyone. Therefore he is truly Christ. Since there is one common blessing for the weak and the firm in faith, for the strong in Christian conduct and for the erring, one should not esteem another more lightly than himself, nor reject him. He is to recognize his fellow as an equal. Then shall praise to God arise harmoniously, and emanate as from one heart and one

mouth. For so each individual praises God, and heart and mouth are actuated by the same impulse common to his fellows. All recognize Christ and render thanksgiving for what they receive through him; as prophesied in Psalm 72, 15: "Men shall pray for him continually; they shall bless him all the day long." But he who offers thanks simply for his own advantages or possessions, destroys unanimity of purpose and expression, and belongs not to the communion of saints. Thus the Papists and sects do. From them we never hear praise of Christ, but praise of their own works.

58. That Paul calls us to praise "the Father of our Lord Jesus Christ," and not to confine our praise to Christ, is worthy of special notice in our day when we extol the honor of the saints so highly that we trust in them and fail to press into God's very presence. We find one satisfied in calling upon St. Barbara and obtaining her favor, while there is no certain knowledge that she is a saint. Another is satisfied with Christofel, which is without doubt one of the greatest fictions and lies. But scarcely anyone is satisfied to honor the Virgin Mary and have her favor.

59. I fear abominable idolatry will thus gain ground, because we place in the saints the confidence and trust that should be placed in God alone, and expect from them what we can receive from God alone; and if no other evil were involved, it is a question whether the worship and honor of saints is supported by a passage or example in Scripture, and whether it is not contrary to this and like sayings of Paul, which teach us to press into the presence of God and place all our trust in him and expect everything we need for him. Christ, too, through the whole Gospel, points us to the Father. He came into the world that we should through him come to the Father.

60. To come to the Father does not mean to walk on bodily feet to Rome or to fly to heaven on wings. It means to rely upon God with sincere confidence as upon a gracious parent; as the opening of the Lord's Prayer implies. In proportion as we have such confidence of heart, do we come

nearer to the Father. Both reason and experience must confess, if the heart trusts in God, the Creator, that all trust in creatures vanishes, whether in saints in heaven or upon earth. Therefore Peter says: "Knowing that ye were redeemed, not with corruptible things, with silver or gold, . . . but with precious blood, as of a lamb without blemish and without spot, even the blood of Christ . . . so that your faith and hope might be in God." 1 Pet 1, 18-21. And Paul says, "Through whom [Christ] also we have had our access by faith into this grace," etc. Rom 5, 2.

61. I admit that some can make a proper use of honoring the saints and the virgin Mary; though it is seldom they do. The example is dangerous and it should not be introduced into the congregation as a practice. The teaching of Christ and of all the apostles is, that we should cheerfully approach God the Father alone through Christ. For it soon happens, because of man's terrible fall, that people seek comfort more from the saints than from God, and pray to their names for help rather than to God. It is a perverted, an unchristian, state of things that exists at present. I fear the world is full, yes, full, of idolatry.

62. God permits the worshiper of saints at times to receive help and perform wonders; yet, he does so through the agency of the devil. For it is God who gives to the servants of Satan their bodies and lives, their possessions and honor, and this he does through the agency of Satan. This is plainly evident; like a rich prince may give a treasure to one knave through another knave. Hence we are not to build upon miraculous signs nor upon the example of the multitude, but alone upon the teachings of Christ, or of his apostles, in this and all cases.

63. Now, while Christ is our common blessing, as before said, we should at the same time ascribe all to the Father; for Christ is the Father's gracious manifestation whereby our hearts are drawn to himself. So we should confidently love and praise the Father for his lavish blessings. With such exercise our hearts will learn to comfort themselves in him and to look to him for every blessing in life or death;

but this through Christ and not through merit in ourselves. Christ was given that by him we might thus confidently approach the Father. John 14, 6 declares: "No one cometh unto the Father, but by me."

64. Notwithstanding Christ is truly God and one might safely repose confidence in him, yet he constantly points to the Father; for he would not have mankind continue to trust in his humanity as the disciples did before his suffering, instead of lifting its thoughts above his humanity, up to his divinity. We must look upon Christ's humanity as enabling him to be a way, an evidence, a work of God, whereby we come to God. We are to place our whole confidence in God, and in him alone, being very careful not to devote any portion of it to the mother of God or any saint and so set up an idol in our hearts.

"Wherefore receive ye one another, even as Christ also received you, to the glory of God."

65. What is the significance here of that word "wherefore?" "There are two reasons," the apostle would say to the Romans, "why ye should receive one another. The first is, because of Christ's example. As ye have heard, the Scripture presents Christ to us as one upon whom fell the infamy of our sins—for us he was ignominious in God's sight—and who did not despise, reject or revile us, but received us that he might redeem us from our sins. We are, then, under particular obligation to receive one another."

66. The other reason the apostle presents for our receiving one another is that thus we contribute to the praise and honor of God. This we learn from Christ. He everywhere testifies that all he does is in obedience to his Father's will, and that he came for no other purpose than to do the will of God. It is certain, then, he bore the ignominy of our sins simply because it was his Father's will.

67. Mark the exceeding mercy of the Father's controlling will in placing upon his beloved and only Son our sins, and permitting him to bear the shame of them, merely that we might escape condemnation therefor. Now, a true recognition of this, God's gracious will, must evoke sincere

love and praise to him and gratitude for his mercy. For, once the individual glimpses the Father's merciful will, he has a conscience so happy and serene he cannot restrain himself but must honor and praise God for his priceless blessings.

68. Note, Paul says Christ has in himself upheld the honor of God by receiving us and bearing, yes, exterminating, our sins. So should we likewise take upon ourselves the burdens, the sins and imperfections, of our neighbors, and bear with and help to reform them. When such Christian conduct is manifest before sinners and the spiritually weak, their hearts are attracted to God and forced to exclaim: "Truly, he must be a great and gracious God, a righteous Father, whose people these are; for he desires them not to judge, condemn nor reject us poor, sinful and imperfect ones, but rather to receive us, to give us aid and to treat us as if our sins and imperfections were their own. Should we not love and exalt such a God? Should we not praise and honor him and give him the implicit confidence of our hearts in all things? What must be the character of that God who desires his people to be so noble?"

69. Mark you, this is the praise God would have from us, that we receive one another and regard our neighbor's condition as our own. Such conduct on our part would encourage others to believe and would strengthen the faith of believers. But where will we find in all the world any who follow Christ's example in this respect? Only tyrants, yes, devils, rule in church offices, who do nothing but excommunicate and condemn, drive and hound the people.

MISSIONS TO THE HEATHEN.

> "Now I say that Christ hath been made a minister of the circumcision for the truth of God, that he might confirm the promises given unto the fathers, and that the Gentiles might glorify God for his mercy."

70. The apostle has submitted to the Romans his sentiment that, in obedience to the example of Christ, they should receive one another, to the honor of God, and make no distinction between Christ's people, whether saints or

sinners, strong or weak, rich or poor, since all are entitled to the same privileges. For all have the same blessings in Christ, who creates unity of heart, spirit, mind and word and renders common all things, whether spiritual or temporal, and however diverse they may be. Now Paul goes on to establish his position with strong passages of Scripture. Standing between Jews and gentiles as an arbitrator and mediator, he by the use of scriptural authority dissipates all causes of discord. He would say: "You Jews cannot reject the gentiles, even though they do not follow your customs in eating and drinking, for they have the very same Christ you have, according to Scripture prophecy." Again, "You gentiles cannot despise the Jews for not conforming to your ways in the matter of eating and drinking, for the Scripture promises to them the same Christ you profess."

"Now," Paul's argument is, "since the Scripture gives to all equal privileges in Christ, and Jews and gentiles are brought together under his authority, and since outside of Christ is naught for anyone, but in him everyone has all things—in view of these facts, why contend, why judge one another and stir up factions? Why not much rather receive one another in kindness as Christ received you? No one is favored over another and no one has less than another. Why then contend, and create schisms, over the question of meats, drink, clothing; over observance of time and place; over manners and such things? These are not vital in any respect; they are temporal things, outside of Christ, and contribute nothing to salvation. Let every man exercise the liberty he desires in these matters. If any is still weak in faith and has not freedom of conscience, patiently bear with him till he becomes strong, for your lenience will cost you nothing; you will still have Christ unreservedly."

71. To understand Paul's words here we must remember he is wont to refer to the Jewish people as "the circumcision." For they practiced the rite. Circumcision was a token whereby they were distinguished from other peoples. Such metaphors are often employed; for instance, we refer to women when we say, "Misfortune is oft woven with a

weft of tresses"; to monks in the words, "Observe, what the cowl may not do"; or designate the priests when we exclaim, "How avaricious the bald pate!" And horsemen are indicated by the words "spurs" and "stirrups." It is in this metaphorical sense Paul, referring to a characteristic sign, terms the Jews "the circumcision" and the gentiles "præputium," "the uncircumcision": "They saw that I had been intrusted with the Gospel of the uncircumcision, [that is, of the uncircumcised gentiles] even as Peter with the Gospel of the circumcision [that is, of the Jews]." Gal 2, 7-8. And again: "Remember, that once ye, the Gentiles in the flesh, who are called Uncircumcision by that which is called Circumcision," etc. Eph 2, 11. So here he says, "I say that Christ hath been made a minister of the circumcision"; that is, of the Jewish people.

Using a convenient term, he calls Christ a "minister," as he calls all preachers and apostles ministers. "What then is Apollos? and what is Paul? Ministers through whom ye believed." 1 Cor 3, 5. The substance of the apostle's words is this: Jesus Christ was a minister of the circumcision. That is, a preacher, teacher, apostle, messenger, sent from God to the Jewish people. For Christ never preached to the gentiles. He was not sent to them, but to the Jews only.

72. But Christ was a minister to the Jews, not because of their merit, but as here stated, "for the truth of God." And what do we understand by those words? God promised Abraham, Isaac and Jacob that Christ should be born of their seed. To maintain God faithful in his promises, Christ came in fulfilment thereof. Thus is the truth of God proven; God keeps his promises. For the sake of God's truth, or in other words, that God might be proven truthful, and not for the sake of merit on the part of anyone, Christ became an apostle and a minister of the circumcision. This explanation is necessary to satisfy the succeeding phrase, "that he might confirm the promises given unto the fathers." Observe the apostle's meaning in the words "the truth of God"—the fulfilment and establishment of the divine promise made to the patriarchs concerning Christ.

73. True, Jews and gentiles have Christ in common, yet the promise was not to the gentiles; it was to the Jews exclusively. Paul tells us in Romans 3, 2 that the Jews "were intrusted with the oracles of God"; and again, in Romans 9, 4, that the Law was given to them. So, too, Christ came to the Jews alone, as he says himself: "I was not sent but unto the lost sheep of the house of Israel." Mt 15, 24. It was the peculiar privilege of the Jews to have Christ promised to them, and to be able to await his coming. But to the gentiles was nothing promised, and they awaited nothing. At the same time, Jews and gentiles are on common ground in the fact that, Christ being promised of pure grace, he was given to the gentiles also. After the promise was made to the Jews, the gentiles had just reason to regard the coming Messiah as given to them also.

74. The Jews, then, have Christ not only through grace in the promise, but also because of the truth of God in fulfilment of his promise. But the gentiles have neither the grace of the promise nor the truth of fulfilment. They have merely the naked, unpromised, unexpected mercy Christ gives to them. There is no promise, and no obligation for fulfilment of the truth of God. Yet, the Scriptures having revealed that the gentiles should obtain Christ, though without promise, hope or expectation, the Scriptures must be fulfilled. Therefore, one people is not favored over the other. But Christ was given to the Jews through divine promise and divine truth, and to the gentiles through pure, unexpected mercy.

Since the Scriptures contain a promise to the Jews and a prediction concerning the gentiles, the two peoples have a common bond in Christ. Hence each should receive the other as a participant in the common blessing. The Jews are not to despise the gentiles; because the Scriptures say the gentiles shall praise God for his mercy, and how shall the Jews despise those who enjoy God's mercy and praise him for it? On the other hand, the gentiles should not despise the Jews; for to the latter was Christ promised, and in fulfilment of the promise he became their minister and preacher, making God faithful to his word.

75. Let us see what is Paul's intent in declaring: "I say that Christ hath been made a minister of the circumcision for the truth of God, that he might confirm the promises given unto the fathers." Why this claim? Doubtless that none may despise the Jews, but rather receive them, in obedience to the example of Christ. Christ did not despise them; nay, he was even publicly promised and given to them as their own minister, preacher and apostle. But what do you say, Paul, in regard to the gentiles? "I do not say they are promised aught, but I say they enjoy and praise the mercy of God given them without promise, as the Scriptures imply. So, too, none should despise the gentiles, but rather receive them, in obedience to Christ's example." As Christ is a common bond between Jews and gentiles, though not given to each people in just the same way; so should there be unity among us. We must receive one another, bear one another's burdens and have patience with imperfections, regardless of personal appearance, name, condition or anything else.

"Therefore I will give praise unto thee among the Gentiles, and sing unto thy name."

76. Now the apostle goes on to quote some Scripture passages revealing the fact that the gentiles shall praise God for his mercy. This first quotation is found in Psalm 18, 49, and also in Psalm 108, 3. The words are spoken by the prophet for Christ, as in both cases the whole Psalm makes plain. Now, if this declaration is to be verified, Christ must be present with the gentiles, not physically but spiritually. For unless Christ is present spiritually, praise of him is not forthcoming; but the singing of his praise is guarantee of his spiritual presence. So this quotation forces us to conclude that the gentiles shall believe in Christ and possess him; in other words, enjoy the mercy of God. Yet the verse makes no promise to them. It is merely a revelation concerning their future conduct.

77. We have before mentioned what constitutes true service of God. Here the prophet refers to it as praising and singing unto God's name. And so is it defined throughout

the Scriptures. Now, praise is simply a confession of blessings received. The Hebrew and apostolic word in this verse is "confitebor," "I will confess thee"; meaning, "I will thank and praise thee and declare, All have I received from thee."

"And again he saith, Rejoice, ye Gentiles, with his people."

78. These words are quoted from Deuteronomy 32, 43, where Moses says, "Rejoice, O ye nations, with his people." The Hebrew, however, admits of the rendering, "Rejoice, ye Gentiles, with him" (understand "his people"). It is with this thought of God, it seems to me, the apostle introduces the quotation. Yet, whether we read it thus or otherwise, clearly no one praises the people of God, nor rejoices with him, unless he be partaker of God's blessings and own him God. For he who does not possess God and his blessings is an enemy to God's people, cursing and persecuting them, as God says in Genesis 12, 3, "I will bless them that bless thee, and him that curseth thee will I curse." Here you see, they who bless God's people are partakers of his blessings. So this second quotation teaches conclusively that the gentiles shall become Christians.

"And again, Praise the Lord, all ye Gentiles; and let all the peoples praise him."

79. This verse is Psalm 117, 1-2. It also has reference to true service of God. Therefore it, too, teaches that the gentiles shall be the people of God. For only they serve (praise and honor) God who are his people.

"And again, Isaiah saith, There shall be the root of Jesse, and he that ariseth to rule over Gentiles, on him shall the Gentiles hope."

80. We have this declaration in Isaiah 11, 10. In Hebrew it reads: "And it shall come to pass in that day that the root of Jesse, that standeth for an ensign of the people, unto him shall the nations seek; and his resting-place shall be glorious." The meaning evidently is that the gentiles shall possess Christ and he shall reign over them. Paul makes a slight change in the words, following the rendering of the old translators who wrote the Bible in the Greek

language. The meaning of the quotation is the same, however. The "root" of Jesse should not be understood here as "stem" or "tree" in the genealogical sense, as the artist would delineate the "tree" of Jesse, the father of David, with its many branches; and as we understand when we sing of the blessed Virgin, "the stem of Jesse has sprung forth." That would be altogether a forced construction. Christ himself, and none other, is the "stem" or "root." The construction of this passage from Isaiah makes that meaning plain, for it says practically, "The gentiles shall hope for the stem or root of Jesse, which is to rule the nations," etc. This prophecy cannot be made to refer to the human Jesse or to our blessed Virgin.

81. Christ is the root of Jesse. He descended from the lineage of Jesse, through David, but in him physical descent ceased. He suffered and was buried in the grave as an ill-favored root, concealed from the world, and out of him grew that beautiful tree, the Christian Church, spreading out into all the world. The root of Jesse is properly delineated when portrayal includes the sufferings of Christ and their fruits.

82. Paul's assertion "and he that ariseth to rule over the Gentiles" is equivalent to the Hebrew "that standeth for an ensign of the people." It shows Christ's government a spiritual one. The Gospel raises him as a standard before the whole world, an ensign to which we must be loyal through faith. We do not see him physically; we behold him only through the ensign, the Gospel. And it is through the Gospel he reigns over men; not in a physical presence.

83. Again, the expression "on him shall the Gentiles hope" does not materially differ from the Hebrew rendering "to it shall the Gentiles seek." The meaning is, the gentiles shall look unto the root of Jesse and cleave only to him, placing all confidence and hope in him and finding in him their consolation. They shall seek for and desire naught else.

But the phrase "and his grave [resting-place] shall be glorious," contained in the quotation from Isaiah but omitted by the apostle, is not well rendered by Jerome, who thinks Isaiah refers to the glorious grave of Christ. Isaiah's thought was of Christ's rest being glorious; that is, his death should mean something more than that of ordinary mortals, to whom death is the end of glory. The glory of the root of Jesse had its beginning in his death. For not until then was he raised to true life and power, to real glory and honor—an ensign for the gentiles, and ruler of them. Indeed, then he was seated at the right hand of God, Lord over all things.

> "Now the God of hope fill you with all joy and peace in believing, that ye may abound in hope, in the power of the Holy Spirit."

84. Paul concludes this passage with a noble prayer, desiring the Romans to be filled with joy and peace. He calls upon the "God of hope," referring to the hope God alone gives through Christ and in Christ.

85. The way we possess peace and joy we have before spoken of; the secret is in perceiving the will of God, how he gave Christ to bear our sins, which we are under obligation to believe. The more clearly we perceive his will, the stronger will be our faith, our hope and love. Hence we must continually preach the Gospel—receive it and meditate upon it. For faith comes through no other medium than the Gospel.

The apostle says, in effect: "May God, who through the Gospel effects hope, grant you grace, enabling you to appropriate the Gospel and believe. Through believing, you first perceive Christ. Thereupon follow perfect peace and an assured conscience. These are blessings common to all, and you will have harmony among yourselves." The Christian's peace and joy is something received, not as the gift of the world is received, through mortal sense, but through faith. He who is the source of your good, and from whom you derive your peace and joy, is not recognized by sight or touch. However, in the world you will have disquietude and grief. But learn that Christ is the common blessing of all and you will enjoy blessed peace. For all being alike rich, no one can begrudge another anything. This is what it means to have peace and joy through faith or in faith.

86. "That ye may abound in hope," continues the prayer. In other words, "that your hope may ever increase." Now, suffering and persecution contribute to the increase of hope. We are not given increased hope to decrease adversity; no, adversity is increased that hope may not rely on human power, but be established through the power of the Holy Spirit. For the Holy Spirit aids us, fortifying our hope and enabling us not to fear nor to flee from the disasters of the world; but to stand firm even unto death, and to overcome all evil; so that evil must flee from us and cease its attacks. Remember, it is hope in the power of the Holy Spirit, not in human weakness, that must do all this through the medium of the Gospel. As before said, "Through patience and through comfort of the Scriptures we have hope." Where the Gospel is not, there is neither hope, comfort, peace, joy, faith, love, Christ, God, nor anything good. Evidence of this fact is before us in the wretched, spiritless, carnal clerical orders, notwithstanding their much praying and holding of masses. From these things, O thou God of hope, of patience and of comfort, graciously preserve us. Amen.

Third Sunday in Advent

Epistle Text: First Corinthians 4, 1-5.

1 Let a man so account of us, as of ministers of
Christ, and stewards of the mysteries of God. 2 Here,
moreover, it is required in stewards, that a man be found
faithful. 3 But with me it is a very small thing that
I should be judged of you, or of man's judgment; yea,
I judge not mine own self. 4 For I know nothing
against myself; yet am I not hereby justified: but he
that judgeth me is the Lord. 5 Wherefore judge
nothing before the time, until the Lord come, who will
both bring to light the hidden things of darkness, and
make manifest the counsels of the hearts; and then
shall each man have his praise from God.

STEWARDS OF THE MYSTERIES OF GOD.

1. This epistle selection illustrates the Gospel lesson for the first Sunday in Advent, wherein we learned the disciples did not themselves ride on the colt, but led it to Christ and set him thereon. That is what the apostle does here. The Corinthians had come to divisions among themselves and to boasting of certain apostles as their leaders. With one party it was Peter, with another Paul, and with yet another Apollos. Each one exalted the apostle by whom he was baptized or was taught, or the one he regarded most eminent. Now comes Paul and interposes, permitting no one to boast of any apostle, and teaching them to laud Christ alone. He tells them it matters not by whom they were baptized and taught, but it is of the utmost importance that they all hold to Christ together and own allegiance to him alone. Paul beautifully teaches how the apostles are to be regarded.

The whole passage is a fierce thrust at Popery and the clerical government, as we shall see.

"Let a man so account of us, as of the ministers of Christ, and stewards of the mysteries of God."

2. The reference is to all apostles and all heirs to the apostolic chair, whether Peter, Paul or any other. Let us, then, be very careful how we regard the apostles and bishops; we must attach neither too much nor yet too little importance to them. Not without reason did Paul—the Holy Spirit, in fact—make this restriction; and without doubt we are under obligation to follow it. The same limit here made concerning apostles applies to bishops. It designates the character of their office and the extent of their power. So when we see a bishop assuming more than this text gives him warrant for, we may safely regard him as a wolf, and an apostle of the devil, and avoid him as such. Unquestionably he must be Antichrist who in ecclesiastical government exceeds the authority here prescribed.

3. First, Paul warns us against receiving apostles or bishops as anything but "ministers of Christ;" nor should they desire to be regarded otherwise. But the term "minister of Christ" must not in this connection be understood as one who serves God, in the present acceptation of the phrase —praying, fasting, attendance upon Church services, and all the things styled "divine service" by ecclesiastical rites, institutions and cloisters, and by the whole clerical order. Theirs are merely humanly devised works and words, whereby Paul's teaching here and elsewhere is wholly obscured, even to the extent of making it impossible to know what he means by the "ministry of Christ." He has reference to the ministry that is an office. All Christians serve God but all are not in office. In Romans 11, 13, also, he terms his office a ministry: "Inasmuch as I am an apostle of Gentiles, I glorify my ministry." And in the epistle selection preceding this (Rom 15, 8) he says: "I say that Christ hath been made a minister of the circumcision." Again (2 Cor 3, 6): "Who also made us sufficient as ministers of a new convenant; not of the letter, but of the spirit."

4. What language is forcible enough to serve me in the attempt to eradicate from the hearts of all Christians that error so deeply impressed of Popery wherein they interpret the ministry of Christ—or the service of God—in no other light than as their own works, performed to Christ without any authority to do them? Mark you, beloved, to serve Christ, or to serve God, is defined by Paul himself as to fulfil a Christ-ordained office, the office of preaching. This office is a service or ministry proceeding from Christ to us, and not from us to Christ. Note this carefully; it is important. Otherwise you cannot understand the design of the Pauline words, "ministry, ministration, to minister." So he always has it. Seldom does he speak of the service or ministry rendered primarily above them to God; it is usually of the ministry beneath them, to men. Christ, too, in the Gospel bids the apostles to be submissive and servants of others. Lk 22, 26.

To make himself clearly understood in this matter of service, or ministry, Paul carefully adds to the word "ministers" the explanatory one "stewards," which can be understood in no other way than as referring to the office of the ministry.

5. He terms his office "service or ministry of Christ" and himself "minister of Christ," because he was ordained of God to the office of preaching. So all apostles and bishops are ministers of Christ; that is preachers, messengers, officers of Christ, sent to the people with his message. The meaning of the verse, then, is: "Let every individual take heed not to institute another leader, to set up another Lord, to constitute another Christ. Rather be unanimously loyal to the one and only Christ. For we apostles are not your lords, nor your masters; we are not your leaders. We do not preach our own interests, nor teach our own doctrines. We do not seek to have you obey us, or give us allegiance and accept our doctrine. No, indeed. We are messengers and ministers of him who is your Master, your Lord and Leader. We preach his Word, enlist men to follow his commandments, and lead only into obedience. And in this light

should you regard us, expecting of us nothing else than to bring the message. Though we are other persons than Christ, yet you do not receive through us another doctrine than his; another word, another government, nor another authority than his. He who so receives and regards us, holds the right attitude toward us, and receives, not us, but Christ, whom alone we preach. But he who does not so regard us, does us injustice, discards Christ, the one true Leader, sets up another in his stead and makes gods of us."

6. In Judges 8, 22-23 we read that the children of Israel said to Gideon: "Rule thou over us, both thou, and thy son, and thy son's son also," to which Gideon answered, "I will not rule over you, neither shall my son rule over you: Jehovah shall rule over you." And in First Samuel 8, 7 we are told that when the children of Israel desired a king of Samuel, God said: "They have not rejected thee, but they have rejected me, that I should not be king over them." Thus we see God cannot permit any authority to usurp his own among his people.

7. But perhaps you ask: "Where was the sin of the people when they desired Gideon to rule over them? Had not God given Gideon leadership in the contest, and did he not later provide many holy kings expressly for them?" I reply it was not a sin for the children of Israel to have sovereigns; it was not contrary to God's will; for there must be temporal authorities. But the sin consisted in the fact that, not content with God's government, they chose human government instead. Gideon and the holy kings did not extend their authority as rulers a hair's breadth farther than God's command warranted, and they did not regard themselves in any other light than as the servants or ministers of God; that is, they ruled according to God's direction and not according to their own. Thus was perpetuated God's government in its purity, and they were servants in it; as were the apostles servants in the word of Christ. Hence David sings of his own kingdom as identical with God's. He says: "Arise, O Jehovah, in thine anger: lift up thyself against the rage of mine adversaries, and awake for me; thou hast

commanded judgment. And let the congregation of the peoples compass thee about; and over them return thou on high. Jehovah ministereth judgment to the peoples." Ps 7, 6-8.

8. But where more authority is assumed than God's command gives, and where the magistrate attempts to rule according to human doctrines, or the subjects seek such leadership, idolatry results and the leader assumes a new character. The magistrate is no longer a servant or minister, but rules arbitrarily, without command of God. God says of them as he said to Samuel concerning the children of Israel: "They have not rejected the magistrate, but they have rejected me, that I should not reign over them." I refer here to spiritual matters, to the sovereignty of the soul, which must stand before God. Civil government is a matter that does not pertain to nor concern the soul.

9. Where divine leadership is shared with any other than God or Christ, there must also be doctrine and commandments differing from the doctrine and command of Christ. Service of Christ must immediately fail; Christ must be rejected for the establishment of a new sovereignty. Plainly enough, no one can be servant of Christ and at the same time teacher of his own message. The two conditions cannot exist at the same time. How can one be a servant of Christ if he does not teach Christ's message? Or how can he teach his own message when he is under obligation to teach only Christ's? If he advocates his own counsels, he makes himself lord and does not serve Christ. If he advocates Christ's counsels, he cannot himself be lord.

10. From this you may judge for yourself whence arises Popery and its ecclesiastical authority, with all its priests, monks and high schools. If these can prove they teach nothing but the message of Christ, we must regard them as his ministers or servants. But if we can prove they do not so teach, we must regard them as not his servants. Now it certainly is clear that their teaching is not the doctrine of Christ, but their own doctrine. Hence it is evident they constitute the kingdom of Antichrist and are servants of the

devil. For Paul makes a firm stand here and declares: "Let a man so account of us as of the ministers of Christ."

11. Their claim that in addition to the teachings of Christ, the commandments of the Church may be taught—and they intimate that their teachings are the doctrines of the Church—is of no significance. Paul's teaching here continues to stand, that the Church belongs neither to Peter nor Paul, but to Christ only, and acknowledges none but the servants or ministers of Christ. You see, then, the blasphemy of the Pope in crying obedience to his doctrines as the road to salvation, and disobedience to them the road to damnation. Paul here makes obedience to these things a work of the devil; as he does also in First Timothy 4, 1-3: "But the Spirit saith expressly, that in later times some shall fall away from the faith, giving heed to seducing spirits and doctrines of demons, through the hypocrisy of men that speak lies, branded in their own conscience as with a hot iron; forbidding to marry, and commanding to abstain from meats, which God created to be received with thanksgiving by them that believe and know the truth." And Christ says: "My sheep hear my voice, and a stranger will they not follow, but will flee from him; for they know not the voice of strangers. I know mine own, and mine own know me." Jn 10, 5-14.

12. Note the harmony between Paul's teaching and this statement of Christ's that any other than the voice of Christ is a strange voice, the doctrine of the devil, and to be avoided. You see here Christ's own verdict in regard to doctrines, what his Church hears and teaches, and what are and what are not the commandments of the Church. The Church has no other doctrine than that of Christ, and no other obedience than to obey him. All the Papists say, then, concerning obedience to the commandments of the Church is in the same class with what Paul calls speaking lies in hypocrisy, moved by false spirits and doctrines of devils.

13. The same is the meaning of the phrase "stewards of the mysteries of God." The word "steward" here signifies

one who has charge of his lord's domestics; one whose office is the same as that of stewards in monasteries at the present day, or provosts in nunneries, or governors, managers and overseers of the sort. For "oekonomus" is Greek and signifies in English a steward, or one capable of providing for a house and ruling the domestics. Christ in Matthew 24, 45 calls such a one simply a servant: "Who then is the faithful and wise servant, whom his lord hath set over his household, to give them their food in due season?" Such a servant was Eliezer, the steward of Abram's house. Gen 15.

14. Now, God's household is the Christian Church—ourselves. It includes pastors and bishops, overseers and stewards, whose office is to have charge of the household, to provide nourishment for it and to direct its members, but in a spiritual sense. Paul puts a distinction between the stewards of God and temporal stewards. The latter provide material nourishment, and exercise control of the physical person; but the former provide spiritual food and exercise control over souls. Paul calls the spiritual food "mysteries." The practice of providing it has so long been discontinued we do not now know what a steward is nor what is meant by "mysteries." Church officials imagine that when they baptize, celebrate mass and administer other sacraments, they exercise the mysteries, and that now there is no proper mystery but the mass. At the same time they know not the meaning of the term in this connection.

15. I cannot just now find a word in German equivalent to "mysterion," and it will be well to retain the Greek form, as we have with many other words. It is equivalent to "secret," something hidden from our eyes, invisible to all, and generally pertaining to words. For instance, a saying not easily understood is said to contain a hidden meaning, a secret, a "mysterion"—something is concealed therein. The concealment itself may properly be termed "mystery"; I call it a secret.

16. What, then, constitutes the mysteries of God? Simply Christ himself; that is, faith and the Gospel concerning Christ. The whole Gospel teaching is far beyond the grasp

of our reason and our physical sense; it is hidden to the world. It can be apprehended only by faith; as Christ says in Matthew 11, 25: "I thank thee, O father, Lord of heaven and earth, that thou didst hide these things from the wise and understanding, and didst reveal them unto babes." And as Paul tells us (1 Cor 2, 7-8): "We speak God's wisdom in a mystery, which none of the rulers of this world hath known."

17. Expressed in the clearest manner possible, "mystery" is the reception of the things of faith—that Christ the Son of God was born of a virgin, died and rose again, and all this that our sins might be forgiven. These things eye sees not nor reason comprehends. Indeed, as Paul says (1 Cor 1, 23), they are mere foolishness to the wise, and simply an offense to the self-righteous saints.

How can the natural man perceive, or reason acknowledge, that the man Christ is our life and salvation, our peace, our righteousness and redemption, our strength and wisdom, Lord of all creatures—that he is even God—and everything else the Scriptures testify of him? None can apprehend these truths except he hears and believes them through the Gospel. They are too far beyond sense and reason to be grasped by the natural man.

18. So, then, the mysteries of God are simply the blessings in Christ as preached through the Gospel and apprehended and retained by faith alone. Paul says relative to the matter, speaking on how men should behave themselves in the house of God: "Without controversy great is the mystery of godliness; he who was manifested in the flesh, justified in the spirit, seen of angels, preached among the nations, believed on in the world, received up in glory." 1 Tim 3, 16. This is spoken of Christ, who was manifest in the flesh. He dwelt among men who had flesh and blood like himself, yet he was still a mystery. That he was Christ, the Son of God, the life, the way, the truth and all good, was hidden.

19. Yet he was "justified in the Spirit;" that is, through the Spirit's influence believers received, acknowledged and

retained him as all we have mentioned. "To justify" means simply to pronounce just, or at least to admit as just; as we have in Luke 7, 29: "All the people when they heard, and the publicans, justified God." Again, in Psalm 51, 4: "That thou mayest be justified when thou speakest." This is equivalent to saying: The believer in Christ justifies him, and acknowledges the truth that Christ alone is our life and righteousness and wisdom, and that we are sinners, condemned and perishing. For such Christ is, and such is his claim. He who acknowledges this his claim justifies him in the Spirit; but he who does not justify him relies upon his own works; he does not see himself condemned but contends against and condemns Christ. [This justification of Christ is effected by no one unless he possesses the Holy Spirit, whose work alone it is. Flesh and blood cannot do it, even if it be publicly presented to our eyes and preached into our ears.]

20. The statement in Romans 1, 4, "Christ was declared to be the Son of God with power, according to the spirit of holiness," has reference to justification. As if to say: "In unbelievers Christ is nothing; not only despised, but utterly condemned. But the saints whose life is in the Spirit who sanctifies them, strongly and boastfully maintain that he is the Son of God. To them it is proved and firmly settled."

21. Paul might have said: "We are the the stewards of the wisdom of God, or of the righteousness of God," and so on. For all this Christ is; as he says (1 Cor 1, 30): "Who was made unto us wisdom from God, and righteousness and sanctification, and redemption." But this would have been specifying, and he desired to embrace in one word all the blessings in Christ which the preaching of the Gospel brings; so he styles them "mysteries." We may understand it as if he said: "We are spiritual stewards whose duty it is to minister the grace of God, the truth of God—but who can enumerate all? Let us briefly sum them up and say, the mysteries of God; mysteries and hidden things because faith alone can attain them."

He adopts the same style in Romans 1, 4 when he comprises in one word how Christ was manifest in the flesh, justified in the Spirit, preached to the gentiles, and so on. Similarly, in First Timothy 3, 16 he expresses it briefly in Greek, "oristheis," determined. In short, Christ was declared and determined, was received and regarded, as the Son of God, by angels, gentiles, the world, heaven and all things; since for this purpose he was manifested, justified, revealed, preached, believed, received, and so on. Hence he indicates it here by the plural word "mysteries," and in First Timothy 3, 16 by the singular "mystery." The words are, however, equivalent in this connection. Christ is all in all, one mystery, and many mysteries, as expressed in the many mysterious blessings we have from him.

22. It is worthy of note that Paul adds to "mysteries" the modifier "of God;" he means the hidden things God grants and which exist in him. For the devil also has his mysteries, as Revelation 17, 5 says: "Upon her forehead a name written, Mystery, Babylon the Great," etc. And again, in the seventh verse, "I will tell thee the mystery of the woman." The things over which the Pope and his priests now preside as stewards are mysteries of the latter class; for they intimate that their doctrine and deeds win heaven, when in reality they but conceal death and hell for all who trust therein. But the mysteries of God enfold life and salvation.

23. Thus we arrive at the apostle's meaning in the assertion that a minister of Christ is a steward in the mysteries of God. He should regard himself and insist that others regard him as one who administers to the household of God nothing but Christ and the things of Christ. In other words, he should preach the pure Gospel, the true faith, that Christ alone is our life, our way, our wisdom, power, glory, salvation; and that all we can accomplish of ourselves is but death, error, foolishness, weakness, shame and condemnation. Whosoever preaches otherwise should be regarded by none as a servant of Christ or a steward of the divine treasurer; he should be avoided as a messenger of the devil. So it follows:

FAITHFULNESS IN STEWARDS.

"Moreover, it is required in stewards, that a man be found faithful."

24. Upon this all depends. After faithfulness God inquires. Angels, men and all creatures look for and demand it; not the mere name or honor of steward will answer. The question is not whether one's bishopric be large or small; nor is it particularly important whether or no he be outwardly pious. The question is, does he faithfully execute the duties of his office, acting as a steward in the blessings of God? Paul here permits us much liberty to judge the doctrines and lives of our bishops, cardinals and all Papists. The same faithfulness is also required by Christ: "Who then is the faithful and wise servant, whom his lord hath set over his household, to give them their food in due season?" Mt 24, 45.

25. What is the nature of the faithfulness of the Papists—how does it measure up? Tell me, who would be reformed or profited were any one bishop to have prominence and power enough to possess every bishopric, as the Pope tries to do? Who would be benefited if a bishop were so holy that his shadow would raise the dead? Who would be the gainer if he had wisdom equal to all the apostles and prophets? But none of these things are inquired after; the question is, Is he a faithful bishop? does he administer to the household of faith the Word of God? does he preach the Gospel and dispense the mysteries of God? Emphatically the inquiry is made upon these points. Here is where the individual is benefited. Above all things, then, faithfulness is demanded of stewards.

26. Now, measure the Pope and all the ecclesiasts by the requirements of this text. Tell me, what is the Pope seeking? Is not the sole purpose of all his grasping and raging to enable him to rule supremely and arbitrarily? His whole concern is for fame, power, position and wealth, for authority over all men. Through the Pope's blasphemous lips the devil deceitfully endeavors to emphasize the importance of obedience to popish laws, and the danger to the

soul's salvation from disobedience. The Pope is not concerned about faithfulness to the Christian household. For tell me where in all his innumerable laws and commands—a veritable flood of them—where in the whole extent of his government, did you ever learn of his touching with a single word upon the mysteries of God? or where has he preached the Gospel? All his utterances relate to quarrels, to prebends, or at best to the matter of pates and apparel. Indeed, he openly condemns the Gospel and the mysteries of God. And the bishops and ecclesiasts follow him with their endowments, cloisters and high schools.

27. They have so perverted apostolic faithfulness that with them a faithful bishop, abbot or ecclesiastical prelate is one who loyally manages, guards, improves and increases their temporal possessions—the heritage of St. Peter, the Castle of St. Moretz, the land of the holy cross, the interests of the Virgin and other concerns of the Church, in a word, their own emolument—under the name of God and of the saints; the world, even in its most sordid state, bears no comparison to them. Such are the princes, the bishops and prelates who have the credit of having governed well the Church; it matters not whether or no they have, during their whole lives, read or heard the Gospel, not to mention their disregard for their duty to preach it. The blasphemous tongue of the Pope, in its world-wide unrestraint, calls them good stewards of the blessings of God who are utterly useless, unless it be to fill the place of treasurer, assessor, guardian, bailiff, architect, mayor, plowman, butler or kitchen steward for some temporal lord. Such is their apostolic fidelity; this and nothing more.

In the meantime, souls are perishing. Divine interests are going to ruin. The wolf reigns and devours. In spiritual affairs the popish stewards see no danger and afford no security. They sit unconcernedly counting over their profits, attending to the interests of St. Laurence and with extreme faithfulness providing for the property of the Church—a faithfulness in return for which they are certain Christ has prepared for them no inferior seat in heaven. O wretched, lost, blinded multitude, how securely you are going on toward hell!

28. I cannot pass without notice here—for I must relate it as a warning against similar attempts—a trick of the devil which, I heard it said, he exhibited in time past at Merseburg, in our own country. It had to do with the golden cup of Emperor Henry. The Pope's beloved people zealously relate a certain falsehood, for which they obtain indulgences. They assert that the roasted Laurence, by casting the golden cup into the balance, got so much the better of the devil that he was forced to release the soul of the Emperor, in consequence of which he (the devil) was enraged to the extent of breaking an ear off the cup. Such gross, foolish, idle falsehoods are intended to blind us Christians from perceiving the devil's trickery. What is the devil's purpose in this fabrication? The whole thing is a design to establish by the miraculous, the wealth, luxury and delicate faithfulness of the prelates of which we have spoken. Thereby the weak-minded are to be induced to believe they can overcome the devil by presenting gifts to the Church. But Peter says this conquest is only to be effected by the power of faith. These are the signs Christ and Paul predicted would accompany the misleading of the elect from the faith.

29. A fidelity even more beautiful to contemplate exists among unspiritual lords and faithful stewards of the same class actively engaged in directing the spiritual welfare of souls. Certainly these are true stewards and the right sort! So extremely holy are they, St. Peter will have to be on his guard if he holds his place with them. They are our spiritual fathers—priests, monks and nuns—who exercise themselves in obedience to the Pope, the holy Church and every form of human institutions and orders and statutes. Among them are the paragon, the quintessence, the kernel, the marrow, the foundation—and how shall I enumerate all the honorable titles which they assume and hold from custom? Yes, far enough from custom! The beautiful little cat has pretty, smooth fur.

30. Here is where we find our good stewards and our un-

heard-of fidelity. How tenaciously, how rigorously and earnestly, they adhere to that sort of obedience and maintain those traditions. Yes, indeed, they are the proper saints. Few bishops who rigidly observe the holy, spiritual law can rank with them. But when we investigate their cloisters and review their doctrines and conduct, we find that no people on earth are less acquainted with the mysteries of God and farther from Christ. Indeed, they act as if mad, maliciously storming Christ with their own inventions. They are the Gog and Magog of the Revelation of John, contending against the Lamb of God. For they exalt their own works to the extermination of faith, and are termed the faithful stewards of God, as the wolf among the sheep is the shepherd.

31. Now, he that hath ears, let him hear what Paul says: "It is required in stewards, that a man be found faithful"; but he is faithful who is occupied with the mysteries of God. The conclusion, then, is: the Pope, the bishops, monks and nuns, the founders and inmates of universities, and all who with them build upon anything or are occupied with anything but Christ, the Gospel and true faith, though they may have indeed the name of servants and stewards of Christ, are in reality servants and stewards of the devil, their lord, and are engaged with his mysteries or secrets. Christ, in the saying we have quoted from Matthew, tells us further, the servant of the household should be not only faithful, but also wise, able to discern between the mysteries of God and the mysteries of the devil, that he may safely guard and keep himself and those committed to his care. For, as Paul says in Second Corinthians 11, 13-14, false apostles sometimes fashion themselves into true apostles of Christ, even as the devil transforms himself into an angel of light.

32. Where wisdom to discern the mysteries of God is lacking, the greater the faithfulness the greater the danger; as we perceive in the two mentioned cases of false, seductive faithfulness on the part of the unspiritual saints. Paul well knew how the mysteries of the devil would prevail; so, while silent in regard to every other qualification neces-

sary for stewards, he points out faithfulness. Had our bishops remained faithful stewards of God, popery and its peculiar spiritual orders undoubtedly would not have been introduced; the common spiritual order and life of faith would have been maintained. And were they now to return to faithfulness the strange special orders would soon pass, and the true common ones be restored.

MAN'S JUDGMENT AND GOD'S.

"But with me it is a very small thing that I should be judged of you, or of man's judgment."

33. First, we must understand Paul's language here, and explain the terms of the original, with which we need to be as familiar as with our mother tongue. He employs the word "judge," or sentence, in a worthy sense; that is, as carrying the thought of esteem. "Judgment," as generally understood, conveys the idea of condemnation. But this is true: Every public judgment operates in two ways. One party is condemned, the other liberated; one is punished, the other rewarded; one dishonored, the other honored. The same is true in private judgment. While the Pharisee in the Gospel praised himself, he censured the publican and others; while he honored himself, he dishonored others. And the attitude of everyone toward his neighbor is either praise or censure. Judgment must involve these two things. Hence, Paul here says he is judged, or sentenced, by the Corinthians; that is, their judgment renders honor and praise unto him. By extolling Paul above the other apostles, decision is made between him and the others, to his advantage and with prejudice against them. Some, however, judged in favor of Peter, others of Apollos. That "judgment" is here equivalent to "praise" is evident from the conclusion of the passage: "Judge nothing before the time, until the Lord come, then shall each man have his praise from God." What is this but saying, Praise not, let God praise? It is God's prerogative to judge, to praise and to crown man; we are not to perform that office for one another.

34. The expression "man's judgment" ("menschliche

Tag") implies that judgment of approval whereby man exalts and makes illustrious and renowned those he esteems. The thought is suggestive of the illumination or glory of day, which renders visible things unrevealed in darkness. In the Latin, illustrious people—they who are on everyone's tongue—are called "præclari," "nobiles," "illustres." In German, "durchlauchtige" stands for those of high renown, those having name and reputation superior to others. On the other hand, the unrenowned are called "obscuri," "ignobles," humiles"—insignificant, unknown, humble.

The holy Scriptures term kings and princes "doxas," "glorias," "claritates," indicative of glory, splendor and popularity. Peter (2 Pet 2, 10) says of the Pope and his adherents that they tremble not to rail at glories. That means they will curse dignitaries—kings, princes, and all exalted in earthly glory; this when Christ has commanded us to love our enemies, to bless them that curse us, to do good to our persecutors. We see how the Pope defames on Maundy-Thursday in the "Bulla Cænae Domini"; and, indeed, whenever it pleases him.

35. Man's judgment, then, is expressed in the clamor and ostentation men make before the world. Jeremiah says (ch 17, 16), "Neither have I desired the woeful day; thou knowest." In other words, "They accuse me of preaching new doctrines solely to gain a name, and honor and praise before men; to win their esteem. But thou knowest it is not so; I have not sought such honor and praise." Christ says (Jn 5, 41), "I receive not glory from men." That is, "I do not desire men to laud and extol me." And (Jn 8, 50), "I seek not mine own glory." Again (Jn 5, 35), speaking of John the Baptist, "Ye were willing to rejoice for a season in his light." The meaning is, "It would have pleased you to have John's testimony contribute to your honor and praise; you would have liked to enjoy for a short season the esteem of the people. This is what you sought."

36. Paul regards it a very trivial matter to command the clamorous honor and praise of men, to gain a reputation with them. He aptly calls such popularity "man's judg-

ment," or human glory. For it is of human origin and not directed of God; and, with men, it shall pass. Paul would say: "I do not desire your praise, nor the praise of all the world." Let men seek for that. Servants of Christ and stewards of God look to Christ and to a divine glory for their judgment.

37. But the apostle surely manifests ingratitude in not sending the Corinthians a bagful of bulls or letters; in not blessing them nor distributing indulgences among them in recognition of their great honoring of the apostolic see. The Pope would have conducted himself in a manner much more worthy of an apostle. Yes, indeed; he would have anathematized them had they not illumined him with the glory of their judgment. He would have said, "I am a Papist; the Pope is the highest, the holiest, the mightiest." Had Paul so desired he might have become pope, might have held supremacy; he had but to utter a single word. He had only to receive them who desired to join themselves to him; the others would have been obliged to yield. But in his stewardship he strove for faithfulness rather than for exaltation. Hence he had to remain a common tent-maker and to travel on foot.

38. From this verse, clearly the Corinthians judged with distinction of persons, preferring that baptism and Gospel which they had themselves received. They intimated that Paul, or Peter, or Apollos, was supreme. This Paul could not admit. He holds the apostles equal, whatever their individualities. He who is baptized and taught by Paul is as much a Christian as one baptized and taught of Peter, or Apollos, or anyone else. In opposition to this teaching, the Pope fiercely rants, admitting no one a Christian unless instructed of himself. At the same time he teaches mere infidelity and the foolish works of men.

39. Now, Paul condemns undue respect of persons, and in the matter of stewardship for God is concerned only about faithfulness. By these very teachings, he removes every reason for divisions; his Church cannot be disunited, but must remain harmonious, allowing equality in all things.

How can there be divisions when one minister of Christ is like another, when he is equally a steward of God? So long as there is no difference in privilege, even if one does exceed another in faithfulnss, it will not create sects; it will only publish the common Gospel with greater efficiency.

40. Paul's words have reference not to one apostle only, but to every apostle. He does not say, "Let a man so account of me," but "Let a man so account of us;" of "us," mark you. Who is meant by "us"? Himself, Peter, Apollos—they about whom the matter arose. The conclusion necessarily is that Peter and Paul are to be considered equal. Then either Paul's teaching is wrong when he regards all apostles equal servants of Christ and stewards of God, or the claims and proceedings of the Pope must be false and this text a powerful enemy of popedom.

"Yea, I judge not mine own self."

41. You may inquire how it is that Paul should look upon his own judgment of himself as truer than the judgment of any other; for we see how the majority of men praise or highly approve themselves. Naturally one is pleased with himself, but few receive the glory of "man's judgment"—are honored in the sentence of others. We might expect Paul to reverse the statement, saying: "With me it is a very small thing that I should judge myself; I desire neither this human glory of man's judgment, nor the praise of yourselves or of all the world." But he speaks, rather, as a Christian and according to the state of his own conscience before God. The Corinthians exalted Paul in the things acceptable to God. They insisted he was higher, greater and better before God than the other apostles; but certain other Christians extolled Peter.

Now, there is with God no better evidence of the soul's condition than what the conscience reveals. God judges not, like men, according to appearance, but according to the heart; as we learn from First Samuel 16, 7: "Man looketh on the outward appearance, but Jehovah looketh on the heart." So it is plain the evidence of our consciences is of greater weight before God than the testimony of all the world. And this evidence alone will stand; as said in Romans 2, 15: "Their conscience bearing witness therewith, and their thoughts one with another accusing or else excusing them; in the day when God shall judge the secrets of men."

42. Paul would ask: "Why should divisions arise among you concerning us? What if one is preferred of men before another? It is altogether immaterial. For even our own consciences refrain from judging as to who ranks first in God's sight." Solomon says, "He that trusteth in his own heart is a fool." Prov. 28, 26. There are no grounds for divisions. No one knows who ranks first with God. Christ himself does not claim the right to set one soul on the right hand and the other on the left. Mt 20, 23. Since all the apostles are alike before God, since one is a minister of Christ as well as another, and since we may not know who ranks first in God's estimation, let no one presume to judge, much less to exalt himself above another because of temporal power, wealth or popularity. The exaltation of the Pope and the claim that his eminence is from God is in violation of this principle; Paul's words dispute it, teaching that no one is able to know nor judge until the last day.

43. But here the keen tongues of the Papists seek to effect a breach. They assume that Paul does not deny the supremacy of Peter, or of the Pope, but forbids judgment of the person himself as to how good or bad he is in God's sight. I admit that Paul does forbid such judgment, nevertheless the design of the Corinthians for which he rebukes them was to exalt the office, the baptism and the doctrine, wholly because of the person; otherwise they would not have said, "I am a good follower of Paul," "I am a good follower of Peter," and so on. Well they knew that doctrine, baptism and office were the same with all the apostles, but their object was to exalt the office and its efficacy with the standing of the individual. Paul, however, takes the opposite stand; he assumes equality of office upon the very ground of equality of individuals in man's sight, since none can know another's standing before God. Had the Corin-

thians desired to exalt the individual only, and not the office, they would not have created sects and said, "I am of Paul," etc. Just as we may hold St. Peter holier in person than St. Augustine and yet not cause division thereby. But it is creating sects for one to say, "I am of Peter," and another, "I am of Augustine," meaning, "The doctrine taught me is superior to what is taught you."

44. The hypocritical Papists, being well aware that their false claim for the supremacy of the Pope cannot stand unless backed by his personal holiness, proceed to bolster up that falsehood by a greater one. They endeavor to give him the reputation of personal goodness by saying he cannot err, for the Holy Spirit never forsakes him, and Christ is ever with and in him. Some of them, knowing the absurdity of denying that the Pope does openly sin, are so bold in their blasphemous utterances as to declare it is impossible for him to remain in mortal sins for a quarter of an hour. Thus accurately have they measured with hour-glass and compasses the extent of the Holy Spirit's presence in the Pope. Why do they tell such blasphemous falsehoods? Doubtless because they are aware of the futility of attempting to maintain supremacy without personal goodness; they would be compelled to admit that exaltation without piety must be of the devil. It cannot be said the Corinthians exalted the person independently of the office; it was because of his office.

45. Do you ask further concerning Paul, who desired to be regarded a minister of Christ and a steward of God, Why did he not judge himself? I reply: As before stated, the ministry and the office are not his but God's, who enjoined them upon him. As no man can create the Word of God, so no man has authority to send it forth, or constitute an apostle. God has himself accomplished the work; he has constituted the apostles. Hence we should own the work, glory in it, confess it, and give to publish abroad the news of the priceless blessing the one God has bestowed. To illustrate: Though I cannot constitute myself a living soul, I ought to glory in and confess the fact that God has created

me a human being. But just as I am incapable of judging how I stand and will stand in the sight of God, so I cannot judge which apostle or steward is greatest before God.

46. But you object: You teach, however, that a Christian should not doubt his acceptance with God, and he that doubts is no Christian; for faith assures that God is our Father and that as we believe so shall it be unto us. I reply: Indeed, I would have you hold fast the assurance of faith in the grace of God; faith is simply a steadfast, indubitable, sure confidence in divine grace. But this is what I say: the Corinthians' intent was to judge the apostles by their personal goodness and works, that according to one's holiness, rank and merit might his office be exalted and his followers secure some honor above others. But Paul overthrows all works and merit, leaving them to God's judgment, and places every apostle in the same rank as to office and faith. They fill one and the same office and are justified by one and the same faith. The question of who ranks first in goodness, position, merit and achievement must be left to God; it is not an occasion for divisions in the community. Hence follows:

"For I know nothing against myself; yet am I not hereby justified."

47. This verse also implies that the Corinthians judged the apostles in regard to the worthiness of person and works; Paul admits his conscience does not reproach him, and confesses to the truth of their judgment so far as his person and conscience are concerned. But, he teaches that such judgment does not suffice before God; and that all decisions based on the same principle are false.

48. Much might be said on this verse. It shows us all works are rejected and no one is made godly and happy by any of them. The fact that Paul dared say "I know nothing against myself" proves him certainly to have abounded in good works; nevertheless he says, "I am not hereby justified." By what is he justified, then? By faith alone. Could one be justified upon the grounds of a clear conscience —knowing nothing against himself—his confidence would

rest in himself. He could judge and extol his own character, as do presumptuous saints. Then faith and God's grace would be unnecessary; we would have in ourselves all essentials and could easily dispense with God. The fact is, however, all depends on our reliance upon the grace of God. Thereby are we justified. The subsequent judgment of our works and character, of our calling and worthiness, must be left to God. We are certain we are vindicated by none of these things, and uncertain how God will estimate them.

49. It is easily evident to all, I presume, that Paul refers to his character after conversion when he says he knows nothing against himself; for, concerning his previous life, he tells us (1 Tim 1, 13) he was an unbeliever, a blasphemer and a persecutor of the first Christians.

50. The question, however, arises, How can it be that he is not justified by his clear conscience when he declares (2 Cor 1, 12): "For our glorying is this, the testimony of our conscience, that in holiness and sincerity of God, not in fleshly wisdom but in the grace of God, we behaved ourselves in the world, and more abundantly to you-ward"? This quotation contains the answer. The words, "in the grace of God," give it. We are indeed to rejoice in the grace of God, to boast of and glory in it; since it is founded upon the glorying of our conscience. Even had not these words been included, it must necessarily be understood that reference is to the glorying in grace or else to honor before the world.

It is the privilege and the duty of everyone to acknowledge before men his innocence, to rejoice in having injured no one. And he should not call evil what he knows to be good. At the same time such glorying avails nothing before God; he must judge the heart, though men are satisfied with deeds. Before God, then, something more than a good conscience is necessary. Moses says (Ex 34, 7), "Forgiving iniquity and transgression and sin; and that will by no means clear the guilty." We read (Rom 3, 27), "Where then is the glorying?" And again (1 Cor 1, 31),

"He that glorieth, let him glory in the Lord"; that is, in his grace.

"But he that judgeth me is the Lord."

51. The thought here is, "I will wait for God's judgment and praise." Paul says also (2 Cor. 10, 18), "For not he that commendeth himself is approved, but whom the Lord commendeth." His intent, however, is not to deter them from godly living but rather to incite thereto. Although no man is capable of judging and commending another, yet none shall go unjudged and uncommended. God himself will judge and praise right living. We should be so much the more faithful in doing good because God is to be judge; we are not to be remiss here even though uncertain as to how he judges us.

> "Wherefore judge nothing before the time, until the Lord come, who will both bring to light the hidden things of darkness, and make manifest the counsels of the hearts; and then shall each man have praise of God."

52. We may well ask, Are we not to give praise to one another? Paul says (Rom 12, 10), "In love of the brethren be tenderly affectioned one to another." And Christ (Mt 5, 16): "Even so let your light shine before men; that they may see your good works, and glorify your Father who is in heaven." And the apostle also tells us (2 Cor 6, 8) we must here upon earth walk "by evil report and good report." But, we reply our faith alone, not our works, is the chief thing to be honored in all cases. Good works are imperative, and we should extol them in others; but no one is to be judged, justified or preferred because of them. The farmer at his plow sometimes may be better in God's sight than the chaste nun.

53. The five foolish virgins (Mt 25, 2), despite their virginity, are condemned. The widow who threw into the treasury two mites (Mk 12, 42) did more than all the others who cast in much greater amounts. The work of the woman who was a sinner (Lk 7, 37) is extolled above any work of the Pharisees. It is impossible for us mortals to discern

the relative merits of individuals and the value of their works; we ought to praise all, giving equal honors and not preferring one above another. We should humble ourselves before one another, ever esteeming our neighbor above ourselves. Then we are to leave it to God to judge who ranks first. True, he has declared that whoever humbles himself shall be exalted, yet it is not evident who humbles and who exalts himself; for the heart, by which God judges, is not manifest. One may humble himself when secretly in his heart he is haughty, and again the meek-hearted may exalt himself.

54. So Paul says: "The Lord comes, who will both bring to light the hidden things of darkness, and make manifest the counsels of the hearts." Then it will appear who is really worthier, superior and better, and whose works excel.

55. It is most unchristianlike to base our estimation of one upon his outward appearance and visible works; to say, for instance, that the Carthusian leads a life essentially better than the farmer, or than any married man. Indeed, the Carthusian if he does right will esteem his own life inferior to that of the married man. For God judges not according to outward expression, but according to the secrets of darkness and the counsels of the heart, and how can the Carthusian know which is the humbler and holier, his own heart or the farmer's?

56. Applicable here are two instances, in my opinion the best in all the "Lives of the Fathers." One is of St. Anthony, to whom it was revealed that a tanner at Alexandria, a humble, honest mechanic, but one in no wise illustrious, was far superior to the saint because of his humility of heart. The other relates to Paphnutio, who, despite all his austerity of life, was not superior to a fifer nor to either of two married women. It was a special manifestation of grace that God revealed these two incidents at a time when monastic life was most intense, and works prodigious. His purpose was to deter us from judging by outward appear-

ances—by works—and to teach us to value all works alike and to prefer others above ourselves.

57. Now you will say: If all stations are alike and all works of the same value, none to have preference, what advantage is it to us to forsake the world and enter the holiest orders, to become monks, nuns and priests, in the effort to serve God? I reply: Did not Christ and Paul foretell that false Christs and prophets should arise and deceive many? Had the doctrine of equal service to God under all conditions and in all works continued to stand, certainly no monasteries and cloisters would have been established—or at least they would not have increased so rapidly—to create the illusion that service to God consists only in meeting their requirements. Who would have become a priest, who a monk, yes, who a pope and bishop, had he realized that in such capacity his position and its works are no more meritorious than those of the poorest nurse maid who rocks children and washes swaddling clothes?

It would grievously distress, yes, and shame, the Pope had he to humble himself to a nurse maid, esteeming his works inferior to hers—he whose position and works are so meritorious that kings, and even God's saints, are scarce worthy to kiss his feet. The holy Papists, then, must institute something superior to Paul's teaching here. They are compelled to judge themselves, and to proclaim their position and works supreme, else they cannot sell their merits and procure heaven for poor laymen, married persons and individuals in various stations, implying that these do not in their lives serve God.

58. Now, seeing how impossible it is for the present ecclesiastical order to stand unless it disposes of this passage from Paul and exalts its religious life with distinction above that of other Christians, it is certainly clear enough that popery, with its monasteries and cloisters, is based on mere falsehoods and blasphemies. The Papists style themselves "ecclesiastical" or "spiritual" and others "secular," when God sees none as ecclesiasts or churchmen, but as believers; and believers are found for the most part not among the

clergy but among the laity. What greater deception than to call the clerical order spiritual, and to separate it from the class among whom true spiritual life exists? God alone is to judge who is holiest and best. The clerical order assumes the title "spiritual" simply because they have shaved heads and wear long cloaks. What folly—even insanity!

59. You will say: If this be true, it were better for us to leave the cloisters and monasteries. I reply: There are but two things for you. Follow the teaching of this lesson, commending not yourselves. Regard your order and station no better than as if you were not an ecclesiastic, and your chastity not superior to that of an honest, loyal wife and mother; if you are not willing so to humble your ecclesiasticism, then discard caps, bald pates, cloisters and all. Either adopt this course or know that your ecclesiasticism, your spirituality, has its origin, not with a good spirit, but with an evil spirit. You will never overthrow Paul's doctrine here. It is better to be a mother among the common believers in Christ than to remain a virgin in the devil's cause. Paul stands firm on the point that we must not judge ourselves.

60. But you will loudly object: Jerome and many others have highly commended virginity; and Paul, too (1 Cor 7, 38), teaches it is better to be a virgin than to marry. I answer: Let Jerome be here or there, Augustine here or Ambrose there, you have learned what God here says through Paul, that no one shall judge himself or anyone else to be best. God's command should have more weight than the sayings of many Jeromes, were they as numerous as the sand grains upon the seashore or the leaves of the forest. True, Paul says it is better to be continent than to marry, but he does not say "in God's sight." If he did, it would be a contradiction of his words here. He who lives continently, it is true, is freer to publish the Gospel than the married man; and it was with the thought of Gospel furtherance that Paul applauded virginity, or continence. He says: "He that is unmarried is careful for the things of the Lord." 1 Cor. 7, 32.

Christ also applauds the eunuchs (Mt 19, 12), not for the sake of their condition but for the sake of their profit to the kingdom of heaven; that is, for the sake of their furtherance of the Gospel. Now, although none cares less for the Gospel than do these ecclesiasts, they continue to exalt their position above that of others, and to extol continence for the mere sake of the merit in denial, not for the end it serves. To illustrate the advantage of continence: It is better to learn a trade than to be a servant; and why? Not because it is a condition more acceptable to God, but because it offers less hindrances to his service. It is in this light that Paul applauds virginity and continence; but only in those who have a desire for it through the grace of God.

61. At present no one cares whether continence is a help or a hindrance; everyone plunges into it, thinking only of how exalted, worthy and great it makes them. All is done with such pains and danger, unwillingness and impurity, that an adequate cry and protest cannot be raised against the evil. Still they wish to be better than other people. Thus they have brought such reproach upon the marriage state that it is considered an impure and disgraceful life. As a reward God permits their continence to pollute their garments and beds continually. Really there is no greater or more polluted incontinence than theirs, inordinate, imprisoned, restrained and intolerable as it is.

"Bring to light the hidden things of darkness, and make manifest the counsels of the hearts."

62. Paul gives the reason we should refrain from commending ourselves or any other when he declares that the hidden things of darkness and the counsels of the hearts are not yet brought to light. Since God judges according to the secrets of the heart which we cannot know, we should withhold judgment of the various stations and works of men, and not make distinction. The virgin is not to exalt her state of virginity above the station of the wife. The Pope ought to humble his eminence below the position of the plow-boy. No one should presume to regard his own station, or that of another, as better before God than the occupations of other men.

63. Every person should be free to choose and live in the state that suits him, all being alike until the Lord comes. But, were this principle to be carried out where would the holy fathers and the spiritual lords obtain their daily bread, not being accustomed to labor? They secure their subsistence by making the impression that the common man is in error and by separating from him their states and position. They judge themselves to be the best people, confident of enjoying the common man's treasures, because his state is nothing. Hence arise so many institutions, and gifts flow to the cloisters, chapels and churches for the especial benefit of these idle, beloved gluttons and gormandizers. All this would fall were Paul's teachings introduced.

64. By the "hidden things of darkness" and the "counsels of the hearts" Paul refers to the two powers commonly but not very intelligibly termed "will" and "reason." Man possesses in his inmost being two capacities: he loves, delights, desires, wills; and he understands, perceives, judges, decides. I shall term these capacities "motive" and "thought."

65. The motives and desires of man are deep and deceitful beyond recognition; no saint, even, can wholly comprehend them. Jeremiah says (ch. 17, 9-10): "The heart is deceitful above all things, and it is exceedingly corrupt: who can know it? I, Jehovah, search the mind, I try the heart." And David (Ps 32, 2): "Blessed is the man in whose spirit there is no guile."

Many pious individuals perform great works from a selfish motive or desire. They seek their own interests, yet never with assurance. They serve God not purely for love of him, but for the sake of personal honor or profit; of gaining heaven and escaping the tortures of hell. One cannot realize the falseness of his motives until God permits him to endure many severe temptations. So Paul calls such motives "hidden things of darkness," a most appropriate name. Not only are they concealed, but in darkness, in the inmost heart, where they are unperceived by the individual himself and known to God alone.

66. Remembering this deplorable secret motive of the heart, we should be induced to submit ourselves one to another and not to contrast any particular work or station with others. The motive determines the force and judgment of every work, every station, of all conduct, of every life. As solomon says (Prov 16, 2): "Jehovah weigheth the spirits"—God is the weigh-master of the spirits. Since there may be something of good concealed in the secret heart of the wife and likewise something of evil in the virgin's heart, it is absurd and unchristian to exalt a virgin above a wife because of her continence, a purely external virtue. It is just as unreasonable to measure the two by their external life as to compare the weight of eggs by putting the shells into the balance and leaving out the contents.

67. Now, according to our secret motives so are our thoughts—good or evil. Our motives and desires control our aims, decisions and reasonings. These latter Paul terms "counsels of the heart"—the thoughts we arrive at in consequence of our secret motives and desires.

68. Of these two, Mary hints in her song of praise (Lk 1, 51): "He hath scattered the proud in the imagination of their heart." She calls intent or motive of the heart the "hidden things of darkness"—her desire, while the "counsels" and imaginations are the heart's expression. Moses, referring to man's heart, says (Gen 6, 5): "Every imagination of the thoughts of his heart was only evil continually." And Christ (Mt 6, 22-23) earnestly warns us against the same false motive: "The lamp of the body is the eye: if therefore thine eye be single, thy whole body shall be full of light. But if thine eye be evil, thy whole body shall be full of darkness. If therefore the light that is in thee be darkness, how great is the darkness!" The reference in this whole quotation is to the secret workings of darkness, which are not to be overcome in any way but by despair of our own works, and strong faith in the pure grace of God. Nothing is more conducive to this end than sufferings severe and many, and all manner of misfortunes. Under such influences man may learn, to some extent, to know himself; otherwise all is lost.

Fourth Sunday in Advent

Epistle Text: Philippians 4, 4-7.

4 Rejoice in the Lord always: again I will say, Rejoice. 5 Let your forbearance be known unto all men.
The Lord is at hand. 6 In nothing be anxious; but in
everything by prayer and supplication with thanksgiving let your requests be made known unto God. 7 And
the peace of God, which passeth all understanding, shall
guard your hearts and your thoughts in Christ Jesus.

1. The text, though short, is a suggestive and important lesson in Christian faith. It teaches how we should conduct ourselves toward God and our neighbor. It says:

"Rejoice in the Lord always."

OUR CONDUCT TOWARD GOD—REJOICE IN HIM.

2. Joy is the natural fruit of faith. The apostle says elsewhere (Gal 5, 22-23): "The fruit of the Spirit is love, joy, peace, longsuffering, kindness, goodness, faithfulness, meekness, self-control." Until the heart believes in God, it is impossible for it to rejoice in him. When faith is lacking, man is filled with fear and gloom and is disposed to flee at the very mention, the mere thought, of God. Indeed, the unbelieving heart is filled with enmity and hatred against God. Conscious of its own guilt, it has no confidence in his gracious mercy; it knows God is an enemy to sin and will terribly punish the same.

3. Since there exist in the heart these two things—a consciousness of sin and a perception of God's chastisement—the heart must ever be depressed, faint, even terrified. It must be continually apprehensive that God stands behind

ready to chastise. Solomon says (Prov 28, 1), "The wicked flee when no man pursueth." And Deuteronomy 28, 65-66 reads, "Jehovah will give thee there a trembling heart . . . . and thy life shall hang in doubt." One may as well try to persuade water to burn as to talk to such a heart of joy in God. All words will be without effect, for the sinner feels upon his conscience the pressure of God's hand. The prophet's injunction (Ps 32, 11) likewise is: "Be glad in Jehovah, and rejoice, ye righteous; and shout for joy, all ye that are upright in heart." It must be the just and the righteous who are to rejoice in the Lord. This text, therefore, is written, not for the sinner, but for the saint. First we must tell sinners how they can be liberated from their sins and perceive a merciful God. When they have been released from the power of an evil conscience, joy will result naturally.

4. But how shall we be liberated from an accusing conscience and receive the assurance of God's mercy? The question has been sufficiently answered in the preceding postils, and will be again frequently satisfied later on. He who would have a quiet conscience, and would be sensitive of God's mercy, must not, like the apostates, depend on works, still further doing violence to the heart and increasing its hatred of God. He must place no hope whatever in works; must apprehend God in Christ, comprehend the Gospel and believe its promises.

5. But what does the Gospel promise other than that Christ is given for us; that he bears our sins; that he is our Bishop, Mediator, and Advocate before God, and that thus only through him and his work is God reconciled, are our sins forgiven and our consciences set free and made glad? When this sort of faith in the Gospel really exists in the heart, God is recognized as favorable and pleasing. The heart confidently feels his favor and grace, and only these. It fears not God's chastisement. It is secure and in good spirit because God has conferred upon it, through Christ, superabundant goodness and grace. Essentially, the fruits of such a faith are love, peace, joy, and songs of thanksgiv-

ing and praise. It will enjoy unalloyed and sincere pleasure in God as its supremely beloved and gracious Father, a Father whose attitude toward itself has been wholly paternal, and who, without any merit on its part, has richly poured out upon that heart his goodness.

6. Such is the rejoicing, mark you, of which Paul here speaks—a rejoicing where is no sin, no fear of death or hell, but rather a glad and all-powerful confidence in God and his kindness. Hence the expression, "Rejoice in the Lord"; not rejoice in silver or gold, not in eating or drinking, not in pleasure or mechanical chanting, not in strength or health, not in skill or wisdom, not in power or honor, not in friendship or favor, nay, not in good works or holiness even. For these are deceptive joys, false joys, which never stir the depths of the heart. They are never even felt. When they are present we may well say the individual rejoices superficially, and without a heart experience.

To rejoice in the Lord—to trust, confide, glory and have pride in the Lord as in a gracious Father—this is a joy which rejects all else but the Lord, including that self-righteousness whereof Jeremiah speaks (ch. 9, 23-24): "Let not the wise man glory in his wisdom, neither let the mighty man glory in his might, let not the rich man glory in his riches; but let him that glorieth glory in this, that he hath understanding, and knoweth me." Again, Paul enjoins (2 Cor 10, 17), "He that glorieth, let him glory in the Lord."

7. The apostle further commands in our text to rejoice "always." Thus he rebukes those who rejoice in God—who praise and thank him—only a portion of the time. These rejoice when it is well with them; when not, rejoicing ceases. Concerning them Psalm 48 teaches, they will praise God when he favors them. David does not so. He declares (Ps 34, 1): "I will bless Jehovah at all times; his praise shall continually be in my mouth." And David has good reason to do so, for who will harm or distress one favored of God? Sin harms him not; nor death nor hell. David sings (Ps 23, 4): "Yea, though I walk through the valley of the shadow of death, I will fear no evil." And Paul

queries (Rom 8, 35): "Who shall separate us from the love of Christ? shall tribulation, or anguish, or persecution, or famine, or nakedness, or peril, or sword?" And then he goes on (verses 38-39): "For I am persuaded, that neither death, nor life, nor angels, nor principalities, nor things present, nor things to come, nor powers, nor height, nor depth, nor any other creature, shall be able to separate us from the love of God, which is in Christ Jesus our Lord."

"Again I will say, Rejoice."

8. The apostle emphasizes his admonition by repeating it. It is essential that we rejoice. Paul, recognizing that we live in the midst of sin and evil, both which things depress, would fortify us with cheer. Thus rejoicing, even if we should sometimes fall into sin, our joy in God will exceed our sorrow in sin. The natural accompaniment of sin truly is fear and a burdened conscience, and we cannot always escape sin. Therefore we should let joy have rule, let Christ be greater than our sins. John says (1 Jn 2, 1-2): "If any man sin, we have an Advocate with the Father, Jesus Christ the righteous; and he is the propitiation for our sins." Again (1 Jn 3, 20): "Because if our heart condemn us, God is greater than our heart, and knoweth all things."

OUR CONDUCT TO MAN—FORBEARANCE.

"Let your forbearance [moderation] be known unto all men."

9. Having instructed the Corinthians concerning their conduct toward God—their duty to serve him with joyful hearts—Paul proceeds briefly to teach them how to conduct themselves before men, saying, "Let your moderation be known unto all men." In other words: Rejoice always before God, but before men be forbearing. Direct your life so as to do and suffer everything not contrary to the commandments of God, that you may make yourselves universally agreeable. Not only refrain from offending any, but put the best possible construction upon the conduct of others. Aim to be clearly recognized as men indifferent to circumstances, as content whether you be hit or missed, and holding to no privilege at all liable to bring you into

conflict or produce discord. With the rich be rich; with the poor, poor. Rejoice with the joyful, weep with the mourning. Finally, be all things to all men, compelling them to confess you always agreeable, uniformly pleasant to mankind and on a level with everyone.

10. Such is the meaning of the little word here employed by the apostle—"epiikia," equity, clemency, accommodation—and which we cannot better render than by "moderation" or "forbearance." It is the virtue of adapting or accommodating oneself to another; of endorsing that other; of making all equal; of presenting a like attitude toward all men; not setting oneself up as a model and pattern; not desiring mankind to do homage to one, to conform to one's position. Justice may be classified as severe and mild. Too severe justice is often mitigated, and that is the equity, the moderation and clemency of the law. The Latin translator has rendered our word "modestiam," "moderation." This word would properly convey the thought were it not generally understood in its relation to eating, drinking and dressing. Here the intent is to indicate that moderation of life which adjusts and adapts self to the abilities and circumstances of others, yielding, commending, following, mitigating, doing, allowing, forbearing, according as one recognizes what the capacity and condition of a neighbor demands, even to the disparagement of one's own honor and life, and the detriment of his possessions.

11. For the sake of a better understanding, let us illustrate: Paul says (1 Cor 9, 19-22): "For though I was free from all men, I brought myself under bondage to all, that I might gain the more. And to the Jews I became as a Jew, that I might gain Jews; to them that are under the law, as under the law, not being myself under the law, that I might gain them that are under the law; to them that are without law, as without law, not being without law to God, but under law to Christ, that I might gain them that are without law . . . I am become all things to all men, that I may by all means save some." That is, Paul ate and drank with the Jews according to the law, and generally conducted him-

self in harmony with its requirements; though he was not obliged so to do. He also ate and drank with the gentiles regardless of the law, and conducted himself without respect to its requirements and as the custom of the gentiles. For only faith and love are requisite. All else man is free to omit or to observe. Therefore, for the sake of one, all laws may be observed; for another, omitted. Observance must be adapted to the individual case.

Now, suppose some blind, capricious individual intrudes, demanding as necessary the omission of this thing and the observance of that, as did certain Jews, and insisting that all men follow him and he none—this would be to destroy equality; indeed, even to exterminate Christian liberty and faith. Like Paul, in the effort to maintain liberty and truth, everyone should refuse to yield to any such demand.

12. To illustrate further: Christ suffered his disciples to break the Sabbath—and himself frequently broke it—where necessary (Mt 12 and Mark 2); but where necessity did not require otherwise, he observed the day. He assigned as reason for his conduct, "The Son of man is lord even of the sabbath." Mk 2, 28. That is, the law of the Sabbath permits freedom; for the sake of extending love and service to one, it may be broken; and to another, it may be observed.

13. Because of the Jews, Luke says, Paul circumcised Timothy. But he would not permit Titus to be circumcised for the very reason that false brethren insisted upon it and were unwilling to concede it a matter of choice. Paul claimed authority both to observe circumcision and not to observe it, according as would best contribute to the benefit of others. He deemed neither one course nor the other necessary. He did not believe in circumcision for the sake of the work itself—as a thing which must be performed.

14. But to make the application to ourselves: When the Pope commands us to confess, to receive the sacrament, to fast, to eat fish, or to perform any bidding of his, and insists that we must do these things because the Church requires it of us, we should calmly trample upon his in-

junctions, doing what is directly opposed, simply to defy him and maintain liberty. But when he does not insist upon these things, we should honor his desire by observing with observers and omitting with those who omit, presenting Christ's testimony, "The Son of man is lord even of the sabbath," and declaring him much more Lord of human laws. To exercise our liberty in the observance of these commands, works no harm to faith nor to the Gospel; but to observe them by a forced act of obedience, destroys faith and the Gospel.

15. The same rule applies to all external institutions and ordinances, as monastic vows and rules. They are in themselves but a matter of choice and are not opposed to faith or love. We should maintain the privilege of observing them in love and liberty, for the sake of our associates—to preserve harmony with them. But when it is insisted that certain ordinances must be honored, that their observance is an act of obedience essential to salvation, we should forsake cloisters, tonsures, caps, vows and rules, and even take the opposite course, by way of testifying that only faith and love are the Christian essentials and it is our privilege to observe or omit all other things, being controlled by love and our associations. To conform to laws in a spirit of love and liberty works no harm, but to conform through necessity and forced obedience is to be condemned. Let this rule apply to ceremonials, hymns, prayers and all other Cathedral ordinances, so long as they are observed as a matter of love and liberty alone. Only for the service and for the enjoyment of the assembled company are they to be observed, and that when they are works not in themselves evil. When urged as inherently essential, we are to refrain; we must oppose them in order to maintain the liberty of faith.

16. Herein you see the diabolical character of the papal institutions, cloisters, in fact all popedom. For they simply make a matter of liberty and love one of necessity and forced obedience, whereby the Gospel, faith included, is exterminated, not to mention the consequent wretchedness of the

common people who submit to obey for the sake of their appetites. For how many now attend the choral ceremonies and pray specified hours for God's sake? A general destruction of cloisters and other institutions would be the best reformation in this respect. They are of no benefit to Christianity and might easily be dispensed with. Before liberty could be established in one such institution, a hundred thousand souls might be lost in the others. When a thing is not beneficial and serves no purpose, but does unspeakable injury, and is beyond remedy, it is much better to utterly exterminate it.

17. But again, when civil government enjoins laws and demands tribute, we should freely serve, even though we are constrained. In this case our liberty and faith are not endangered. For civil government does not claim that observance of its laws is essential to salvation, but essential to civil dominion and protection. In submitting to it, then, conscience maintains its liberty, and faith is not impaired. To whatever does not do violence to our faith, and benefits others, we should fully conform. But when it is insisted that observation of any material laws is essential to salvation, our course of action should be the same as that already suggested relative to the laws of the Pope and the cloisters.

18. Now, the illustrations given serve as examples to follow in every instance. As Paul here teaches, let one put himself on an equality with all men, being not content to consider simply his own claims and rights, but the wishes and well-being of others. Paul has here in a single word set aside all rights. If your neighbor's condition really demands that you yield a certain personal right or privilege, and you insist upon that privilege, you act at variance with the principle of love and equality and are indeed blameworthy. For in yielding you sustain no injury to your faith, and your neighbor is profited. You would desire him to do thus unto you—a principle of natural law

Indeed, we further add, in the event of one working you harm or injury, you are to put the best construction upon his act, excusing it in the spirit of that holy martyr who, when all his possessions were taken from him, said, "Truly, they can never take Christ from me." Say you likewise: "His act injures not my faith; why not excuse him? why not submit, and accommodate myself to him?"

19. I cannot better illustrate than by citing the conduct of two good friends, whose manner toward each other may serve as an example for us in our conduct toward all men. How did they act? Each did what pleased his fellow. Each yielded, submitted, suffered, wrought and accepted, just in accordance with his conception of what might profit or please the other, and all voluntarily, without constraint. Each adapted and accommodated himself to his friend, never from any selfish motive offering restraint. If one infringed upon the other's property rights, he was kindly excused. In short, in their case was neither law, demand, restraint, nor fear; naught but perfect freedom and good will. Yet all things moved in a harmony the hundredth part of which could not be secured by any laws or restraints.

20. The headstrong and the unyielding, they who excuse none but are determined to control all things by their own wisdom, lead the whole world into error. They are the cause of all the wars and calamities known on earth. Yet they claim justice as their sole motive. Well has it been said by a certain heathen: "Summum jus, summa injustitia"—the most extreme justice is the greatest injustice. Ecclesiastes 7, 16 also warns: "Be not righteous overmuch; neither make thyself overwise." As the most extreme justice is the greatest injustice, so the most extreme wisdom is the greatest folly. The old adage is, "When the wise act the fool, they are grossly foolish." Were God always to execute extreme justice, we could not live a moment. Paul commends gentleness in Christ (2 Cor 10, 1), saying, "I . . . entreat you by the meekness and gentleness of Christ." So we are to moderate our attitude, our demands, our wisdom and wit, adapting ourselves to the circumstances of others in all respects.

21. Observe the beautiful aptness of the words, "Let your forbearance be known unto all men." You may ask:

"How can one become known to all men? And must we boast of our forbearance, proclaiming it to everyone?" God forbid the latter. Paul does not say, boast of and proclaim your forbearance. He says, let it be experimentally known by all men. That is, exercise forbearance in your deeds before men; not think or speak of it, but show it in your conduct. Thus men generally must see and grasp it—must have experience of it. Then no one can do otherwise than admit you are forbearing. Actual experience will defeat every desire to speak of you in any other way. The mouth of the fault-finder will be stopped by the fact that all men know your forbearance. Christ says (Mt 5, 16): "Even so let your light so shine before men; that they may see your good works, and glorify your Father who is in heaven." And Peter (1 Pet 2, 12): "Having your behavior seemly among the Gentiles; that, wherein they speak against you as evil-doers, they may by your good works, which they behold, glorify God in the day of visitation." It lies not in our power to make our moderation acceptable to all men, but it is enough for us to give everyone opportunity to perceive it in our lives.

22. By the phrase "all men" we are not to understand all individuals on earth, but every sort of person—friends and foes, great and humble, lords and servants, rich and poor, native and alien, relatives and strangers. Some there are whose manner toward strangers is most cordial and acquiescent, but toward their own household, their domestics, with whom they are familiar, they manifest only rigor and austerity. How many there are who excuse the harshness of the great and the rich, who wrest to the most favorable construction what they do and say, but with servants, with the poor and the inferior, are severe and unfeeling, placing the most unfavorable construction upon their every word and act. Again, men are affectionate toward children, parents, friends and relatives, always judging them with the utmost lenience. Indeed, how often friend flatters friend, until the practice becomes a public vice as one imitates and regards admirable all acts of the other. But with foes and

adversaries men adopt the opposite course. In them they can find no good, no reason for toleration or favorable construction; rather, they censure according to appearances.

23. In denunciation of such unequal and partial forbearance, Paul here speaks. He would have a Christian's forbearance perfect and complete, manifested toward one as toward another, whether friend or foe. He would that the Christian bear with and excuse everyone, regardless of person or merit. Forbearance is essentially good, inherently kind; just as gold remains gold whether possessed by a godly or an ungodly individual. The silver did not become ashes when Judas the traitor received it. Similarly, all gifts of God are real and remain the same in everyone's possession. That forbearance which is a fruit of the Spirit retains its characteristic kindness whether directed toward friend or enemy, toward rich or poor.

24. But frail, deceptive human nature assumes that gold, though remaining gold in St. Peter's hand, becomes ashes in the hand of Judas. The forbearance of human nature, of natural reason, is kind, not to all men, but to the rich and the great, to strangers and friends. Hence it is false, empty, deceptive; mere dissimulation and treachery before God. Note how impossible it is for human nature to exercise complete spiritual forbearance, and how few individuals are conscious of the imperfections of that supposedly beautiful, transcendent forbearance they manifest toward some persons while they show the reverse to other individuals, presuming they thus act rightly. But such is the teaching of our mean, filthy human nature with that same beautiful reason, which ever decides and proceeds contrary to the Spirit and the things of the Spirit. As Paul says in Romans 8, 5, "They that are after the flesh mind the things of the flesh."

25. In these few words Paul comprehends the Christian's entire conduct toward his neighbor. The forbearing individual treats everyone rightly, in word and act; treats him as he ought, physically and spiritually, bearing with his evils and imperfections. Such conduct may be defined as simply

love, peace, patience, longsuffering, gentleness, goodness, meekness, in fact, everything included in the fruits of the Spirit. Gal 5, 22.

OBJECTIONS ANSWERED.

26. But you will say: "Yes, but in that case who would be left in the enjoyment of a morsel of bread because of the wicked people ready to abuse equality and take our all, not permitting us to live on the earth even?" Note Paul's beautiful answer to your question, in the conclusion of this epistle lesson. He says, first,

"The Lord is at hand."

27. Were there no God, you might well thus fear the wicked. But not only is there a God; he "is at hand." He will neither forget nor forsake you. Only be forbearing to all men, and let him care for you; leave it to him how he is to support and protect you. Has he given you Christ the eternal treasure? how then shall he not give you the necessities of this life? With him is much more than anyone can take from you. Then, too, you possess in Christ more than is represented in all this world's goods. On this subject the psalmist says (Ps 55, 22): "Cast thy burden upon Jehovah, and he will sustain thee"; and Peter (1 Pet 5, 7), "Casting all your anxiety upon him, because he careth for you." And Christ in the sixth chapter of Matthew points us to the lilies of the field and the fowls of the air. The thought of these passages is the same as that of "The Lord is at hand." Now follows,

"In nothing be anxious."

28. Take no thought for yourselves. Let God care for you. He whom you now acknowledge is able to provide for you. It is the heathen, unknowing he has a God, who takes thought for himself. Christ says (Mt 6, 31-32): "Be not therefore anxious, saying, What shall we eat? or, What shall we drink? or, Wherewithal shall we be clothed? For after all these things do the Gentiles seek; for your heavenly Father knoweth that ye have need of all these things." Then, let the whole world grasp, and deal unrighteously, you shall have enough. You shall not die of hunger or

cold unless someone shall have deprived you of the God who cares for you. But who shall take him from you? How can you lose him except you yourself let him go? We have no reason to take thought for ourselves when we have a Father and Protector who holds in his hand all things, even them who, with all their possessions, would rob or injure us. Our duty is to rejoice ever in God and be forbearing toward all men, as becomes those assured of ample provision for body and soul; especially in that we have a gracious God. They without him may well be concerned about themselves. It should be our anxiety not to be anxious, to rejoice in God alone and to be kind to men. On this topic the psalmist says (Ps 37, 25): "I have been young, and now am old; yet have I not seen the righteous forsaken, nor his seed begging bread." And again (Ps 40, 17), "The Lord thinketh upon me."

PRAYER.

"But in everything by prayer and supplication with thanksgiving let your requests be made known unto God."

29. Here Paul teaches us to cast our care upon God. The meaning is: Take no thought for yourselves. Should anything transpire to give you care or anxiety—and such will be the case, for many trials will befall you on earth—make no effort to escape it, be it what it may. Have no care or anxiety. Turn to God with prayer, with supplication, entreating him to accomplish for you all you would seek to effect by care. And do so in thankfulness that you have a God solicitous for you and to whom you may freely come with all your anxieties. Who does not so when misfortune befalls, but endeavors to measure it by his reason and to overrule it by his counsel, and falls into anxiety—this man plunges himself into deep wretchedness, loses his joy and peace in God, and all to accomplish nothing. He but digs in the sand, sinking himself ever deeper, and effects no good. Of this fact we daily have testimony in our own experience and in that of others.

30. It may be necessary to add this, however: Let no

one conclude he will be utterly careless and rest upon God, making no effort, no exertion, not even resorting to prayer. Whoso adopts this course must soon fail and fall into anxiety. We must ever strive. Many care-engendering things befall us for the very purpose of driving us to prayer. Not undesignedly does the apostle contrast the two injunctions, "In nothing be anxious," and, In all things flee to God. "Nothing" and "all" are contrasting terms. Paul thus makes plain that many things transpire which tend to create in us anxiety, but we must not let them make us over-anxious; we must commit ourselves to God and implore his aid for our needs.

31. Now, let us examine Paul's words and learn how to frame our prayers and what attitude to assume. He makes a fourfold division of prayer: prayer, supplication, thanksgiving and petition. By "prayer" we understand simply formal words or expressions—as, for instance, the Lord's Prayer and the psalms—which sometimes express more than our request. In "supplication" we strengthen prayer and make it effective by a certain form of persuasion; for instance, we may entreat one to grant a request for the sake of a father, or of something dearly loved or highly prized. We entreat God by his Son, his saints, his promises, his name. Thus Solomon says (Ps 132, 1), "Jehovah, remember for David all his affliction." And Paul urges (Rom 12, 1), "I beseech you therefore, brethren, by the mercies of God"; and again (2 Cor 10, 1), "I . . . entreat you by the meekness and gentleness of Christ." "Petitioning" is stating what we have at heart, naming the desire we express in prayer and supplication. In the Lord's Prayer are seven petitions, beside prayer proper. Christ says (Mt 7, 7-8): "Ask, and it shall be given you; seek, and ye shall find; knock, and it shall be opened unto you: for every one that asketh receiveth; and he that seeketh findeth; and to him that knocketh it shall be opened." In "thanksgiving" we recount blessings received and thus strengthen our confidence and enable ourselves to wait trustingly for what we pray.

32. Prayer is made vigorous by petitioning; urgent by supplication; by thanksgiving, pleasing and acceptable. Strength and acceptability combine to prevail and secure the petition. This, we see, is the manner of prayer practiced by the Church; and the holy fathers in the Old Testament always offered supplication and thanks in their prayers. The Lord's Prayer opens with praise and thanksgiving and the acknowledgment of God as a Father; it earnestly presses toward him through filial love and a recognition of fatherly tenderness. For supplication, this prayer is unequaled. Hence it is the sublimest and the noblest prayer ever uttered.

33. These words of Paul beautifully spiritualize and explain the mystery of the golden censer whereof Moses has written much in the Old Testament, detailing how the priests should burn incense in the temple. We are all priests, and our prayers are the censer. The first is the golden vessel, which signifies the precious words of prayer; such as the language of the Lord's Prayer, the psalms, and like written prayers. Always in the Scriptures the words are represented by the vessel; for words are a medium for containing and conveying thought, just as the vessel serves to contain wine, water, coals or anything else. Similarly, the golden cup of Babylon mentioned in Revelation 17, 4 typifies human doctrine; and the sacramental cup, containing Christ's blood, is the Gospel.

34. The live coals in the censer stand for thanksgiving, for enumerated benefits in prayer. That coals signify benefits Paul implies where, quoting Solomon's injunction in Proverbs 25, 21-22, which the apostle cites (Rom 12, 20): "If thine enemy hunger, feed him; if he thirst, give him to drink; for in so doing thou shalt heap coals of fire upon his head." Burning coals of fire, the benefits are, and powerful to take captive and enkindle the heart. The Law forbad to take coals from any place but the altar; accordingly, we must not in prayer urge our own works and merits, as did the pharisee in the Gospel (Lk 18, 11-12), but acknowledge the benefits in Christ. He is the altar upon whom we are offered. By this benefit we render thanks and pray. Paul

says (Col 3, 17), "Do all in the name of the Lord Jesus, giving thanks to God the Father through him." God cannot permit us to regard anything but our altar Christ. Thus he teaches, where it is recorded (Lev 10) that Nadab and Abihu, sons of Aaron, were devoured by fire before the altar because they took coals for the censer from elsewhere than that place of sacred offering.

35. The petition whereby prayer is made complete is typified by the smoke ascending at the laying of the thyme —the incense—upon the coals. Paul's exhortation, "Let your requests be made known unto God," recognizes and explains the symbol of the smoke rising from the censer. His meaning is: "If you would offer a sweet savor of incense to God, express your petition in supplication and thanksgiving. This is the precious, sweet incense recognized by God, ascending as straight before him as a taper and a rod." Such prayer penetrates heaven. Grateful recognition of God's benefits induces us to pray voluntarily and fervently, naturally and with delight; just as the coals of fire make strong the volume of smoke. If there be not first the coals to generate heat, if there be not gratitude for benefits to enkindle fervor, prayer will be sluggish; it will be cold and dull.

36. But what is meant by "making known" our prayers to God when he knows them even before we begin, in fact, comes to us first and induces us to pray? I answer, Paul uses this expression by way of teaching us how to really and truly pray—not to pray vainly or at a venture as do they who are indifferent whether God hears them or not, who are ever uncertain of being heard, yes, are inclined to think they will not be heard. That is not praying; it is not petitioning. It is tempting and mocking God. Should one entreat me for a penny and I knew he did not believe, did not have a thought, that I would give it him, I would not be disposed to hear him. I would conclude he was either mocking me or was not in earnest. How much less will God hear mere noise! True prayer is the "making known" of our desires to God. In other words, we must not doubt

that God hears us; that our prayer reaches him; that our requests assuredly shall be granted. If we do not believe we are heard, that our prayer reaches God, undoubtedly it will not reach him. As we believe, so will it be.

The ascending smoke is but our faith when we believe our appeal reaches God and is heard. Paul's words hint at the frequent claims of the psalms: "My cry before him came into his ears." Ps 18, 6. "Let my prayer be set forth . . . before thee." Ps 141-2. Relative to this topic, Christ says, "All things, whatsoever ye shall ask in prayer, believing, ye shall receive." Mt 21, 22. See also Mk 11, 24. And James counsels (ch 1, 6-7): "But let him ask in faith, nothing doubting; for he that doubteth . . . let not that man think that he shall receive anything of the Lord."

37. Easily, then, we recognize the bawling in the cloisters and cathedrals all over the world as mere mockery, a tempting of God. Prayer of that sort is well enough made known to men, considering the constant loud outcry and bellowing of them who offer it. But to God it is unknown. It fails to reach him because the offerers do not believe, or at least are uncertain, that it will. As they believe, so is it. Time indeed it is for such mockery and tempting of God to be rejected and the mock-houses, as Amos calls them in the seventh chapter, to be exterminated. Oh, if we would but pray aright, what could we not accomplish! As it is, we pray much and obtain nothing; for our prayers never reach God. Wo to unbelief and distrust!

THE PEACE OF GOD.

> "And the peace of God, which passeth all understanding, shall guard your hearts and your thoughts in Christ Jesus."

38. Note the beautiful logic and order of Paul's teaching. The Christian is first to rejoice in God through faith and then show forbearance or kindness, to men. Should he ask, "How can I?" Paul answers, "The Lord is at hand." "But how if I be persecuted and robbed?" Paul's reply is, "In nothing be anxious. Pray to God. Let him care." "But meanwhile I shall become weary and desolate." "Not

so; the peace of God shall keep vou." Let us now consider the last thought.

39. By the phrase, "the peace of God," we must understand, not that calm and satisfied peace wherein God himself dwells, but the peace and contentment he produces in our hearts. It is called the "peace of God" in the same sense that the message of God which we hear and believe and speak is styled "the Word of God." This peace is the gift of God, and is called the "peace of God" because, having it, we are at peace with him even if we are displeased with men.

40. This peace of God is beyond the power of mind and reason to comprehend. Understand, however, it is not beyond man's power to experience—to be sensible of. Peace with God must be felt in the heart and conscience. How else could our "hearts and minds" be preserved "through Christ Jesus"? To illustrate the difference between the peace of God and the peace comprehensible by reason: They who know nothing of fleeing to God in prayer, when overtaken by tribulation and adversity and when filled with care and anxiety proceed to seek that peace alone which reason apprehends and which reason can secure. But reason apprehends no peace apart from a removal of the evil. Such a peace does not transcend the comprehension of reason; it is compatible with reason. They who pray not, rage and strive under the guidance of reason until they obtain a certain peace by fraudulent or forcible removal of the evil. Just as the wounded seeks to be healed. But they who rejoice in God, finding their peace in him, are contented. They calmly endure tribulation, not desiring what reason dictates as peace—removal of the evil. Standing firm, they await the inner strength wrought by faith. It is not theirs to inquire whether the evil will be short or long in duration, whether temporal or eternal; they give themselves no concern on this point, but ever leave it to God's regulation. They are not anxious to know when, how, where or by whom termination of the evil is to come. In return, God affords them grace and removes their evils, bestowing blessings beyond their expectations, or even desires.

41. This, mark you, is the peace of the cross, the peace of God, peace of conscience, Christian peace, which gives us even external calm, which makes us satisfied with all men and unwilling to disturb any. Reason cannot understand how there can be pleasure in crosses, and peace in disquietude; it cannot find these. Such peace is the work of God, and none can understand it until it has been experienced. Relative to this topic, it is said in the epistle for the second Sunday in Advent: "The God of hope fill you with all joy and peace in believing." What the apostle there terms "peace in believing" he here calls "peace of God."

42. In this verse Paul implies that for him who rejoices in God and exercises forbearance in his life, the devil will raise up a cross calculated forcibly to turn his heart from that way. The Christian should therefore be well fortified, placing his peace beyond the devil's reach—in God. Let him not be anxious to rid himself of what the devil has forced upon him. Let him suffer Satan's wantonness until God's coming shall exterminate it. Thus will the Christian's heart, mind and affection be guarded and preserved in peace. His patience could not long endure did not his heart exist above its conditions, in a higher peace—were it not satisfied it has peace with God.

43. "Heart" and "mind" here must not be supposed to mean human will and understanding. We are to take Paul's explanation—heart and mind in Christ Jesus; in other words, the will and understanding resultant in Christ, from Christ and under Christ. Faith and love are meant—faith and love in all their operations, in all their inclinations toward God and men. The reference is simply to a disposition to trust and love God sincerely, and a willingness of heart and mind to serve God and man to the utmost. The devil seeks to prevent this state by terror, by revealing death and by every sort of misfortune; and by setting up human devices to induce the heart to seek comfort and help in its own counsels and in man. Thus led astray, the heart falls from trust in God to a dependence upon itself.

44. Briefly, this text is a lesson in Christian living, in the attitude of the Christian toward God and man. It teaches us to let God be everything to us, and to treat all men alike, to conduct ourselves toward men as does God toward us, receiving from him and giving to them. It may be summed up in the words "faith" and "love."

First Christmas Sermon

Christmas Eve Service.

Epistle Text: Titus 2, 11-15.

11 For the grace of God hath appeared, bringing
salvation to all men, 12 instructing us, to the intent
that, denying ungodliness and worldly lusts, we should
live soberly and righteously and godly in this present
world; 13 looking for the blessed hope and appearing
of the glory of the great God and our Saviour Jesus
Christ; 14 who gave himself for us, that he might redeem us from all iniquity, and purify unto himself a
people for his own possession, zealous of good works.
15 These things speak and exhort and reprove with
all authority. Let no man despise thee.

THE APPEARING OF THE GRACE OF GOD.

1. It is written in the book of Nehemiah (ch 4) that the Jews, in rebuilding Jerusalem, wrought with one hand and with the other held the sword, because of the enemy who sought to hinder the building. Paul in Titus 1, 9 carries out the thought of the symbol in this teaching that a bishop, a pastor, or a preacher, should be mighty in the Holy Scriptures to instruct and admonish as well as to resist the gainsayers. Accordingly, we are to make a twofold use of the Word of God: as both bread and weapon; for feeding and for resisting; in peace and in war. With one hand we must build, improve, teach and feed all Christendom; with the other, oppose the devil, the heretics, the world. For where the pasture is not defended, the devil will soon destroy it; he is bitterly opposed to God's Word. Let us then, God granting us his grace, so handle the Gos-

pel that not only shall the souls of men be fed, but men shall learn to put on that Gospel as armor and fight their enemies. Thus shall it furnish both pasture and weapons.

2. The first consideration in this lesson is, Paul teaches what should be the one theme of Titus and of every other preacher, namely, Christ. The people are to be taught who Christ is, why he came and what blessings his coming brought us. "The grace of God hath appeared," the apostle says, meaning God's grace is clearly manifest. How was it manifested? By the preaching of the apostles it was proclaimed world wide. Previous to Christ's resurrection, the grace of God was unrevealed. Christ dwelt only among the Jews and was not yet glorified. But after his ascension he gave to men the Holy Spirit. Concerning the Spirit, he before testified (Jn 16, 14) that the Spirit of truth, whom he should send, would glorify him.

The apostle's meaning is: Christ did not come to dwell on earth for his own advantage, but for our good. Therefore he did not retain his goodness and grace within himself. After his ascension he caused them to be proclaimed in public preaching throughout the world—to all men. Nor did he permit the revelation to be made as a mere proclamation of a fact, as a rumor or a report; it was appointed to bring forth fruit in us. It is a revelation and proclamation that teaches us to deny—to reject—ungodly things, all earthly lusts, all worldly desires, and thenceforward lead a sober, righteous and godly life.

3. In the first verse, the true essence of the text, "The grace of God hath appeared, bringing salvation to all men," Paul condemns the favors of the world and of men as pernicious, worthy of condemnation, ineffectual; and would incite in us a desire for divine grace. He teaches us to despise human favor. He who would have God's grace and favor must consider the surrender of all other grace and favor. Christ says (Mt 10, 22), "Ye shall be hated of all men for my name's sake." The Psalmist says (Ps 53, 5,), "God hath scattered the bones of him that campeth against

thee." And Paul declares (Gal 1, 10), "If I were still pleasing men, I should not be a servant of Christ." Where the saving grace of God comes, the pernicious favor of men must be ignored. He who would taste the former must reject and forget the latter.

4. According to the text, this grace has appeared, or is proclaimed, to all men. Christ commanded (Mk 16, 15) that the Gospel be preached to all creatures throughout the whole world. And Paul in many places—for instance, Colossians 1, 23—says, "The Gospel, which ye heard, was preached in all creation under heaven." The thought is, The Gospel was preached publicly in the hearing of all creatures, much more of all men. At first Christ preached the Gospel and only in the land of the Jews, knowledge of the Holy Scriptures being confined to that nation, as Ps 76, 2 and Ps 147, 19 declare. But afterward the Word was made free to all men; not confined to any particular section. Psalm 19, 4 declares, "Their line is gone out through all the earth, and their words to the end of the world." This is spoken of the apostles.

5. But you may object, "Surely the words of the apostles did not, in their time, reach the end of the world; for nearly eight hundred years elapsed after the apostolic age before Germany was converted, and also recent discoveries show there are many islands and many countries where no indication of the grace of God appeared before the fifteenth century." I reply: The apostle has reference to the character of the Gospel. It is a message calculated, from the nature of its inception and purpose, to go into all the world. At the time of the apostles it had already entered the greater and better part of the world. Up to that day, no message of like character was ever ordained. The Law of Moses was confined to the Jewish nation. Universal proclamation of the Gospel being for the most part accomplished at that time, and its completion being inevitable—as it is today—the Scripture phraseology makes it an accomplished fact.

In the Scriptures we frequently meet with what is called "synecdoche;" that is, a figure of speech whereby a part is made to stand for the whole. For instance, it is said that Christ was three days and three nights in the grave, when the fact is he passed one entire day, two nights, and portions of two other days in that place. Mt 12, 40. Again, we read (Mt 23, 37) of Jerusalem stoning the prophets, yet a large proportion of the inhabitants were godly people. Thus, too, the ecclesiastics are said to be avaricious, but among them are many righteous men. This way of speaking is common to all languages; especially is it found in the Holy Scriptures.

6. So the Gospel was in the apostolic day preached to all creatures; for it is a message introduced, designed and ordained to reach all creatures. To illustrate: A prince, having despatched from his residence a message and seeing it started upon the way, might say the message had gone to the appointed place even though it had not yet reached its destination. Similarly, God has sent forth his Gospel to all creatures even though it has not so far reached all. Note, the prophet says the voice of the apostles has "gone out through all the earth." He does not say their voice has reached the entire world, but is on the way—"is gone out." And so Paul means the Gospel is continuously preached and made manifest to all men. It is now on the way; the act is performed though the effect is not complete.

FIRST EVIL—UNGODLINESS.

7. The appearing of grace, Paul says, instructs us in two things: one is described as "denying ungodliness and wordly lusts." We must explain these terms. The Latin word "impietas," which the apostle renders in the Greek "asebia" and which in Hebrew is "resa," I cannot find any one German word to express. I have made it "ungœttlich wesen," "ungodliness." The Latin and Greek terms do not fully convey the Hebrew meaning. "Resa," properly, is the sin of failing to honor God; that is, of not believing, trusting, fearing him, not surrendering to him, not submit-

ting to his providence, not allowing him to be God. In this sin, those guilty of gross outward evils are deeply implicated indeed; but much more deeply involved are the wise, sainted, learned ecclesiasts who, relying upon their works, think themselves godly and so appear in the eyes of the world. In fact, all men who do not live a life committed to the pure goodness and grace of God are "impious," ungodly, even though they be holy enough to raise the dead, or perfect in continence and all other virtues. "Graceless" or "faithless" would seem to be the proper adjective to describe them. I shall, however, use the term "ungodly." Paul tells us that saving grace has appeared to the graceless to make them rich in grace and rich in God; in other words, to bring them to believe, trust, fear, honor, love and praise him, and thus transform ungodliness into godliness.

8. Of what use would be the appearing of saving grace were we to attempt to become godly in life through some other means? Paul here declares grace was revealed and proclaimed to the very end that we might deny ungodliness and thereafter live righteously; not through or of ourselves, but through grace. No one more disparages divine grace, and more gainsays its appearing, than do hypocrites and ungodly saints; for, unwilling to regard their own works ineffectual, sinful and faulty, they discover in themselves much good. Measuring themselves by their good intentions, they imagine they deserve great merit independently of grace. God, however, regards no work good—nor is it—unless he by his grace effects it in us. It was for the sake of accomplishing in us all many such works, and of deterring us from our own attempts, that God manifested his saving grace to men.

9. Now, the foremost evil of men is their godlessness, their unsaved state, their lack of grace. It includes first a faithless heart, and then all resultant thoughts, words, works and conduct in general. Left to himself, the individual's inner life and outward conduct are guided only by his natural abilities and human reason. In these his beauty and brilliance sometimes outshine the real saints. But

he seeks merely his own interest. He is unable to honor God in life and conduct, even though he does command greater praise and glory in the exercise of reason than do the true saints of frequent Scripture mention. So world-wide and so deeply subtile an evil is this godless, graceless conduct, it withholds from the individual the power to perceive the evil of his way, to believe he errs, even when his error is held up to him. The prophet (Ps 32, 2) looks upon this blindness as not that of reason, or of the world, or of the flesh, but as a spiritual deception, leading astray not only the reason but the spirit of man.

10. In fact, that ungodliness is sinful must be believed rather than felt. Since God permitted the manifestation of his grace to all men to lead them to deny ungodliness, we ought to believe him a Being who knows our hearts better than we do ourselves. We must also confess that were it not for the ungodliness and faulty character of our deeds, God would not have ordained the proclamation of his grace for our betterment. Were one to administer remedies to an individual not ill, he would be looked upon as lacking sense. Accordingly, God must be regarded in the same light by them who, measuring themselves by their good intentions and their feelings, are unwilling to believe all their deeds ungodly and worthy of condemnation, and that God's saving grace is necessary. To them this is a terrible doctrine. Christ (Mt 21, 32) charges the chief priests, doctors and ecclesiasts (elders) with disbelieving John the Baptist, who called them to repentance; they refused to know their sin. All the prophets met death for accusing the people of the sin of ungodliness. No one believed the prophets. No one of the people thought himself guilty of such sin. They judged themselves by their feelings, their intentions and works; not by God's Word, not by his counsel delivered through the prophets.

11. Paul employs a strong Greek term, "pædeusa," meaning "to instruct"—such elementary instruction as we give children concerning a thing whereof they have no knowledge at all. The children are guided, not by their reason,

but by the instructing word of their father. According to his representation they regard a certain thing as useful or as harmful. They believe in and are guided by him. With intelligent and learned individuals, however, we explain in a way comprehensible to their reason why a certain thing is profitable and a certain other thing unprofitable. God designs that we, as childish pupils, be instructed by his saving grace. Then if we cannot feel we may yet believe that our natures are godless and faulty, and so receive grace and walk therein. Well does Christ testify (Mt 18, 3), "Except ye turn, and become as little children, ye shall in no wise enter into the kingdom of heaven;" and Isaiah (ch. 7, 9), "If ye will not believe, surely ye shall not be established." Divine, saving grace, then, has appeared, not only to help us, but also to teach us our need of grace. For the fact of its coming shows all our works godless, graceless, condemned. The psalmist (Ps 119, 5-8) fervently entreats God to teach him his judgments, laws and commandments, that he may not be guided by his own ideas and feelings, a thing God has forbidden (Deut 12, 8), saying: "Ye shall not do . . . . every man whatsoever is right in his own eyes."

SECOND EVIL—WORLDLY LUSTS.

12. The other evil in man Paul terms "worldly lusts." Therein is comprehended all disorderly conduct the individual may be guilty of, touching himself and his neighbor; while the first evil—ungodliness—comprehends all wrongs toward God. Observe Paul's judicious choice of words—"lusts," "worldly lusts." By the use of "worldly" he would include all evil lusts, whether it be for goods, luxuries, honor, favors or aught of the world wherein one may lustfully sin. He does not say, however, we must deny ourselves worldly goods, or must not make use of them. They are good creatures of God. We must avail ourselves of food, drink, clothing and other necessaries of life. No such thing is forbidden; it is only the lust after them, the undue love and craving for them, that we must deny, for it leads us into all sins against ourselves and our neighbors.

13. In this expression is also condemned the conduct of godless hypocrites, who, though they may be clad in sheep's clothing and sometimes refrain from an evil deed through cowardice or shame or through fear of hell's punishment, are nevertheless filled with evil desires for wealth, honor and power. No one loves life more dearly, fears death more terribly and desires more ardently to remain in this world than do they; yet they fail to recognize the worldly lusts wherein they are drowned, and their many works are vainly performed. It is not enough to put away wordly works and speech; worldly desires, or lusts, must be removed. We are not to place our affections upon the things of this life, but all our use of it should be with a view to the future life; as follows in the text: "Looking for the . . . appearing of the glory," etc.

14. Observe here, the grace of God reveals the fact that all men are filled with worldly lusts, though some may conceal their lustfulness by their hypocrisy. Were men not subject to such desires, there could be no necessity for the revelation of grace, no need for its benefits, no occasion for its manifestation to all men, no need it should teach the puttihg off of lusts. For whosoever is not subject to lusts is not called upon to forsake them. Paul's statement here has no reference to such a one. Indeed, he cannot be a human being; hence he has no need of grace, and so far as he is concerned its manifestation is not essential. What, then, must he be? Unquestionably, a devil, and eternally condemned with all his holiness and purity. Could the hypocrites, however, wholly hide their worldly lusts, they could not conceal their ardent desire to hold to this life, and their unwillingness to die. Thus they reveal their lack of grace, and the worldliness and ungodliness of all their works. Nevertheless, they fail to perceive their graceless condition and their perilous infirmity.

15. Further, Paul speaks of "denying," or renouncing. Therein he rejects many foolish expedients devised by men for attaining righteousness. Some run to the wilderness, some into cloisters. Others separate themselves from so-

ciety, presuming by bodily flight to run away from ungodliness and worldly lusts. Yet others resort to tortures and injuries of the body, imposing upon themselves excessive hunger, thirst, wakefulness, labor, uncomfortable apparel. Now, if ungodliness and worldly lusts were but something painted upon the wall, you might escape them by running out of the house; if they were knit into a red coat, you might pull off the coat and don a gray one; did they grow in your hair, you might have it shaved off and wear a bald pate; were they baked in the bread, you might eat roots instead. But since they inhere in your heart and permeate you through and through, where can you flee that you will not carry them with you? What can you wear under which you will escape them? What will you eat and drink wherein they will not be with you? In a word, what can you do to escape yourself, since you cannot get out of yourself? Dear man, the great temptations are within you. To run away from them would necessitate, first, fleeing from yourself. James says (ch 1, 14), "Each man is tempted, when he is driven away by his own lust, and enticed."

16. The apostle means, not simply that we must flee the outward temptations to sin, but, as he says, that we must "deny" them, must mortify the lusts, or desires, within ourselves. Our lusts being mortified, no external temptation can harm. By such subjection do we truly flee. If we fail to mortify our desires, it will not avail to flee outward temptations. We must remain amidst temptations and there learn through grace to deny lusts and ungodliness. It is written (Ps 110, 2), "Rule thou"—or apply thyself—"in the midst of thine enemies." Conflict and not flight, energy and not rest, must be the order in this life if we are to win the crown.

17. We read of an ancient father who, unable to endure temptation in a cloister, left it that he might in the wilderness serve God in peace. But in the desert one day his little water-jug overturned. He set it up, but it overturned a second time. Becoming enraged, he dashed the vessel into pieces. Then, saying within himself, "Since I cannot

find peace when alone, the defect must be in myself," he returned to the cloister to suffer temptations, from that time forward teaching that we must obtain the victory, not by fleeing worldly lusts, but by denying them.

THE CHRISTIAN LIFE.

18. Paul goes on to show another thing wherein we are instructed of grace—the Christian's manner of life after ungodliness and worldly lusts are denied:

> "We should live soberly and righteously and godly in this present world."

What an excellent general rule of life he gives us! one adapted to all conditions. He offers no occasion for sects. He introduces no differing opinions of men, as the case is with human doctrines.

First, he mentions "soberness," wherein is indicated what should be the nature of man's conduct toward himself in all respects. It calls for the subjection of the body, the keeping of it well disciplined. In every place of our text where the term "soberness" is used, Paul has the Greek word "sophron," which signifies, not only soberness, but temperance in every recognition of the body, in every ministration to the flesh; in eating, drinking and sleeping, for instance; in apparel, speech, manner and movement. Such soberness represents what is known in German as honorable living and good breeding. The sober man knows how, in all physical relations, to conduct himself temperately, discreetly and bravely; not leading a wild, shameless, unrestrained, disorderly life, lax in regard to eating, drinking, sleeping, and to speech, manner and movement. In the earlier part of the chapter, Paul devises that aged women teach the young women to be "sober-minded" and chaste.

19. Excessive eating and drinking truly does greatly impede our efforts to lead an honorable life. On the other hand, temperance contributes much to accomplish it. The moment one indulges his appetite to excess, he loses perfect control of himself; his five senses become unmanageable. Experience teaches that when the stomach is filled with meat and drink, the mouth is filled with words, the ears with

the lust of hearing, the eyes with the lust of seeing. The whole system either becomes indolent, drowsy, dull, or else it grows wild and dissolute, all the members overleaping the bounds of reason and propriety, until no discipline nor moderation remains. The word in our text, therefore, is not inaptly Latinized "sobrius," "soberness." In Greek, the word "sophron" is the opposite of "asotos," just as in German "vœllerei" and "mæszigkeit," "drunkenness" and "soberness," are contrasting terms. Examining the Latin "sobrius," we find it does not signify total abstinence from food and drink. "Sobrius" and "ebrius" are also contrasting terms, like the German "trunkenheit oder vœllerei" and "nuechterkeit," "drunkenness or ebriety" and "soberness." We Germans also call that individual "nuechtern," "sober," who, though he may have eaten and drunk, is not intoxicated, but has perfect control of himself.

20. You see now the manner of good works advocated by the apostle. He does not require us to make pilgrimages; he does not forbid certain foods; nor does he prescribe a particular garb, nor certain fast days. His teaching is not that of the class who, in obedience to human laws, separate themselves from men, basing their spirituality and goodness upon the peculiarity of their garb and diet, their manner of wearing the hair, their observance of times; who seek to become righteous by not conforming to custom in the matter of clothing, diet, occupation, seasons and movements. They are given an appropriate name in the Gospel—"pharisæi," meaning "excluded" or "separated." In Psalm 80, 13, the prophet calls them "monios," signifying "a solitary one." The name primarily is applied to a wild hog of solitary habits. We shall hereafter designate this class as "solitary." As the psalmist complains, they make terrible havoc of God's vineyard. These pharisees, or solitary ones, make great show with their traditions, their peculiar garb, their meats, days and physical attitudes. They easily draw away the multitude from the common customs of life to their ways. As Christ tells us (Mt 24, 24), even the elect can scarce resist them.

21. Let us learn here from Paul that no meats, drinks, apparel, colors, times, attitudes, are forbidden and none are prescribed. In all these things, everyone is given freedom, if only they be used in soberness, or moderation. As said before, these temporalities are not forbidden. Only the abuse of them, only excess and disorder therein, is prohibited. Where there is distinction and emphasis on such matters, there you will surely find human laws; not evangelical doctrine, not Christian liberty. Without soberness, or moderation, the ultimate result must be dissimulation, and hypocrisy. Therefore, make use of all earthly things when and where you please, giving thanks to God. This is Paul's teaching. Only guard against excess, disorder, misuse and licentiousness relative to temporal things and you will be in the right way. Do not permit yourself to be misled by the fact that the holy fathers established orders and sects, made use of certain meats and certain apparel, and conducted themselves thus and so. Their object was not peculiar eminence—therein they would have been unholy—but their conduct was of preference, and as a means for exercising moderation. Likewise do you exercise moderation as you see fit, and maintain your freedom. Confine not yourself to manners and methods, as if godly living consisted in them. Otherwise you will be solitary and deprived of the communion of saints. Diligently guard against such narrowness. We must fast, we must watch and labor, we must wear inferior clothing, and so on; but only on occasions when the body seems to need restraint and mortification. Do not set apart a specified time and place, but exercise your self-denial as necessity requires. Then you will be fasting rightly. You will fast every day in denying worldly lusts. So the Gospel teaches, and they who follow this course are of the New Testament dispensation.

22. Secondly, Paul says we should be "righteous" in our lives. No work, however, nor particular time, is here designated as the way to righteousness. In the ways of God is universal freedom. It is left to the individual to exercise his liberty; to do right when, where and to whom

occasion offers. Herein Paul gives a hint of how we should conduct ourselves toward our neighbor—righteously. We owe him that righteousness which consists in doing to him as we would have him do to us; in granting to him all we would have him grant us. We are to do our neighbor no bodily harm, no injury to his wife, children, friends, possessions, honor or anything of his. Rather we are obligated, wherever we see he needs our assistance, to aid him, to stand by him, at the risk of our bodies, our property, our honor and everything that is ours. Righteousness consists in rendering to each one his due. What a little word to comprehend so much! How few walk in this way of righteousness, though otherwise living blamelessly! We do everything else but what saving grace reveals to us as our duty to do.

23. The word "neighbor" must be construed to include even an enemy. But the way of righteousness is entirely obliterated. It is much more overgrown in neglect than the way of moderation, which itself is almost wholly untrodden and effaced because of the introduction of certain meats and apparel, certain movements and display. These things have been superabundantly, more than profusely, insinuated. We ape after set forms, and make fools of ourselves with rosaries, with ecclesiastical and feudal institutions, with hearing of masses, with festivals, with self-devised works concerning which is no divine command. O Lord God, how wide hell has opened her mouth (see Isaiah 5, 14); and how narrow has the gate of heaven become in consequence of the accursed doctrines and devices of these solitary and pharisaical persons! The prophets unwittingly paint the picture of present-day conditions. They represent hell by the wide-open mouth of a dragon, and heaven by a closed door. Oh, the wretchedness of the picture!

24. It is not necessary to inquire what outward works you can perform. Look to your neighbor. There you will find enough to do, a thousand kind offices to render. Do not suffer yourself to be misled into believing you will reach heaven by praying and attending church, by contribut-

ing to institutions and monuments, while you pass by your neighbor. If you pass him in this life, he will lie in your way in the life to come and cause you to go by the door of heaven as did the rich man who left Lazarus lying at his gate. Wo to us priests, monks, bishops and Pope! What do we preach? what teach? How we lead the pitiable multitude from the way! The blind leading the blind, both shall fall into the ditch. Such doctrines as Paul declares in the conclusion of this lesson—these are what we should teach.

25. In the third place, we are taught we must live "godly" lives. Here we are reminded of how to conduct ourselves toward God. Now we are fully instructed concerning our duty to ourselves, to our neighbors and to God. As before said, impiety signifies wickedness, ungodliness, lack of grace. Piety, on the other hand, means having faith, godliness, grace. Godly living consists in trusting God, in relying on his grace alone, regarding no work not wrought in us by him, through grace. If we are godly, we will recognize, honor, adore, praise and love God. Briefly in two words, to live godly is to fear and trust God. As it is written (Ps 147, 11), "Jehovah taketh pleasure in them that fear him, in those that hope in his lovingkindness." See also Ps 33, 18. To fear God is to look upon our own devices as pure ungodliness in the light of his manifest grace. These being ungodly, we are to fear God and forsake them, and thereafter guard against them. To trust in God is to have perfect confidence that he will be gracious to us, filling us with grace and godliness.

26. The individual yields to God when he gives himself wholly to God, attempting nothing of himself but permitting the Lord to work in and to rule him; when his whole concern and fear, his continual prayer and desire, are for God to withhold him from following his own works and ways, which he now recognizes as ungodly and deserving of wrath, and to rule over and work in him through grace. Thus the individual will obtain a clear conscience and will love and praise God. Observe, they are pious and filled

with grace, who do not walk by reason, do not trust in human nature, but rely only on the grace of God, ever fearful lest they fall from grace into dependence upon their own reason, their self-conceit, good intentions and self-devised works. The theme of the entire one-hundred-and-nineteenth psalm is trust in God. In every one of its one hundred and seventy-six verses, David breathes the same prayer. Reliance upon God is a subject of such vital importance, and so numerous are the difficulties and dangers attending human nature and reason and human doctrine, we cannot be too much on our guard.

27. The way of God does not require us to build churches and cathedrals, to make pilgrimages, to hear mass, and so on. God requires a heart moved by his grace, a life mistrustful of all ways not emanating from grace. Nothing more can one render God than such loyalty. All else is rather his gift to us. He says (Ps 50, 14-15), in effect: "Think not, O Israel, I inquire after thy gifts and offerings; for everything in heaven and earth is mine. This is the service I require of thee: to offer unto me thanksgiving and pay thy vows. Call upon me in the day of trouble and I will deliver thee, and thou shalt glorify me." In other words: Thou hast vowed that I should be thy God. Then keep this vow. Let me work; perform not thine own works. Let me help thee in thy need. For everything, look to me. Let me alone direct thy life. Then wilt thou be able to know me and my grace; to love and praise me. This is the true road to salvation. If thou doest otherwise, performing thine own works, thou wilt give thyself praise, wilt disregard me and refuse to accept me as thy God. Thou wilt prove treacherous and break thy vow.

28. Note, such obedience to God is real, divine service. For this service we need no bells nor churches, no vessels nor ornaments. Lights and candles are not necessary; neither are organs and singing, images and pictures, tables and altars. We require not bald pates nor caps, not incense nor sprinkling, not processions nor handling of the cross; neither are indulgences nor briefs essential. All

these are human inventions, mere matters of taste. God does not regard them, and too often they obscure with their glitter the true service of God. Only one thing is necessary to right service—the Gospel. Let the Gospel be properly urged; through it let divine service be made known to the people. The Gospel is the true bell, the true organ, for divine service.

29. Further, Paul says we are to live as he describes "in this present world." First: the perfect life cannot be accomplished by works; our whole life, while we remain here, must be sober, righteous and godly. Christ promises (Mt 10, 22), "He that endureth to the end, the same shall be saved." Now, there are some who, it must be admitted, occasionally accomplish good; but occasional accomplishment is not a complete life of goodness, nor does it mean endurance to the end. Second: No one can afford to leave this matter of a godly life until death, or until another world is reached. Whatever we would have in the life to come must be secured here.

30. Many depend upon purgatory, living as it pleases them to the end and expecting to profit by vigils and soul-masses after death. Truly, they will fail to receive profit therein. It were well had purgatory never been conceived of. Belief in purgatory suppresses much good, establishes many cloisters and monasteries and employs numerous priests and monks. It is a serious drawback to these three features of Christian living: soberness, righteousness and godliness. Moreover, God has not commanded, nor even mentioned, purgatory. The doctrine is wholly, or for the most part, deception; God pardon me if I am wrong. It is, to say the least, dangerous to accept, to build upon, anything not designated by God, when it is all we can do to stand in building upon the institutions of God which can never waver. The injunction of Paul to live rightly in this present world is truly a severe thrust at purgatory. He would not have us jeopardize our faith. Not that I, at this late day (when we write 1522), deny the existence of purgatory; but it is dangerous to preach it, whatever of truth

there may be in the doctrine, because the Word of God, the Scriptures, make no mention of a purgatory.

31. Paul's chief reason, however, for making use of the phrase "in this present world" is to emphasize the power of God's saving grace. In the extreme wickedness of the world, the godly person is as one alone, unexampled as it were, a rose among thorns; therefore he must endure every form of misfortune, of censure, shame and wrong. The apostle's thought is: He who would live soberly, righteously and godly must expect to meet all manner of enmity and must take up the cross. He must not allow himself to be misled, even though he has to live alone, like Lot in Sodom and Abraham in Canaan, among none but the gluttonous, the drunken, the incontinent, unrighteous, false and ungodly. His environment is world and must remain world. He has to resist and overcome the enticements of earth, censuring worldly desires. To live right in this present world, mark you, is like living soberly in a saloon, chastely in a brothel, godly in a gaiety hall, uprightly in a den of murderers. The character of the world is such as to render our earthly life difficult and distressing, until we longingly cry out for death and the day of judgment, and await them with ardent desire; as the next clause in the text indicates. Life being subject to so many evils, its only hope is in being led by grace. Human nature and reason are at a loss to direct it.

"Looking for the blessed hope."

32. With these words the apostle makes the godly life clearly distinct from every other life. Here is the text that enables one to perceive how he measures up to the life of grace. Let all who presume to think they live godly, step forward and answer as to whether or no they delight in this hope, as here pictured; whether they are so prepared for the day of judgment that they await it with pleasure; whether they regard it as more than endurable, as even a blessed event to be contemplated with longing and with cheerful confidence. Is it not true that human nature ever shrinks from the judgment? Is it not true that if the ad-

vent of that day rested upon the world's pleasure in the matter, it would never come? and particularly in the case of hypocritical saints? Where, then, does human nature stand? where reason? where the free-will so much extolled as inclined to and potent for good? Why does free-will not only flee from good but shrink from that honor to the God of salvation which the apostle here refers to as a "blessed hope" and in which hope we shall be blessed? What is to prevent the conclusion here that they who shrink from the judgment lead lives impious, blamable and devoid of grace, the evils and ungodliness of which they might, but for the approach of that day, conceal? What is more ungodly than to strive against God's will? But is not that just what the individual does who would flee from the day wherein the honor of God shall be revealed, who does not await the event with a loving and joyful heart? Mark you, then, he who desires not that day and does not with delight and with love to God await it, is not living a godly life, not though he is able even to raise the dead.

33. "Then it must be," you say, "that few lead godly lives, particularly among those solitary, spiritual ones who above all men flee death and the judgment." That is just what I have said. These separated individuals simply lead themselves and others from the true path, obliterating the ways marked out of God. Plainly we see now how little reason and nature can accomplish; they but strive against God. And we see how necessary is saving grace. For when our own works are abandoned, God comes and alone works in us, enabling us to rise from ourselves, from our ungodly conduct, to a supernatural, grace-filled, godly life. Then we not only do not fear the day of judgment, but cheerfully, even longingly, await it, contemplating it with joy and pleasure. This point has been further treated in the Gospel lesson for the second Sunday in Advent.

34. True godliness, you note, is not taught by human nature or mortal reason, but by the manifest grace of God. By grace are we enabled to deny worldly lusts, even to feel aversion to them, to desire liberation from them, to be

dissatisfied with our manner of life in general. More than that, it creates in us a disposition essential to godliness, a disposition to entreat God with perfect confidence and to await with pleasure his coming. So should we be disposed.

35. Now, let us carefully weigh the words "blessed hope." A contrast is presented to that miserably unhappy life wherein, when we attempt to walk uprightly, we are only harassed by misfortune, danger and sin. All in this life serves but to vex, while we have every reason to be encouraged in that hope. Such is the experience of them who earnestly endeavor to live soberly, righteously and godly. The world cannot long endure this class; it soon regards them as repulsive. Paul testifies (Rom 5, 3): "We also rejoice in our tribulations: knowing that tribulation worketh stedfastness; and stedfastness, approvedness; and approvedness, hope: and hope putteth not to shame." Thus our eyes remain closed to the wordly and visible, and open to the eternal and invisible. All this transformed condition is the work of grace, through the cross, which we must endure if we attempt to lead a godly life, the life the world cannot tolerate.

"And appearing of the glory."

36. Paul's word for "advent" here is "epiphaniam," "appearing" or "manifestation." Similarly, he spoke above of the "appearance" or "manifestation" of grace. The word "advent" in the Latin, therefore, does not express all. The apostle would make a distinction between the first appearing and the last. The first appearing was attended by humility and dishonor, with intent to attract little attention and occasion no manifestation but that made in faith and through the Gospel. Christ is at present not manifest in person, but on the day of judgment he will appear in effulgent splendor, in undimmed honor; a splendor and honor eternally manifest to all creatures. The last day will be an eternal day. Upon the instant of its appearing every heart and all things will stand revealed. Such is the meaning of "the appearing of glory" mentioned, the appearance of Christ's honor. Then there will be neither preaching nor

faith. To all men everything will be manifest by experience, and by sight as in a clear day. Hence Paul adds,

"Of the great God and our Saviour Jesus Christ."

Not that another and lesser God exists; but that God has reserved unto the last day the displaying of his greatness and majesty, his glory and effulgence. We behold him now in the Gospel and in faith—a narrow view of him. Here he is not great because but slightly comprehended. But in the last appearing he will permit us to behold him in his greatness and majesty.

37. The words of this verse afford comfort to all who live soberly, righteously and godly. For the apostle therein declares the coming glory, not of our enemy or judge, but of our Saviour, Jesus Christ, who will at that time give us perfect happiness. For the day of that glorious appearing he will make the occasion of our liberation from this world wherein we must endure so much in the effort to lead a godly life in response to his will. In view of his coming and our great and glorious redemption, we ought firmly and cheerfully to bear up under the persecution, murders, shame and misfortunes the world effects, and to be courageous in the midst of death. With these joys before us, we ought the more stedfastly to persevere in a godly life, boldly relying upon the Saviour, Jesus Christ.

38. On the other hand, the words of this verse are terrible to the worldly-minded and wicked who are unwilling to endure, for the sake of godliness, the persecutions of the world. They prefer to make their godliness go no farther than to live without friction in the world and thus avoid incurring enmity and trouble. But the dissolute, the reckless, the obdurate, utterly disregard those words. They never give a thought to the fact of having to appear on the final day. Like frenzied animals, they run blindly and heedlessly on to the day of judgment and into the abyss of hell. You may ask, "How shall I obtain the godliness fitted to enable me to confidently await that day, since human nature and reason flee from a godly life and cannot accomplish it?" Observe what follows,

"Who gave himself for us."

39. The things the apostle has been so carefully presenting are laid before you to enable you to perceive and acknowledge your helplessness, to utterly despair of your own power, that you may sincerely humble yourself and recognize your vanity, and your ungodliness, impiety and unsaved state. Note, the grace appearing through the Gospel teaches humility; and being humbled, one desires grace and is disposed to seek salvation. Wherever a humble desire for grace exists, there is open to you the door of grace. The desire cannot be without provision for its fulfilment. Peter says (1 Pet 5, 5), "God resisteth the proud, but giveth grace to the humble." And Christ frequently in the Gospel declares: "Whosoever shall exalt himself shall be humbled; and whosoever shall humble himself shall be exalted."

40. So the blessed Gospel is presented to you. It permits saving grace to appear in and shine forth from you, teaching you what more is required to keep you from falling into despair. Now, the Gospel, the appearance of the light of grace, is this which the apostle here declares, namely, that Christ gave himself for us, etc. Therefore, hearken to the Gospel; open the windows of your heart and let saving grace shine forth, to enlighten and teach you. This truth, that Christ gave himself for us, is the message spoken of as proclaimed to all men. It is the explanation of what is meant by the appearing of grace.

41. Banish from your mind, then, the error into which you may have fallen, of thinking that to hear the epistles of Paul and Peter is not to hear the Gospel. Do not allow yourself to be misled by the name "epistle." All Paul writes in his epistles is pure Gospel. He says so in Romans 1, 1 and in First Corinthians 4, 15. In fact, I venture to say the Gospel is more vividly presented in the epistles of Paul than in the four books of the evangelists. The latter detail the life and words of Christ, which were understood only after the advent of the Holy Spirit, who glorified Christ. Thus the Saviour himself testifies. Paul, though he records no account of the life of Christ, clearly

explains the purpose of our Lord's coming, and shows what blessings his advent brings to us. What else is the Gospel but the message that Christ gave himself for us, to redeem us from sin, and that all who believe it will surely be saved?

So we are to despair of our own efforts and cleave to Christ, relying upon him alone. Gracious, indeed, and comforting is this message, and readily welcomed by hearts despairing of their own efforts. "Evangelium," or Gospel, implies a loving, kind, gracious message, fitted to gladden and cheer a sorrowing and terrified heart.

42. Take heed to believe true what the apostle, through the Gospel, declares—that Christ gave himself for you for the sake of redeeming you from all unrighteousness and of purifying you for a peculiar inheritance. It follows that, in the first place, you must believe and confess all your efforts, impure, unrighteous; and that your human nature, reason, art and free-will are ineffectual apart from Christ. Unless you so believe, you make void the Gospel; for, according to the Gospel, Christ did not give himself for the righteous and the pure. Why should he? With righteousness and purity existent, he would be giving himself in vain. It would be a senseless giving.

In the second place, you must believe that Christ gave himself for you, to put away your impurity and unrighteousness and make you pure and righteous in himself. If you believe this, it will be so. Faith will accomplish it. The fact that he gave himself for you can make you pure and righteous only through faith on your part. Peter (Acts 15, 9) speaks of the cleansing of hearts by faith. Observe, Christ is not put into your hand, not given you in a coffer, not placed in your bosom nor in your mouth. He is presented to you through the Word, the Gospel; he is held up before your heart, through the ears he is offered to you, as the Being who gave himself for you—for your unrighteousness and impurity. Only with your heart can you receive him. And your heart receives when it responds to your opened mind, saying, "Yes, I believe." Thus through the medium of the Gospel Christ penetrates your heart by way of your hearing, and dwells there by your faith. Then are you pure and righteous; not by your own efforts, but in consequence of the guest received into your heart through faith. How rich and precious these blessings!

43. Now, when faith dwelling within you brings Christ into your heart, you cannot think him poor and destitute. He brings his own life, his Spirit—all he is and commands. Paul says the Spirit is given, not in response to any work of man, but for the sake of the Gospel. The Gospel brings Christ, and Christ brings the Spirit—his Spirit. Then the individual is made new; he is godly. Then all his deeds are well wrought. He is not idle; for faith is never inactive. It continually, in word and act, proclaims Christ. Thus the world is roused against Christ; it will not hear, will not tolerate, him. The result is crosses for the Christian, and crosses render life loathsome and the day of judgment desirable. This, mark you, explains the Gospel and the appearing of the saving grace of God.

44. How can death and the day of judgment terrify the heart that receives Christ? Who shall injure such a one when the great God and Saviour, Jesus Christ, who orders the day of judgment, stands by with all his glory, greatness, majesty and might? He who gave himself for us, he and no other, will control that day. Assuredly he will not deny his own testimony, but will verify your faith by declaring he gave himself for your sins. And what have you to fear from sin when the judge himself owns he has taken it away by his own sacrifice? Who will accuse you? Who may judge the Judge? who exercise authority over him? His power outweighs that of all the world with its sins innumerable. Had he purchased your salvation with anything but himself, there might be great error in this doctrine. But what can terrify when he has given himself for you? He would have to condemn himself before sin could condemn the souls for whom he died.

45. Here is strong, unquestionable security. But our connection with it depends upon the stedfastness of our

faith. Christ certainly will not waver. He is absolutely stedfast. We should, then, urge and enforce faith by our preaching and in our working and suffering, ever making it firm and constant. Works avail nothing here. The evil spirit will assail only our faith, well knowing that upon it depends all. How unfortunate our failure to perceive our advantage! for we ignore the Gospel with its saving grace. Wo unto you, Pope, bishops, priests and monks! Of what use are you in the churches and occupying the pulpits? Now let us analyze the words,

"That he might redeem us."

46. He gave himself to redeem—not himself, but us. Evidently, we are naturally captives. Then how can we be presumptuous and ungrateful enough to attribute so much merit to our free-will and our natural reason? If we claim there is aught in us not bound in sin, we disparage the grace whereby, according to the Gospel, we are redeemed. Who can do any good thing while captive in sin, while wholly unrighteous? Our own efforts may seem to us good, but in truth they are not; otherwise, the Gospel of Christ must be false.

"From all iniquity."

47. The word Paul uses for "iniquity" is "anomias," the specific meaning of which is, anything not conforming to the Law, whether transgression of soul or body, the former transgression being ungodliness or impiety, and the latter worldly lusts. He is careful to add the word "all," to make plain the inclusion of the sins of the body and the unrighteousness of soul wherefrom Christ has completely redeemed us. This teaching is a blow at the self-righteous and separate, who redeem themselves, and others as well, from certain forms of unrighteousness by means of the Law, or by their own reason and free-will. In reality they do avoid the outward act of transgression, being restrained by prohibitions, or fear of pain and penalty, or expectation of reward or gain. But this is only ridding of the scum of unrighteousness; the heart remains filled with ungodly, unregenerate inclination and worldly lusts, and neither body nor soul

is righteous. But through faith Christ redeems us from all unrighteousness. He liberates us, enabling us to live godly and heavenly, a power we had not when in the prison of unrighteousness.

"And purify unto himself."

48. Sin is attended by two evils: First, it takes us captive. In its power we are incapable of doing good, of desiring or even recognizing good. Sin thus robs us of power, freedom and light. The second evil attendant upon sin is the natural outcome of the first: we forsake good to engage only in iniquity and impurity, tilling with hard and heavy labor the land of wicked Pharaoh in Egypt. But when, through faith, Christ comes, he liberates from the bondage of Egypt and gives power to do good. That power is our first gain.

49. Afterward, the effort of our entire lives should be to purge from body and soul unrighteous, unregenerate, and worldly conduct. Until death our lives should be nothing but purification. While it is true that faith instantly redeems from all legal guilt and sets free, yet evil desires remain in body and soul, as odor and disease cling to a dungeon. Faith occupies itself with purifying from these. Typical of this principle, Lazarus in the Gospel was raised from the dead by a single word (Jn 11, 44), but afterward the shroud and napkin had to be removed. And the half-dead man whose wounds the Samaritan bound up and whom the Samaritan carried home, had to remain in the inn until he was restored.

"A people for his own possession."

50. The thought is of ownership—a peculiar inheritance or possession. The Scriptures term God's people his inheritance. As a landholder cultivates, nourishes and improves his inheritance, so, through the medium of our faith, Christ, whose inheritance we are, cultivates us, or impels us to daily grow better and more fruitful. Thus you see, faith liberates from sin, but more than that, it makes us Christ's inheritance, which he accepts and protects as his own. Who can injure us when we are the inheritance of the mighty God?

"Zealous of good works."

51. As ungodliness is opposed by inheritance, so zeal or diligence in our efforts after good opposes worldly lusts. By inward godliness we become Christ's heritage, and by sober and righteous living are good works wrought. As his heritage we serve him, and by good works we serve our neighbors and ourselves; first the heritage, then the good works. For good works are not wrought without godliness, and we are taught we must be zealous—zelotæ—that is, must emulate one another in doing good, or vie with one another in the effort to work universal good, disputing who was the best and who did the most good. This is the real meaning of the word "zelotæ." Where are these now?

"These things speak and exhort."

52. Truly, O Lord God, it is a vital charge, this—not only to preach the principles taught in this lesson, but continually to urge, admonish and arouse the people, leading them to faith and actually good works. Though we may have taught, we must follow it up with persevering exhortation, that the Word of God may have its sway.

53. O Pope, bishops, priests and monks now flooding the Church with fables and human doctrines, let these things sink into your minds. You will have more than enough to preach if you attempt only what this text contains, provided you continually admonish the people and enforce it. It beautifully portrays the life of the Christian. Its teaching, and only this, are you to preach and enforce. God grant it! Amen.

54. Note, the office of a minister calls for two things—teaching and exhortation. We must teach the uninformed, and must admonish the already informed lest they go backward, grow indolent or fall away entirely instead of persevering against all temptations.

THE ARMOR FURNISHED BY THE TEXT.

55. First, the text gives us authority to maintain that without grace no good can be wrought and all human efforts are sinful. This principle is established by Paul's statement, "Grace hath appeared." Evidently, previous to the advent mentioned, no grace existed among men. If

no grace existed, plainly there was only wrath. Therefore, without grace, there is in ourselves nothing but unregeneracy and wrath, instead of good.

56. Again, Paul's reference to saving grace clearly indicates that whatever is devoid of grace is already condemned and beyond the power of procuring help and salvation. Where, then, is free will? Where are human virtues, human reason and opinions? All are without saving grace, all are condemned, sinful and shameful before God, even though precious in our sight.

57. Still more impressive is the phrase "to all men." None are excepted. Manifestly, then, until recognition of the Gospel, naught but wrath ruled in all men. The apostle says (Eph 2, 3), "We were by nature children of wrath, even as the rest." Here he repels with safe armor, and stops the mouths of, all who boast of reason, works, opinions, free-will, light of nature, etc., as efficacious without grace. He makes them all corrupt, impious, ungodly and devoid of grace.

58. Further, Paul declares the grace of God appeared to "all men" to enable them to "deny ungodliness and worldly lusts." Who can stand before the armor he uses? What is the inevitable conclusion but this: without the grace of God, the works of all men are ungodliness and worldly lusts? For were there godliness, or spiritual aspirations, in any individual, there would be no reason for "all men" to deny ungodliness and worldly lusts; neither would the saving appearance of grace be called for in all cases. In this way, mark you, we should use the Scriptures as armor against false teachers. Not only are they for the exercise of our faith in our daily living, but for the open defense and battle of faith against the attacks of error.

59. Before the testimony of this text, all hypocrites, all ecclesiastics, must lie prostrate in defeat, no matter how much they may have fasted, prayed, watched and toiled. These exertions will avail naught; ungodliness and worldly lusts will still survive in them. Though shame may cause them to conceal evil expression, the heart is still impure.

Could our works, apparel, cloisters, fasting and prayers render us godly, the apostle might more properly have said that a prayer or a fast, a pilgrimage or an order, or something else, had appeared teaching us to be godly. But emphatically it is none of these; it is the appearing of saving grace. This, this alone, nothing else, renders us godly.

60. The danger and error of human laws, orders, sects, vows, and so on, is easily apparent. For they are not grace; they are merely works, by their false appearance leading the whole world into error, distress and misery. Under their influence, the world forgets grace and faith, and looks for godliness and happiness in these errors.

61. Again, Paul's admonition to us to look for the blessed and glorious appearing of the great God establishes the fact of another life beyond this. Plainly, it is evident that the soul is immortal; yes, that even the body must rise again. We say in the creed, "I believe in the resurrection of the body and in the life everlasting."

62. Further, it may be logically inferred from Paul's language—"the great God and our Saviour Jesus Christ"—that Christ is true God. Clearly, then, it follows that the Being to come in glory on the judgment day is the great God and our Saviour, Jesus Christ.

63. Should one in a caviling spirit apply to the Father alone the reference here to "the great God," his theory would not hold. For this glorious appearing is shared by the great God and our Saviour, Jesus Christ. Were Christ not true God, the glory and splendor of God would not be attributed to him. Since mention is made of the splendor, the glory, the work, of "the great God and our Saviour" the latter must be God with the former. Through the mouth of Isaiah, God has more than once said, "My glory will I not give to another," and yet here he shares it with Christ. Hence Christ can be no other than God. The glory of God is his. Yet he is a person distinct from the Father.

64. Once more, a strong argument against human doctrine is afforded us in Paul's words, "These things speak and exhort." Had Paul designed anything further to be

taught than the things he mentions, he surely would have said so. Our bishops and popes today think they have done enough when they permit these Paul's injunctions to be written in books and on slips of paper, enforcing them by no commands of their own; but the fact is, their own voices should be heard in constant preaching and enforcing of the Gospel. Wo unto them!

Second Christmas Sermon

Early Christmas Morning Service.

Epistle Text: Titus 3, 4-8.

4 But when the kindness of God our Saviour, and his
love toward man, appeared, 5 not by works done in
righteousness, which we did ourselves, but according
to his mercy he saved us, through the washing of regeneration and renewing of the Holy Spirit, 6 which he
poured out upon us richly, through Jesus Christ our
Saviour; 7 that, being justified by his grace, we might
be made heirs according to the hope of eternal life.
8 Faithful is the saying, and concerning these things I
desire that thou affirm confidently, to the end that they
who have believed God may be careful to maintain good
works. These things are good and profitable unto men.

GOD'S GRACE RECEIVED MUST BE BESTOWED.

1. This epistle selection inculcates the same principle taught in the conclusion of the Gospel lesson pertaining to contentment, good will and love for our neighbor. The substance of the text is: Why should we be unwilling to do for others what has been done for us by God, of whose blessings we are far less worthy than anyone can be of our help? Since God has been friendly and kindly disposed toward us in bestowing upon us his loving kindness, let us conduct ourselves similarly toward our neighbors, even if they are unworthy, for we too are unworthy.

2. It is necessary to a ready understanding of this epistle that we know the occasion of these words. In the verses immediately preceding, Paul says to Titus, his disciple:

"Put them in mind to be in subjection to rulers, to authorities, to be obedient, to be ready unto every good work, to speak evil of no man, not to be contentious, to be gentle, showing all meekness toward all men. For we also once were foolish, disobedient, deceived, serving divers lusts and pleasures, living in malice and envy, hateful, hating one another."

Note that Paul here indicates the relation we sustain to God and man. He would have us obedient to magistrates and kind to neighbors. Though our neighbors may be blind, erring and wicked, yet we should be charitable in our judgment and cheerfully endeavor to please them, remembering God's similar attitude toward us when we were as they.

3. The word "appeared," implying the revelation of the Gospel, or Christ's appearance to the whole world, is sufficiently defined in the preceding epistle lesson. Though in that case it refers to the birth of Christ, little depends on the circumstance so far as the meaning of the word is concerned. Paul does not employ here the little word "grace" used there, but he described the God of grace with two other pleasing words—"kindness" and "love." The first is, in Greek, "Chrestotes" (friendliness), implying that friendly, lovable demeanor which makes the individual attractive and gives his society a gracious influence moving everyone within its circle to love and affection. Such a one is capable of bearing with all men. He is not inclined to neglect any nor to repel with harshness. In him everyone may repose confidence. All men can approach him and deal with him. He resembles Christ, whom the Gospel portrays as always friendly to everyone, repelling none but gracious unto all.

4. God, too, shows himself to us through the Gospel as wholly lovable and kind, receiving all, rejecting none, ignoring our shortcomings and repelling no soul by severity. The Gospel proclaims naught but grace, whereby God sustains us and through which he kindly leads us, regardless of our worthiness. This is the day of grace. All men may confidently draw near to the throne of his mercy, as it is

written in Hebrews 4, 16. And we read in Psalm 34, 5: "They looked unto him, and were radiant; and their faces shall never be confounded." That is, God will not permit us to ask in vain, or to come unto him and go away empty and ashamed.

5. The second Word is, in Greek, "Philanthropia" (Philanthropy)—love of mankind. Avarice is the love of money. David (2 Sam 1, 26) refers to "the love of women." But naturalists term certain animals—the dog, the horse, the dolphin—philanthropic or humane, because they have a natural love and fondness for man; they adapt themselves to his service as if endowed with reason enabling them to understand him.

6. It is an attitude of love for mankind the apostle here attributes to our God. Moses has done likewise in Deuteronomy 33, 2-3, where he says of God: "At his right hand was a fiery law for them. Yea, he loveth the people." This quotation indicates that God does more than show himself, through the Gospel, with a kindly bearing, desiring to draw men unto himself, and tolerant of their shortcomings; he would give them of himself, would bestow his presence, and he extends his grace and friendship.

7. These two words descriptive of God, "kindness" and "love," are indeed pleasant and consoling. They represent him as offering grace, following us, ready to receive most graciously all who draw near to him and desire him. What more could he do? Note now why the Gospel is termed a gracious, comforting message concerning God revealed in Christ. What can be conceived more gracious to a poor, sinful conscience than what these words convey? Oh, how wretchedly the devil, through the laws of the Pope, has perverted for us these pure words of God!

8. These two words are to be accepted with their full and broad import. No distinction of person, as prevails among men, is to be made: for divine love and kindness is not secured by human merit; it is of God's grace alone and given to all that bear the name of man, however insignificant. God loves not what is characteristic of one person,

but of all. He is partial not to one, but kind to all. Therefore a man's honor is perfectly maintained, and no one can boast of his worthiness, or need despair because of his unworthiness. All mankind may be equally comforted in the unmerited grace God kindly and humanely offers and applies.

Had there ever been a meritorious individual or a work worthy of consideration, it surely would have been found among the doers of "works of righteousness." But Paul rejects especially these, saying, "not by works of righteousness which we have done." How much less reason have we to think the kindness and love of God has appeared in consequence of man's wisdom, power, nobility, wealth and the color of his hair! The grace which cancels all our boasted honor, ascribing glory alone to God who freely bestows it upon the unworthy, is pure as well as great.

9. This epistle instills the two further principles of believing and loving—receiving favors from God and granting favors to our neighbors. The entire Scriptures enforce these two precepts, and the practice of one requires the practice of the other. He who does not firmly believe in God's grace assuredly will not extend kindness to his neighbor, but will be tardy and indifferent in aiding him. In proportion to the strength of his faith will be his willingness and industry in helping his neighbor. Thus faith incites love, and love increases faith.

10. Now we see how utterly we fail to walk in faith when we presume to arrive at goodness and happiness by any other good works than those done to our neighbor. So numerous are the new works and doctrines daily devised, everything like a correct conception of a truly good life is wholly destroyed. But the fact is, all Christian doctrines and works, all Christian living, is briefly, clearly and completely comprehended in these two principles, faith and love. They place man as a medium between God and his neighbor, to receive from above and distribute below. Thus the Christian becomes a vessel, or rather a channel, through which the fountain of divine blessings continuously flows to other individuals.

11. Mark you, the truly godlike are they who receive from God all he offers through Christ, and in return accredit themselves by their beneficence, performing for others the part God performs for them. Psalm 82, 6 is in point here: "I said, Ye are gods, and all of you sons of the Most High." Sons of God are we, through the faith that constitutes us heirs of all divine blessings. But we are also "gods" through the love that makes us beneficent toward our neighbor. The divine nature is simply pure beneficence, or as Paul here says, kindness and love, daily pouring out blessings in abundance upon all creatures; as we everywhere witness.

12. Take heed, then, to embrace the message of these words presenting the love and kindness of God to all men. Daily exercise your faith therein, entertaining no doubt of God's love and kindness toward you, and you shall realize his blessings. Then you may with perfect confidence ask what you will, what your heart desires, and whatever is necessary for the good of yourself and your fellow-men. But if you do not so believe, it were far better you had never heard the message. For by unbelief you make false these precious, comforting, gracious words. You conduct yourself as if you regarded them untrue, which attitude is extreme dishonor to God; no more enormous sin could be committed.

13. But if you possess faith, your heart cannot do otherwise than laugh for joy in God, and grow free, confident and courageous. For how can the heart remain sorrowful and dejected when it entertains no doubt of God's kindness to it, and of his attitude as a good friend with whom it may unreservedly and freely enjoy all things? Such joy and pleasure must follow faith; if they are not ours, certainly something is wrong with our faith. This act of faith the apostle in Galatians terms "receiving the Holy Spirit" in and through the Gospel. The Gospel is a message concerning the love and mercy of God so gracious as to bring with it to preacher and hearer the presence of the Holy Spirit; just as the rays of the sun bear in themselves, and transmit, heat.

14. How could Paul have presented words conveying more love and graciousness? I venture to assert I have never read, in the entire Scriptures, words more beautifully expressive of the grace of God than these two—"Chrestotes" and "Philanthropia," friendliness and philanthropy. They represent grace not only as procuring for us remission of sins, but as God ever present with us, embracing us in his friendship, ever ready to help us and offering to do for us according to all we desire; in short, as a good and willing friend, to whom we may look for every favor and accommodation. Picture to your imagination a sincere friend and you will have an idea of God's attitude toward you in the person of Christ, though a very imperfect representation of his superabundant grace.

15. Now, if you steadfastly believe, if you rejoice in God your Lord, if you are alive and his grace satisfies, if your wants are all supplied, how will you employ yourself in this earthly life? Inactive you cannot be. Such a disposition of love toward God cannot rest. Your zeal will be warm to do everything you know will be to the praise and glory of a kind and gracious God. At this point there is no longer distinction of works. Here all commands terminate. There is neither restraint nor compulsion, but a joyful willingness and delight in doing good, whether the intended achievement be insignificant or difficult, small or great, requiring short service or long.

16. Your first desire will be that all men may obtain the same knowledge of divine grace. Hence your love will not be restrained from serving all to the fullest extent, preaching and proclaiming the divine truth wherever possible, and rejecting all doctrine and life not in harmony with this teaching. But take note, the devil and the world, unwilling that their devices be rejected, cannot endure the knowledge of what you do. They will oppose you with everything great, learned, wealthy and powerful, and represent you as a heretic and insane.

Mark you, you will be brought to the cross for the sake of the truth, as was Christ your Lord. You will have to endure the extremity of reproach. You must endanger all your property, friends and honor, your body and life, until thrust out of this life into eternity. In the midst of these trials, however, rejoice, cheerfully enduring all. Regard your enemies with the utmost charity. Act kindly, ever remembering you yourself were once as they are in the sight of God. Faith and love certainly can do it. Note this: the truly Christian life is that which does for others as God has done for itself.

17. Such is the apostle's meaning when he tells us the kindness of God did not appear unto us, or save us, because of our righteousness. His thought is: If we, though unworthy, were received through mercy, to enjoy the favors of God in spite of our great demerits and the enormity of our sins, why should we withhold our favors from others, whose merits have claims upon us? Let us not withhold; no, let us rather be children of God, doing good even to our enemies and to evil-doers: for so God has done, and still does, to us, evil-doers and his enemies. This teaching is in harmony with Christ's (Mt 5, 44-46): "Love your enemies . . . that ye may be sons of your Father who is in heaven; for he maketh his sun to rise on the evil and the good, and sendeth rain on the just and the unjust. For if ye love them that love you, what reward have ye? do not even the publicans the same?"

18. Paul not only forcibly rejects us for our evil deeds, but goes so far as to say, "Not by works of righteousness which we have done." He means the works regarded by ourselves as good—our righteousness in our own eyes and in the eyes of others—but which only render us more unfit to receive God's grace because they are in themselves deceitful and because we commit a twofold sin in looking upon them as good and in relying upon them; an attitude to provoke God's displeasure.

19. Similarly do our enemies, who while in the wrong yet maintain, in opposition to us, their faultlessness, for the most part provoke us to anger. Yet we are not to refuse them kindness. God, solely for his mercy's sake, re-

fused not kindness to us in similar errors, when we foolishly imagined all we did was right. As he dealt not with us according to our imagined righteousness, so should we in return not deal with our enemies according to their merits or demerits, but assist them from pure love, looking for thanks and reward, not from them, but from God. Let this be sufficient for a summary of this epistle.

20. Now let us consider the words Paul employs to define and advocate grace. In the first place he exalts it to the rejection of all our righteousness and good works. We are not to conclude it is a trivial thing he is rejecting here. It is man's best earthly achievement—righteousness. Were all men to concentrate their united efforts to attain wisdom and virtue by their natural reason, knowledge and free will—as we read, for instance, of the illustrious virtues and wisdom of certain pagan teachers and princes, Socrates, Trajan, and others, to whom all the world gives written and oral applause—were all men so to do, yet such wisdom and virtue are, in the sight of God, nothing but sin, and altogether reprehensible. The reason is, they are not attained in the grace of God; the achievers know not God and have not honored him in the effort, for they consider they have wrought by their own abilities. Righteousness is not taught otherwise than by grace, in the Gospel.

Paul boasts that he once led a life altogether irreproachable, and superior to the lives of his intellectual equals (Gal 1, 14), wherein he presumptuously thought he did right in persecuting the Christians who rejected that sort of piety. But after he had learned to know Christ, he declared he regarded his righteousness but filth and refuse that he might be found, not in his own righteousness, but in Christ and in faith, as he further shows in Phil 3, 9 and Gal 1, 14.

21. So he discards all boasted free will, all human virtue, righteousness and good works. He concludes they all are nothing and are wholly perverted, however brilliant and worthy they may appear, and teaches that we must be saved solely by the grace of God, which is effective for all believers who desire it from a correct conception of their own ruin and nothingness.

22. Now, it is essential that we accustom ourselves to interpret rightly the Scripture teaching of two kinds of righteousness. There is a human righteousness, to which Paul here and often elsewhere refers, and a divine righteousness—or divine grace—which justifies us through faith. Paul so expresses it in the conclusion of this epistle: "That, being justified by his grace, we might be made heirs according to the hope of eternal life." You see, the grace of God, and righteousness, become ours; we say "righteousness of God" because he gives it, and "our righteousness" because we receive it.

In Romans 1, 17 Paul tells us that the Gospel declares the righteousness of God is obtained through faith; "as it is written, The righteous shall live by faith." And it is stated of Abraham in Genesis 15, 6: "And he believed in Jehovah; and he reckoned it to him for righteousness." So the Scripture conclusion is, no one is justified before God except the believer; witness the quotation just given and that other by Paul from Habakkuk 2, 4, "The righteous shall live by his faith." So faith, grace, mercy and truth are one thing, wrought in us by God, through the Gospel of Christ; as it is written: "All the paths of Jehovah are lovingkindness and truth." Ps 25, 10.

23. We walk in "the paths of Jehovah," and he is in us when we observe his commandments. To be God's, the way must proceed in divine mercy and truth; not in our own ability or strength, for such are, in the eyes of God, ways of wrath and falsehood. He says (Is 55, 9): "For as the heavens are higher than the earth, so are my ways higher than your ways." In other words, "Your ways are earthly and ineffectual; you must walk in my heavenly ways if you are to be saved."

"But according to his mercy he saved us."

24. How are these words, reading as if we were already saved, to pass criticism? Are we not still on earth, in the midst of afflictions? I answer: The statement is made in just this way to emphasize the power of divine grace and the character of faith as opposed to the erring self-righteous,

who essay to obtain salvation through their works, as if it were not right at hand. But salvation is not so to be attained. Christ has saved us once for all, and in a twofold manner: First, he has done all that is necessary for our salvation—conquered and destroyed sin, death and hell, leaving no more there for anyone to do. Secondly, he has conveyed all these blessings unto us in baptism. He who confidently believes Christ has accomplished these things, immediately, in the twinkling of an eye, possesses salvation. All his sins and the reality of death and hell are removed. Nothing more than such faith is necessary to salvation.

25. Take note, God pours out upon us in baptism superabundant blessings for the purpose of excluding the works whereby men foolishly presume to merit heaven and gain happiness. Yes, dear friend, you must first possess heaven and salvation before you can do good works. Works never merit heaven; heaven is conferred purely of grace. Good works are to be performed without any thought of merit, simply for the benefit of one's neighbor and for the honor of God; until the body, too, shall be released from sin, death and hell. The true Christian's whole life after baptism is but a waiting for the manifestation of the salvation already his. He is certainly in full possession of the eternal life yet concealed in faith.

When faith is removed by fulfilment, salvation is manifest in the believer. This takes place at physical death. It is written (1 Jn 3, 2-3): "Beloved, now are we children of God, and it is not yet made manifest what we shall be. We know that, if he shall be manifested, we shall be like him; for we shall see him even as he is. And every one that hath this hope set on him purifieth himself, even as he is pure."

26. Therefore, let not the work-righteous who disregard faith mislead you, placing your salvation far ahead of you and compelling you to obtain it by works. It is within you, dear friend; it is already obtained. Christ says (Lk 17, 21): "The kingdom of God is within you." Hence the life we

live after baptism is but a tarrying, a waiting and longing for the manifestation of what is within ourselves, an apprehension of that for which we are apprehended. Paul declares (Phil 3, 12), "I follow after, if that I may apprehend that for which also I am apprehended of Christ Jesus"; that is, that he may see the blessings given in the shrine of faith. The apostle is eager to behold the treasure that baptism has granted and sealed to him in faith.

In this same third chapter of Philippians Paul says: "Our citizenship is in heaven"—that is, now—"whence also we wait for a Saviour, the Lord Jesus Christ: who shall fashion anew the body of our humiliation, that it may be conformed to the body of his glory." In Galatians 4, 9, when saying, "Now that ye have come to know God," he recalls the words and adds, "or rather to be known by God." While both these things are in point, there is a difference in their meaning: we are known of God, already apprehended; but we do not yet know and apprehend him. Our knowledge is hidden and withholden in faith.

Again, the apostle tells us (Rom 8, 24-25) we are saved in hope; that is, our salvation is not yet manifest. "Hope that is seen is not hope," he says, "for who hopeth for that which he seeth? But if we hope for that which we see not, then do we with patience wait for it." And Christ (Lk 12, 35-36) commands: "Let your loins be girded about, and your lamps burning; and be ye yourselves like unto men looking for their lord, when he shall return from the marriage feast; that, when he cometh and knocketh, they may straightway open unto him." Paul also said in the preceding epistle lesson (Tit 2, 12-13): "We should live soberly and righteously and godly in this present world; looking for the blessed hope and appearing of the glory of the great God and our Saviour Jesus Christ."

27. These and similar passages prove we are even now saved and that a Christian should not seek works as a means of salvation. The delusive doctrine of works blinds the Christian's eyes, perverts a right understanding of faith and forces him from the way of truth and salvation. Sal-

vation by grace is implied in the words, "According to his mercy he saved us," and again in the latter part of the lesson where it reads, "that we might be made heirs according to the hope of eternal life." We are heirs—though the fact is unrevealed in faith—and wait in hope for the manifestation of our inheritance.

28. The life of waiting we must live after we are baptized is designed to subdue the flesh and to display the power of grace in the conflict against the flesh, the world and the devil; and thus ultimately to enable us to serve our neighbors, by our preaching and example bringing them also into the faith. Though God might convert men through angels, he desires to accomplish it by human beings—by us, so that faith might be established and completed in a more congenial way through a kindred agency. Were angels constantly to dwell with us, faith would cease here. The instrumentality of angels would not be so congenial as that of our fellow-creatures, whom we are familiar with and understand. If we all were taken to heaven immediately after baptism, who would convert the others and bring them to God by means of the Word and a good example?

29. The fact that we expend so much by reason of purgatory and, forgetful of faith, presume to secure ourselves against purgatory or to liberate us from it by good works, unquestionably indicates we are under the influence of the devil and of Antichrist. We proceed as if our salvation were not already secured but we must gain it in some other way than by faith; and this even though plainly in contradiction of the Scriptures and of the principles of Christianity. He who does not receive salvation purely through grace, independently of all good works, certainly will never secure it. And he who makes his good works serve his own advantage, seeking to profit himself and not his neighbor thereby, performs no good work. All his doctrine is without faith and is such harmful error and deceit that I wish purgatory had never been instituted or introduced into the pulpit, for it is very destructive of Christian truth and true faith.

So great has been the devil's influence, nearly all institutions, cloister ceremonials, masses and prayers have reference simply to purgatory, leading us to the pernicious inference that through works we must improve our condition and secure salvation. So the blessings of baptism and faith must be obscured, and Christians must ultimately become pure heathen.

30. O Lord God, what abominable wickedness! When we should, like Christ and Paul, teach Christians to consider themselves, after baptism or absolution, ready for death at any hour and waiting for the manifestation of the salvation already theirs, we by relying on purgatory afford them indolence-fostering security. In such security they consider only this life, deferring and procrastinating in the matter of salvation until they come to their death-beds, there to effect sorrow and repentance and to presume, by ceremonials, soul-masses and bequests, to liberate themselves from purgatory. They will surely become conscious of their mistake. Now follows:

"Through the washing of regeneration, and renewing of the Holy Spirit."

31. How beautifully the apostle in these strong words extols the grace of God bestowed in baptism! He refers to baptism as a washing, whereby not our feet only, not our hands, but our whole bodies are cleansed. Baptism perfectly and instantaneously cleanses and saves. For the vital part of salvation and its inheritance, nothing more is necessary than this faith in the grace of God. Truly, then, are we saved by grace alone, without works or other merit. So, eternally pure love, praise and gratitude for, and honor unto, divine mercy shall possess us; we will not boast of nor delight in our own powers or achievements: as has already frequently and sufficiently been declared.

32. The righteousness of man, however, is a different sort of cleansing, simply a washing of garments and vessels, as recorded of hypocrites in Matthew 23, 25. Externally they appear clean, but internally remain full indeed of filth. Paul terms baptism not a bodily cleansing, but a "washing

of regeneration." It is not a superficial washing of the skin, a physical cleansing; it converts the whole nature, destroying the first birth, that of the flesh, with all inherited sin and condemnation.

This verse clearly indicates that salvation is not to be secured by works, but is an instantaneous gift. In physical birth we are given, not one member alone—hands or feet—but the entire body and the life; our life operates, not to effect birth, but because we are born. Similarly works do not render us pure and godly or save us: we are first made clean and godly, and receive salvation; then we freely perform good works to the honor of God and the benefit of our neighbor.

33. This, mark you, is the true knowledge of the pure grace of God. Thus we learn to know God and ourselves, to praise him and reject ourselves, to seek consolation from him and despair of ourselves. This doctrine is an occasion of much stumbling to them who presume to compel men to seek salvation by laws, commands and works.

34. For the sake of conveying a clearer understanding of this washing and this regeneration, Paul adds the word "renewing," because the individual is a new man, with a new nature. He is a new creature, with an altogether different disposition. He loves in a different way, and speaks, acts and lives in a manner unlike his former self. The apostle says (Gal 6, 15): "For neither is circumcision anything, nor uncircumcision"—that is, no work of the Law has significance—"but a new creature." The thought is: It will not do to patch up, or mend, the life here and there with works. An entirely new disposition is necessary; the nature must be changed. Then works will follow spontaneously.

35. Concerning this birth, Christ also declares (Jn 3, 3): "Except one be born anew, he cannot see the kingdom of God." Here we are taught that works will not answer; the individual must himself die and obtain a different nature. This takes place in baptism when he believes, for faith is this renewing. The damned will also be born again in the last day, but theirs will be a birth without a renewing.

They will remain unclean, as here in the old Adamic life. So, then, this washing, this regeneration, makes new creatures.

36. Much is said at various places in the Scriptures relative to the new birth. God refers to his Word and Gospel as the womb ("matricem" and "vulvam") of the new birth: "Hearken unto me, O house of Jacob, and all the remnant of the house of Israel, that have been borne by me from their birth, that have been carried from the womb" (Is 46, 3), or under my heart, as women speak of bearing children. Whosoever believes the Gospel, is conceived and born of God. But more on this subject at some other time.

37. We see how all these sayings overthrow works and presumptuous human mandates, and make clear the nature of faith, how the individual instantaneously and fully receives grace and is saved, works not aiding him in the matter but following as a result. Salvation by grace would be perfectly illustrated were God to produce from a dry log a live, green tree, the tree then to bring forth natural fruit. God's grace is powerful and effective. It does not, as visionary preachers presume to teach, lie dormant in the soul; nor is it an accessory to works, as the paint is an accessory to the wood. No, not so; it carries, it leads, drives, draws, changes. It effects all in man, making itself felt. Though concealed, its works are manifest. Words and works show where it is present, as the leaves and the fruit indicate the nature of the tree.

38. To make faith no more than an aid or ornament to works, as the sophists Thomas and Scotus, and the people, erroneously and perversely do, is a doctrine wherein faith falls far short of its real significance. For it not only aids in the accomplishment of works, but effects them unaided. Indeed, more than that, it changes and renews the whole being. Its object is to alter the character of the individual rather than to accomplish works by him. It claims to be a washing, a regeneration, a renewing, not only of works, but of the whole man.

39. Note, Paul here freely and fully preaches the grace

of God. He does not say God has saved us by works. He loudly proclaims that God has saved us by a regeneration and a renewing. To patch up with works is unavailing; conversion of our whole nature is necessary. Therefore, believers must suffer and die before grace can manifest itself and reveal its nature. Observe, David says in this connection: "The works of Jehovah are great, sought out of all them that have pleasure therein," Ps 111, 2. Who are these, his works? We are, sought out through grace in baptism. We are great works, new works, new born. It is indeed great that man is instantly saved, forever liberated from sin, death and hell. Hence, David says, "They are sought out of all them that have pleasure therein" or desire what God designs to accomplish through them, and God does all that man desires. But what can man desire more than to be saved, to be delivered from sin, death and hell?

40. Finally: the apostle terms this washing a "regeneration," a "renewing of the Holy Spirit," to fully express the power and efficacy of grace. This washing is a thing so vitally important it must be effected, not by a creature, but by the Holy Spirit. How completely, O holy Paul, thou dost reject the free will, the good works and the great merits of presumptuous saints! How high thou exaltest our salvation, at the same time bringing it so near to us! yes, even within ourselves. How plainly and purely thou dost preach grace. Let works, then, be here or there, to renew the man, to change the life, is impossible except by the washing of regeneration of the Holy Spirit.

41. That fact is plainly evident in the self-righteous. None are more intolerant, presumptuous, proud and faithless than they. In their old Adamic nature, which they clothe and adorn with good works, they remain intractable, unrenewed and obdurate, hardened and immovable; their evil nature is unchanged. They possess only outward works. Oh, they are a people of pernicious influence, and in the sight of God wholly destitute of grace, though they imagine themselves his nearest friends.

42. Paul's teaching here accords with that of Christ in

John 3, 5, where he says, referring to the washing of regeneration: "Except one be born of water and the Spirit, he cannot enter into the kingdom of God." Note here, the water answers to the washing; to be born again, to regeneration and renewing; and the Spirit, to him whom Paul mentions as the Holy Spirit.

43. Note here also the apostle's apparent ignorance of the sacrament of confirmation. He teaches, as does Christ, the giving of the Holy Spirit in baptism; in baptism we are indeed born of the Holy Spirit. True, we read (Acts 8, 17) how the apostles laid their hands upon those who had been baptized, that they might receive the Holy Spirit. This incident has been construed to sanction confirmation, but its real purpose was to invoke the Holy Spirit as external evidence, and the gift of divers tongues for the preaching of the Gospel. But in course of time the ceremony was abandoned. It no longer exists except in ordination or consecration to the ministerial or preaching office. Even there it is deplorably abused. But more of this at some other time.

"Which he poured out upon us richly, through Jesus Christ our Saviour."

44. Observe, the Holy Spirit is not merely given, but "poured out"; not only that, but "abundantly poured out." The apostle seems unable to sufficiently magnify grace and its works, while we, alas, estimate it so low in comparison to our works. It would be absurd for God to pour out upon us the Holy Spirit in such measure and yet to expect from us, and in us, something whereby we might be justified and saved; as if the superabundant divine works were insufficient.

45. Were such the case, Paul here must have spoken inconsiderately and might justly be accused of falsehood. But so bountifully does he represent to us the measure of grace, clearly no one can rely too much upon the washing of regeneration; it is of unlimited importance. No one can place too much confidence in it; there is always occasion for more. For God has embraced, in the Word and in faith, blessings too great for mortal life to comprehend or to receive were

they to manifest themselves. As revelation begins, the individual dies; he passes out of this life, swallowed up in the blessings he now by faith apprehends in very limited measure. Thus more than abundantly are we justified and saved without works if we only believe.

Peter says: "Through Christ he hath granted unto us his precious and exceeding great promises; that through these ye may become partakers of the divine nature." 2 Pet 1, 4. He does not say "will be granted" but "hath granted." And Christ says: "For God so loved the world, that he gave his only begotten Son, that whosoever believeth on him should not perish, but have eternal life." Jn 3, 16. Notice, all who believe have eternal life. That being true, believers certainly are just and holy without works. Works contribute nothing to justification. It is effected by pure grace richly poured out upon us.

46. "But," you say, "how is it, then, the Scriptures so frequently speak of salvation for them who do good? For instance, Christ says (Jn 5, 29): 'And shall come forth; they that have done good, unto the resurrection of life; and they that have done evil, unto the resurrection of judgment.' And Paul declares (Rom 2, 7-8) that honor and glory are the reward of them who do good; indignation and wrath, of evil-doers. And he makes many similar declarations." I answer: How are these passages to be interpreted? Not otherwise than as they read—without additions: He who does good shall be saved; he who does evil shall be damned. The difficulty lies in our error in judging according to external appearances in the matter of good works. The Scriptures teach not that way, but that no one can do good until he is himself good. He does not become good through works, but his works are good because he is good. He becomes good through the washing of regeneration and in no other way. This is the meaning of Christ's words (Mt 7, 17): "Every good tree bringeth forth good fruit; but the corrupt tree bringeth forth evil fruit." And (Mt 12, 33): "Either make the tree good, and its fruit good; or make the tree corrupt, and its fruit corrupt."

47. True, the self-righteous perform works similar to those of the regenerated; indeed, their works are frequently the more brilliant. They pray, fast, contribute money, erect institutions, make pilgrimages and conduct themselves with great ostentation. But Christ calls their works "sheep's clothing" (Mt 7, 15) wherein move ravening wolves. None of the self-righteous are really humble, mild, moderate and good in their hearts. This fact is revealed when one crosses them and rejects their works. Then they bring forth their natural and identifying fruits: temerity, impatience, arbitrariness, obstinacy, slander and many other evil propensities.

48. Therefore it is true that he who does good shall be saved—his salvation shall be revealed; but he could do nothing good were he not already saved in the new birth. The Scriptures sometimes have reference to the external conduct of the good, and at others to their inner nature that prompts the outward works, teaching present salvation because of the inner nature, and a future salvation if good is done; that is, if the individual remains steadfast, his salvation shall be revealed in the future.

49. The works we performed in our old, unregenerate state, our Adamic nature, the apostle in this lesson rejects when he says "not by works done in righteousness, which we did ourselves." These may be good works, but not before God, who looks first for personal goodness and afterward for the works. In Genesis 4, 4-5, he had respect first unto Abel, and then unto his offering; and first rejected Cain, and then his offering. Cain's offering, however, was in external appearance good like that of Abel.

50. Paul significantly adds "through Jesus Christ our Savour." The intent is to shelter us all under Christ, as young chickens are gathered under the wings of the hen. Christ himself says (Mt 23, 37): "O Jerusalem . . . how often would I have gathered thy children together, even as a hen gathereth her chickens under her wings, and ye would not!"

51. In the phrase above is taught the nature of true, liv-

ing faith. Such is the character of faith that it is not sufficient to salvation for you to believe in God after the manner of the Jews and many others, upon whom, however, he conferred many blessings and temporal advantages; but it is through Jesus Christ you must believe in God. In the first place, you must not doubt that he is your gracious God and Father, that he has forgiven all your sins and has saved you in baptism. In the second place, you must know, too, that all this has not been effected without cause—without satisfaction having been rendered to his righteousness. There is no reason for mercy and grace to operate upon and in us, to aid us to obtain eternal blessings and salvation. Justice must first be satisfied to the fullest extent. Christ says (Mt 5, 18: "One jot or one tittle shall in no wise pass away from the law till all things be accomplished."

Whatever is promised of the grace and goodness of God must be understood as only for those who perfectly fulfil his commands. He says (Mic 2, 7) in reply to the Jews, when they presumed they were great in the sight of God and continually cried "Peace, peace!" and "Why should God be so angry? Why should his benign Spirit have departed from us?"—he replies, "Do not my words do good to him that walketh uprightly?" No one, therefore, can attain God's abundant grace unless he shall have rendered full satisfaction to God's commands.

52. Now, enough has been said to show our works of no value in God's sight, and ourselves unable to fulfil the least of his commands, to perform a single work. How much more impossible is it, then, for us to render full satisfaction to his justice and become worthy of his grace! Even though we were able to keep all his commandments and to make full satisfaction to his justice, yet we would not for that reason be worthy of his grace and of salvation. He would not be under any obligation to confer them upon us. He might require it all as obligatory upon his creatures, who must serve him. Whatever he grants is of pure grace and mercy.

This Christ clearly taught in the parable in Luke 17, 7-10:

"But who is there of you, having a servant plowing or keeping sheep, that will say unto him, when he is come in from the field, come straightway and sit down to meat; and will not rather say unto him, Make ready wherewith I may sup, and gird thyself, and serve me, till I have eaten and drunken; and afterward thou shalt eat and drink? Doth he thank the servant because he did the things that were commanded? Even so ye also, when ye shall have done all the things that are commanded you, say, We are unprofitable servants; we have done that which it was our duty to do."

53. Now, if through grace and not of necessity heaven is given to those who do all they are under obligation to do; if to such—provided, such there be—heaven is given not by merit but through divine and gracious promises like that of Matthew 19, 17, "If thou wouldest enter into life, keep the commandments": shall we then presume upon our wretched good works? Why extol them as if their nature and not the pure promise, the gracious Word of God, makes them worthy of the kingdom of heaven?

54. In the first place, God has given a Being to fully satisfy divine justice for us all. In the second place, he has, through this same Being, poured out his grace and his rich blessings. So, then, notwithstanding grace is received by us without price and without merit on our part—indeed, in spite of great demerit and unworthiness—yet it is not bestowed without cause and deserved merit somewhere. As Paul teaches (Rom 5, 18), we fell into sin not of our own act or deserving, it being born in us from Adam in our natural birth; and on the other hand, in the new birth we enter into grace and salvation through Christ, without our merit or works.

55. Hence the apostle is careful in every place where he mentions grace and faith to add "through Jesus Christ," that no one may be able to say, "I believe in God and am satisfied with that." No, beloved friend, your belief must include a knowledge of how and through whom you believe. You must know that God requires you to fulfil all his commandments, to satisfy his justice, before he accepts your

faith unto salvation; and that though you were able to render full satisfaction you would still have to await salvation through grace alone, and not receive it on account of any duties you perform, but rather your pride and presumption must fall to the ground before God.

56. Observe the advantages you have in Christ. Through him grace and salvation are conferred upon you, he having rendered full obedience to all the commandments of God, and satisfied God's justice, in your stead and for you. Grace and salvation are conferred upon you because he is worthy. This is true Christian faith.

No faith is sufficient but the Christian faith, the faith that believes in Christ and accepts solely through him the two principles—satisfaction of divine justice, and the gracious bestowal of eternal salvation. Paul, speaking of Christ (Rom 4, 25), says, "Who was delivered up for our trespasses, and was raised for our justification." Not only was he given to put away sin and to fulfil the commandments of God, but also to render us worthy, through him, of possessing righteousness and of being children of grace.

Again, Paul says of Christ (Rom 3, 25), "Whom God set forth to be a propitiation, through faith in his blood." It is not just "faith" but "faith in his blood." With his blood, and in our nature, he has rendered full satisfaction and become for us a throne of grace. We receive absolution and grace at no cost or labor on our part, but not without cost and labor on the part of Christ.

57. We must, then, shelter ourselves under his wings (Mt 23, 37) and not fly afar in the security of our own faith, else we will soon be devoured by the hawk. Our salvation must exist, not in our righteousness, but, as I have often said, in Christ's righteousness, which is an outspread wing, or a tabernacle, to shelter us.

58. Our faith and all we may have received from God is insufficient to salvation, wholly inadequate, unless faith rests beneath the wings of Christ and firmly trusts that not we but he can render, and has rendered, full satisfaction to the justice of God for us; and that grace and salvation

are not conferred upon us because of our faith but because of the will of Christ. The pure grace of God, promised, procured and bestowed upon us in Christ and through Christ, must be perfectly recognized.

This is the teaching implied in John 14, 6, "No one cometh unto the Father but by me." Christ's sole effort in the whole Gospel is to draw us out of ourselves into himself; he spreads out his wings and calls us together beneath their shelter. To emphasize the grace of Christ is also Paul's design in the conclusion of this lesson, where he says:

> "That, being justified by his grace, we might be made heirs according to the hope of eternal life. This is a faithful saying."

59. He does not say "justified by our faith" but "justified by the grace of Christ." Christ alone has favor with God. No one but he has done the will of God and merited eternal life. In view of the fact that he did it not for his own sake but for ours, all believers should be so perfectly one with Christ that all he has done for them will, through him and his grace, be regarded as if the believer himself had accomplished it. See what an inexpressibly beneficent thing Christian faith is—what inconceivably great blessings it brings to all believers!

60. Let us learn from this epistle how precious is the Gospel that proclaims these benefits, and what injury and destruction of souls they effect who silently ignore the Gospel and preach the works of the Law, yes, their own human doctrines. Guard, then, against false preachers and also against false faith. Rely not upon yourself, nor upon your faith. Flee to Christ; keep under his wings; remain under his shelter. Let his righteousness and grace, not yours, be your refuge. You are to be made an heir of eternal life, not by the grace you have yourself received, but, as Paul says here, by Christ's grace.

Again, it is said in Psalm 91, 4, "He will cover thee with his pinions, and under his wings shalt thou take refuge." And in the Song of Solomon 2, 14, "O my dove, that art in the clefts of the rock, in the covert of the steep place." That is, in the wounds of Christ the soul is preserved. Observe, true Christian faith does not take refuge in itself, as the sophists dream, but flees to Christ and is preserved under him and in him.

61. It has been sufficiently stated that we are heirs of eternal life in hope, and that grace, regardless of works, instantaneously confers salvation, inheritance and all; yet, as said, "in hope." They are not revealed until death. Then we shall see what, in faith, we have received and possess.

THE ARMOR OF THIS EPISTLE.

62. This epistle lesson forcibly and in express terms contends against all humanly-devised righteousness, as well as against all human powers and free will. These are plain words, "Not by works done in righteousness, which we did ourselves, but according to his mercy he saved us." In fact, the words of the whole lesson oppose the righteousness of man. Paul attributes all efficacy to the washing of regeneration, to the renewing of the Holy Spirit, to Jesus Christ and his grace. In the face of such thunderbolts, how can there remain in us the least trace of presumption?

63. It matters not how brilliant may be secular and ecclesiastical laws; how attractive the station of priests, monks and nuns; how dazzling the titles of gentlemen of honor and ladies of uprightness, even if the wearers of them could raise the dead: without faith in Christ all is vain. Such hypocrisy as that just mentioned blinds and misleads the whole world, and obscures for us the holy Gospel and the Christian faith.

These brilliant works and attractive stations of men assist as little in procuring our salvation as do the works of beasts or the common trades of mankind. Indeed, they perniciously obstruct salvation. Therefore, you should guard against wolves in sheep's clothing, and learn to cleave to Christ in true and firm faith.

Third Christmas Sermon

Christmas Morning Service.

Epistle Text: Hebrews 1, 1-12.

1 God, having of old time spoken unto the fathers in
the prophets by divers portions (at sundry times) and in
divers manners, 2 hath at the end of these days spoken
unto us in his Son, whom he appointed heir of all things,
through whom also he made the worlds; 3 who being the
effulgence of his glory, and the very image of his substance, and upholding all things by the word of his power,
when he had made purification of sins, sat down on
the right hand of the Majesty on high; 4 having become by so much better than the angels, as he hath inherited a more excellent name than they. 5 For unto
which of the angels said he at any time,

Thou art my Son,
This day have I begotten thee? and again,
I will be to him a Father,
And he shall be to me a Son?

6 And when he again bringeth in the firstborn into the
world he saith, And let all the angels of God worship
him. 7 And of the angels he saith,

Who maketh his angels winds,
And his ministers a flame of fire:

8 but of the Son he saith,

Thy throne, O God, is for ever and ever;
And the sceptre of uprightness is the sceptre of
thy kingdom.
9 Thou hast loved righteousness, and hated iniquity;
Therefore God, thy God, hath anointed thee
With the oil of gladness above thy fellows.

10 And,

Thou, Lord, in the beginning didst lay the foundation of the earth,
And the heavens are the works of thy hands:
11 They shall perish; but thou continuest:
And they all shall wax old as doth a garment;
12 And as a mantle shalt thou roll them up,
As a garment, and they shall be changed:
But thou art the same,
And thy years shall not fail.

THE DIVINITY OF CHRIST.

1. This is a strong, forcible, noble epistle, preëminently and emphatically teaching the great article of faith concerning the Godhead, or the divinity of Christ. The presumption that it was not written by Paul is somewhat plausible, because the style is unusually ornamental for him. Some are of the opinion it was written by Luke; others by Apollos, whom Luke represents as "mighty in the Scriptures," opposing the Jews. Acts 18, 24 and 28. Certain it is, no epistle enforces the Scriptures with greater power than does this. Hence it is evident the author was an eminent apostolic individual, whoever he was. Now, the object of the epistle is to establish and promote faith in the divinity of Christ, and, as already stated, scarce any portion of the Bible more strongly enforces this article of our creed. We must, therefore, confine ourselves to its words and treat it in regular order, item by item.

2. In the first place, it was the apostle's design to bring the Jews to the Christian faith. As we shall learn, he presses them so closely they cannot deny that Christ is true God. Now, if he is God and the Son of God, and if he himself has spoken unto us and suffered for us, justice necessarily demands our faith. We have much more reason to believe in him than had the fathers who in time past believed when God spoke simply through the prophets.

3. Paul contrasts the ancient preachers and disciples with those of later times. The prophets and Christ are the preachers, the fathers and ourselves the disciples. The Son, the Lord himself, speaks unto us; his servants the

prophets spoke unto the fathers. If the fathers believed the servants, how much more readily would they have believed the Lord himself! And if we believe not the Lord, how much more reluctant would we have been to believe the servants! Thus he makes one condition argue for the other: our unbelief contrasted with the faith of the fathers is an awful disgrace; again, the faith of the fathers in contrast with our unbelief is deserving of very great honor.

Our disgrace is yet greater when we recall the fact that God spoke to the fathers, not only once, but at different times, and not only in one way, but in different ways; and yet they always believed; while we are not induced by their example to believe, even in one instance, the message of the Lord himself. Observe, Paul proceeds with a powerful discourse in the effort to convert the Jews, yet the attempt avails nothing.

"By divers portions (at sundry times) and in divers manners."

4. To me the particular and unlike meaning of these two phrases is this: "By divers portions" implies the succession of many prophets, and that all prophecies were not made through one man nor at one time; "in divers manners" signifies that through each individual prophet, to say nothing of the many, God spoke in different ways at different times. For instance, at times he expressed himself in plain, definite terms; and at other times figuratively or through visions. Ezekiel portrayed the four evangelists by the four beasts. Isaiah sometimes clearly states that Christ shall be a king; at other times he alludes to him as a rod and a branch from the stem of Jesse; again, as excellent fruit of the earth.

5. Thus the prophets speak of Christ in "divers manners." This latter phrase, moreover, may also be understood as implying that God spoke in various ways when he gave the people of Israel temporal aid. His leading them out of Egypt by Moses was one way of speaking, and his bringing them through the Red Sea another. In his direc-

tions to David concerning warfare and other matters he spoke in a still different way. Not one declaration, but divers declarations, were made. The objects accomplished differed. But faith was always the same—at all times and with every method.

6. How beautifully and gently the apostle invites and persuades the Jews when he reminds them of the fathers and the prophets, and of God himself! They had unbounded confidence in the record of these as they were in time past. But now they will not believe in God. They will not take to heart the fact of his speaking to the fathers, not once only, but often; not in one way, but in different ways. Yet they know well, and must confess that such was the case. They will not believe him now when he speaks at another time and in another way—a way he never before employed nor will again. The manner of speaking they ardently desire, will never be granted. God has never yet, not even in former time, spoken in a manner designated by them. That would be but to obstruct faith and frustrate God's design. We must leave to him the time, person and manner of speaking, and be concerned only about faith.

7. The phrase "at the end of these days" is significant. From now to the end no other manner of preaching is to be adopted. This is the last time he purposes to speak, and the last method he will employ. He has commanded—left on record—that this Word, and only this, is to be preached until the end. Paul says (1 Cor 11, 26): "For as often as ye eat this bread, and drink the cup, ye proclaim the Lord's death till he come." He also arrests their expectation when he says "in these days;" they are not to look for other days to come. The days when he speaks for the last time and in the last manner are already at hand.

"In his Son."

8. Here Paul begins to extol Christ, the last teacher, speaker and apostle: with forcible and well-grounded Scriptural evidence he shows Christ as the real Son of God and Lord over all. We must first learn to truly understand the

character of Christ, that he exists in a twofold nature—divine and human. This is a point where many err. Sometimes it is to manufacture fables from his words. Men apply to the divine nature the sayings really uttered with reference to his humanity; thus are they deluded by certain passages of Scripture. It is of the utmost importance first to determine which of the statements concerning Christ pertain to his divine nature and which to his human side. This settled, all else will be easily plain.

9. But first we must answer the inquiry liable to be made, "If the voice of God today is the last message, why is it said that Elijah and Enoch shall come, opposing Antichrist?" I answer: Concerning the advent of Elijah, I hold that he will not come in a physical manner. [As to the coming of Elijah I am suspended between heaven and earth, but I am inclined to believe it will not take place bodily. However, I will not contend hard against the other view. Each may believe or not believe it, as he likes. Editions, A, C, D, E.] I well know St. Augustine has somewhere said, "The advent of Elijah and of Antichrist is firmly fixed in the belief of all Christians." But I also know there is no statement of Scripture to substantiate his assertion. Malachi's prophecy concerning the coming of Elijah (ch 4, 5) the angel Gabriel makes refer to John the Baptist (Lk 1, 17), and Christ does the same even more explicitly where he says (Mk 9, 13): "But I say unto you, that Elijah is come, and they have also done unto him whatsoever they would, even as it is written of him." Now, if John is the Elijah of the prophecy, as the Lord here says he was, the prediction of Malachi is already fulfilled. And there is nothing more prophesied concerning the coming of Elijah. The statement the Lord made just previously to the one quoted, "Elijah indeed cometh first, and restoreth all things," may be fairly interpreted to mean that Christ, referring to the office of John, practically says: "Yes, I well know Elijah must first come and restore all things, but he has already come and accomplished it."

10. This view is demanded by the fact that immediately after his reference to the coming and office of Elijah, Christ speaks of his own sufferings: "It is written of the Son of man, that he must suffer many things, and be set at naught." If this prophecy concerning Christ was to be fulfilled after the coming of Elijah, then certainly Elijah must have already come. I know of nothing more to expect concerning the coming of Elijah unless it might be that his spirit will be manifest again in the power of the Word of God, as now seems probable. For I have no longer any doubt that the Pope, with the Turks, is Antichrist, whatever you may believe.

11. To return to Christ: We assert it is essential firmly to believe Christ true God and true man; and that the Scriptures—including Christ's own words—sometimes have reference to the divine nature of Christ and at other times to his human nature. For instance, the declaration (Jn 8, 58), "Before Abraham was born, I am," relates to his divinity; but the statement (Mt 20, 23), "To sit on my right hand, and on my left hand, is not mine to give," recognizes his humanity, which could not help itself even on the cross. Yet some expounders have desired here to show their great skill by abstruse interpretations made to oppose the heretics. It is his human nature that says: "The Father is greater than I." Jn 14, 28. Also: "How often would I have gathered thy children together, even as a hen gathereth her chickens under her wings." Mt 23, 37. Again, the passage (Mk 13, 32) reading, "Of that day or that hour knoweth no one, not even the angels in heaven, neither the Son, but the Father," has reference to the man Christ.

12. The explanation which some have made, "The Son knew not; that is, he did not choose to reveal," is superfluous. What is the advantage of that addition? The humanity of Christ, like that of any other holy mortal man, did not, at every moment, consider and utter, did not desire and note, how some made him a man with almighty power; they improperly combine the two natures and their opera-

tion. As he did not always see, hear and feel all things, so likewise he did not at every moment contemplate in his heart every matter; he recognized things as God moved him to do, as he brought them before him. Being filled with grace and wisdom, he was able to judge and to teach as occasion demanded; the Godhead, who alone sees and knows all things, was personally present in him. Finally: All reference in the Scriptures to the humiliation and exaltation of Christ must be understood of the man; for the divine nature can neither be humiliated nor exalted.

"Whom he appointed heir of all things."

13. These words refer to Christ's human nature. We must believe in his supremacy in that respect as well as in his divinity. All creatures are subservient to the man Christ. As God, he creates all. As man, he creates nothing, yet all creation is subject to him. David says (Ps 8, 6), "Thou hast put all things under his feet."

14 Christ is our Lord and our God. As God, he creates us; as Lord, we serve him and he rules over us. The apostle refers to him in this epistle as true God, and also Lord over all. Though having two different natures, he is one person. What Christ does and suffers, essentially God does and suffers. In this case only one nature is involved. To illustrate: I speak of a "wounded man" when but a single limb is injured. The soul is not wounded, nor is the body as a whole; only a part of the body. But I speak as I do because body and soul constitute one person. Now, as I must recognize a difference between body and soul when I speak, so must I recognize the two natures of Christ. Again: It is not a misstatement if in the night I say I have no knowledge of the sun, when at the same time I have a thorough mental knowledge of it; for I have no physical vision. Similarly, Christ knows nothing concerning the last day, and at the same time has full knowledge of it.

"Through whom also he made the worlds."

15. Observe, by this same Son who in his human nature

is "appointed heir of all things"—by him as God, the worlds were made. He is but one person, yet with two natures of unlike operation. There is one Christ, of two natures. The terms Paul here employs are in recognition of Christ's highest nature.

Now, the apostle plainly speaks of the Son who is appointed heir when he says that by him the world is made. If everything is made by him, he could not himself have been created. Consequently, it is plain that he is true God. For anything not created and yet existing must be God. Again, whatsoever is made must be a creature and cannot be God; for it does not exist of itself but derives its existence from its Creator. Now, all things are made by Christ, and he is not created. Hence he must have his existence from himself; not from any creature nor any creator.

16. Furthermore, if he is a Son he is not alone, his existence necessitates a Father. Through the Son God made the world, but God cannot himself be that Son. Consequently there must be two distinct persons, the Father and the Son, yet (because) the divine nature is only one; for there cannot be more than one God. Conclusively, then, Christ with the Father is true God. In one divine substance with him, he is Creator and Maker of the world. The only difference is, one is the Son and the other the Father. And Christ is not created by the Father, as the world was created; essentially he was begotten in eternity. Nor is he inferior to the Father. He is the same in every respect except that he is begotten of the Father, and the Father not begotten of him.

17. If these things are beyond the grasp of our reason, reason must surrender as a captive to these and like Scripture words, and believe. Could we comprehend this mystery by human reason, there would be no faith. Clearly enough, the words, "Through whom also he made the worlds," make mentions of two Beings. And it is not less clear that the uncreated one through whom all things were made, also must be God. Just how this can be, the Scriptures do not teach. It must be received by faith.

The Scriptures speak after this fashion: "The world is created through Christ, by the Father, in the Holy Spirit"; and though the meaning is not wholly clear, and easy of comprehension, there is good reason for the language. It is employed more by way of intimation than explanation—to imply that the Father derives not his substance from the Son, but the Son from the Father; and that the latter is the first original person in the Godhead. In the statement that the Father made the world through Christ, not Christ through the Father, the intent is to teach the Father's title to the first person; he from whom, through Christ, all things have existence. John speaks in the same way (Jn 1, 3), "All things were made through him." And Paul again (Col 1, 16), "All things have been created through him, and unto him;" and (Rom 11, 36), "For of him, and through him, and unto him, are all things.

18. Note the aptness of the language where Christ is termed an "heir," in reference to his humanity. For who should be more entitled to inherit the estate of God than his Son? He with the Father created it—created all creatures. But Christ is man and Son, and because of his Sonship he inherits; in both natures is he Son. But as to the origin of the apostle's particular language, we shall learn that in the Gospel.

> "Who being the effulgence [brightness] of his glory and the very image of his substance [person]."

19. Paul uses these figures to express with all possible clearness the fact that Christ is a person distinct from the Father, yet one, real, true God. But the German and Latin words are not just equivalent to the Greek terms employed by the apostle. The apostle speaks of Christ as the effulgence proceeding from the glory of the Father. Just as the illumination of the morning sun, the sun's vital substance, is not a part of the effulgence, but the whole effulgence of the whole sun, proceeding from the sun and yet inherent in it. By the figure, "the effulgence of his glory," is conveyed as in a word the birth of the Son, the unity of

his nature and the Father's, and the distinction of the persons. Christ, without limit of time, is eternally begotten of the Father, and ever proceeds, with that unweariedness represented by the sun in the morning rather than at midday or evening. But Christ is not the person of the Father, as the effulgence is not the sun. He is with and in the Father; not existing before nor after, but co-eternal with him and a part of him, as the effulgence is with and a part of the sun.

20. The apostle terms the Father's effulgence "Doxa," (glory) properly implying honor or glory. Therefore the divine nature is unqualified glory and honor, having all in itself and deriving nothing from another. It has the right to boast of and glory in itself. Now, Paul says Christ is complete light, the full effulgence of God's honor. That is, he too has in himself the unlimited Godhead and has equal right with the Father to boast and glory. The only exception is, he derives his authority from the Father and not the Father from him. He is the effulgence proceeding from the paternal honor, he is God begotten and not God begetting, yet God complete and perfect as the Father is.

21. The Scriptures, you will observe, do not so speak of the saints, though they are also an honor to God; that is, they were created for his honor. But Paul says Christ is the brightness of the paternal honor; the words force the conclusion that the brightness constitutes the Father's honor, else it would not be the effulgence of his honor. But what shall I say by way of explanation? These words are more easily understood by the heart than explained by tongue or pen. They are in themselves clearer than any commentary renders them, and in proportion as they are explained are they obscured. The substance of the clause is this: the whole Godhead is in Christ, and to him as to God all honor is due; yet he does not derive his Godhood from himself, but from the Father. The apostle implies two persons but one God; for the Holy Spirit is not mentioned here. When we have advanced far enough to comprehend

two persons existent in one God, we will readily believe in the third person.

22. In the other figure the apostle styles Christ an image or sign of the substance of God. Despite its clearness I still claim the privilege of speaking plainly and clearly. An image created after the likeness of a person is not an image of the substance or nature of that person. It is not a being; it is mere stone or wood. It is an image formed from stone or wood substance in the likeness of man. But if I could handle the substance of the person as the potter handles clay and make therewith an image of the individual which should also perfectly contain his substance or nature, that would, as you perceive, be an essential image, or a likeness of the human substance. But such would be a creature. An image necessarily is constructed from a different substance than the thing imaged, and differs in nature.

Here the Son is such an image of the Father s substance, that the Father's substance is the image itself. If we may so express it, the image is made from the Father's substance. The image is not only like the Father resembling him, but fully contains his whole substance and nature; as it may be said of "the effulgence of his glory," that the effulgence is constituted of the glory, and not only like it but embodying it perfectly, making the effulgence and the glory identical.

23. Now notice, as I say an image of man is formed of wood or stone, so I say Christ is a divine image: as truly as the former is but a material image, so truly is the latter God. Paul calls Christ the image of the living and invisible God.

In the wooden image, this perfection is lacking. Though a wooden image, it is not an image of the wood but of an individual; it does not represent the wood, but the individual. Though the individual be faithfully reproduced in the wood, yet he himself is not wood; his substance is something different from the substance imaging him. In all cases the image differs in substance from the person imaged. It is impossible to furnish an image actually the substance of the individual. But in this verse we have an image and one imaged who are identical in substance, except that the Father is not an image. The Father is not fashioned from nor like the Son; but the Son from the Father, and is like the Father, in one simple, truly divine substance with him.

24. Such perfection is also wanting in the sun and its effulgence. The sun has its own splendor, and the same is true of its effulgence, but the effulgence derives its splendor from the sun. But in the figure before us, effulgence is splendor; of the splendor, if we may so speak, the effulgence is constituted. The splendor is essentially and perfectly the effulgence itself, with this difference that the effulgence has not its origin in itself but in the paternal splendor.

25. You will notice the verse is even now clearer than the explanation. "The image of his substance," "the effulgence of his glory"—these Paul's sayings are clear enough. The tongue should be silent here to allow the heart to reflect. The Hebrew mode of speaking is thus: "Pauperes sanctorum, i. pauperes sancti; Virtus Dei, i. virtus Deus; Sic, character substantiæ, i. character substantia, subsistens et impsemet Deus; Sic, splendor gloriæ, i. splendor gloria ipsa." Latin scholars may easily comprehend this, but for the Germans and the common people it suffices to call the likeness made from gold an image of gold. Similarly, they are to call Christ an image of God the Father because he is wholly of God in character, and there is no God beside him, though at the same time his Godhead and image have origin from the Father as the first person; but the two are one God. This is not true of creatures. The golden image represents not a golden nature, but the wholly different nature of the individual. Though it is a golden image, it does not image the nature of gold. Another image is necessary to represent the nature of gold; as, for instance, a golden color, or something else not truly gold.

But in our text the image is also the substance of the imaged, and no other image is requisite than its own substance. It is faith that is called for here and not keen speculation. The words are clear enough; they are positive and forcible. He who will not in them recognize the divinity of Christ, will not recognize it in any way. Christ is not here termed a common image in the ordinary sense of the word; the word used is "Character"—an image more characteristic than a portrait or any other likeness. Again, he is called "Apaugasma"—an actual brightness resembling nothing but the glory from which it proceeds.

"And upholding all things by the word of his power."

26. For a third time Christ is represented as God. First, it is stated that the worlds were made by him; second, he is called the brightness and the image of God; and here he upholds all things. If he upholds all, he is not himself upheld. He is supreme, hence he must be God. To uphold all things is to support and maintain them. Not only are all things made by him, as stated in the preceding verse, but they are perpetuated and preserved by him. As Paul says in Colossians 1, 17: "In him all things consist." The word "upholding" is well chosen. Christ neither coerces nor restrains nor disturbs the peace; he gently sustains, permitting all creatures to enjoy his tender goodness. As it is written in the Wisdom of Solomon 8, 1: "Wisdom reacheth from one end to another mightily; and sweetly doth she order all things."

27. I am not fully decided as to the intent of the phrase "by the word of his power." Were these the words of uninspired man, I would think the writer in error; for Christ is himself the Word, as the Gospel teaches, and acts in obedience to no word. Did they refer to the person of the Father, it would be perfect harmony with the Scripture teaching; for the Father made all things through his Word and upholds them in that Word. As said in Psalm 33, 6, "By the word of Jehovah were the heavens made."

28. I withhold my view to give place to another and bet-

ter one. I merely venture the opinion that the apostle's purpose in this manner of speaking may be to emphasize the unity of the persons in one Godhead. Since they are one God, we may understand here reference to the Father; God's action is the action of each of the three persons. God upholds all things by his Word; Christ, or the Word here mentioned, is really God.

29. There are other places in the Scriptures where we have a sudden change of person. For instance, Psalm 2, 6-7: "Yet have I set my king upon my holy hill of Zion. I will tell of the decree: Jehovah said unto me, Thou art my Son." There the first verse represents the Father speaking concerning the Son: and the second verse, the Son concerning the Father. The reason for the sudden change of persons in this brief passage is, the two persons are one God. It may be that when our text declares that one is the image of God, the reference is to Christ; and that when it states one upholds all things by his word, reference is to the Father, no designation being made because the two are one God without distinction.

30. If this is not a satisfactory conclusion, we might regard the expression in this light: we might understand the term "word" as having somewhat the significance of an event or act. For instance, in the Gospel (Lk 2, 15) we read of the shepherds saying: "Let us now go even unto Bethlehem, and see this thing [word—event] that is come to pass"—let us see the event which has taken place there. So, in this phrase declaring Christ upholds all things by the word of his power, we might understand "by the act of his power." By the operation of his power are all things preserved; and all existence and power are derived not from the things themselves but from the active power of God. Further, power and the Word are not to be divorced; they are identical. We may say of an efficient word that its nature and substance are the operating power. Now, each may adopt the view to him most plausible.

"When he had by himself made purification of our sins."

31. Here the apostle touches upon the Gospel proper. Whatever we may be taught concerning Christ is without significance to ourselves until we learn we are the beneficiaries of the doctrine. What would be the advantage to us of preaching were it designed alone for Christ's benefit? The fact is, these words concern only us; they have to do with our salvation. Let us, then, joyfully listen. The language is incomparably beautiful, telling that the supreme Christ, the heir of all things, the effulgence of God's glory and the image of his substance; who upholds all things, not by extraneous power, not with assistance, but by his own power, his own act; who, in short, is all in all—that he has come to serve us, has poured out his love for us and made purification for our sins.

32. The apostle says "our," "our sins;" not his own sin, not the sins of unbelievers. Purification is not for, and cannot profit, him who does not believe. Nor did Christ effect the cleansing by our free-will, our reason or power, our works, our contrition or repentance, these all being worthless in the sight of God; he effects it by himself. And how? By taking our sins upon himself on the holy cross, as Isaiah 53, 6 tells us.

33. But even this answer does not sufficiently explain how he cleanses us "by himself." To go further: When we accept him, when we believe he has purified us, he dwells within us because of, and by, our faith, daily continuing to cleanse us by his own operation; and nothing apart from Christ in any way contributes to the purification of our sins. Note, he does not dwell in us, nor work our cleansing through himself, by any other way than in and through our faith.

34. Hearken, then, ye deceivers of the world and blind leaders of the blind; ye Pope, ye bishops, priests, monks, learned and idle talkers; who teach the purification of sins by human achievements, and that satisfaction for sins may be made by men; who issue indulgences and vend devised purifications of sins. Listen to the teaching here: Purifica-

tion of sins is not effected by human effort, but solely in Christ and through himself. Christ is communicated to us, not through any work of ours, but through faith alone, as Paul teaches in Ephesians 3, 17 that "Christ dwells in your hearts through faith." Plainly, then, the purification of sins is faith, and he who believes that Christ has purged his sins, unquestionably is cleansed through that faith and in no other way. Appropriate, then, is Peter's expression in Acts 15, 9; "cleasing their hearts by faith."

35. Having once possessed faith, and purification being effected in us by Christ, we are then to perform good works, hating our sins and repenting of them. Under these conditions our works are really good. Before faith is present, they avail naught; rather they induce false confidence and trust. So heinous an evil are our sins, and so enormous is the cost of their purification, it was necessary that one exalted as we here read Christ was, must intervene to purge them by himself. What could the poor, vain attempts of us who are creatures, and besides sinful, feeble, corrupt creatures, accomplish where the demand was of such magnitude? One might as reasonably presume to burn heaven and earth with an extinguished brand. Our sins can be expiated only by a price commensurate with the God they offend.

> "Sat down on the right hand of the Majesty on high; having become by so much better than the angels, as he hath inherited a more excellent name than they."

36. This statement refers to the human nature of Christ wherein he effected the purification of our sins; at the same time it is true the cleansing was an achievement of the Son of God. We must not, in making distinction of natures, try to make a distinction of persons. Again, we may truly say the Son of God sits on the right hand of the Majesty, though the passage is to be accepted only in the human sense, for in his divine nature he is himself the only Majesty, in unity with the Father, upon whose right hand he sits. But we will abandon these comments which but

obscure, and keep to the clearer language of the text.

37. To "sit on the right hand of the Majesty" certainly implies a likeness to that Majesty. Wherever it is said that Christ sits at the right hand of God, there is fundamentally established his title to true God; for no one but God himself is like God. So, to say that the man Christ sits on the right hand of God is equivalent to saying he is true God. Psalm 110, 1 declares, "Jehovah saith unto my Lord, Sit thou at my right hand." That is, Jehovah said to Christ the man: Be like me; in other words, Thou shalt be recognized not simply as man but as God. It is with this thought the apostle cites the psalmist.

Again, it is written (Ps 8, 6), "Thou hast put all things under his feet." That is, Thou hast made him equal with thyself. Not that Christ was not God until all things were put under his feet. But his humanity was not yet God and equal with God. For as soon as he began to be man, he began to be God. The Scriptures refer to Christ in terms more appropriately significant than we are accustomed to use. So far at times is the person lost sight of in the nature, or the natures so strongly distinguished, few rightly comprehend the words. I have myself frequently erred in passages of this character, attributing to the nature that which concerns the person, and vice versa. In Philippians 2, 6-8 we read: "Who, existing in the form of God, counted not the being on an equality with God a thing to be grasped, but emptied himself, taking the form of a servant, being made in the likeness of men; and being found in fashion as a man." This passage, however, is obscure.

38. To return to our text: Note, the apostle now begins to cite the Old Testament for Scripture testimony that Christ is God. Up to this time he has given us his own views and used his own language, based on his interpretations of Scripture. He has told us Christ is far superior to the angels for he has become God and has by inheritance obtained a more excellent name than they. His whole design is to show the man Christ, becoming God, being recognized and glorified as God.

"For unto which of the angels said he at any time, Thou art my Son, this day have I begotten thee?"

39. This quotation is from the Second Psalm. To make plainer the apostle's allusion to Christ, we cite the entire Psalm, as follows: "Why do the nations rage, and the peoples meditate a vain thing? The kings of the earth set themselves, and the rulers take counsel together, against Jehovah, and against his anointed, saying, Let us break their bonds asunder, and cast away their cords from us. He that sitteth in the heavens will laugh: the Lord will have them in derision. Then will he speak unto them in his wrath, and vex them in his sore displeasure: Yet I have set my king upon my holy hill of Zion. I will tell of the decree: Jehovah said unto me, Thou art my son; this day have I begotten thee. Ask of me, and I will give thee the nations for thine inheritance, and the uttermost parts of the earth for thy possession. Thou shalt break them with a rod of iron; thou shalt dash them in pieces like a potter's vessel. Now therefore be wise, O ye kings: be instructed, ye judges of the earth. Serve Jehovah with fear, and rejoice with trembling. Kiss the son, lest he be angry, and ye perish in the way, for his wrath will soon be kindled. Blessed are all they that take refuge in him."

40. We see plainly, the reference here is to Christ, against whom raged the Jews, with Pilate, Herod and the chief priests. To Christ, God says, "Thou art my Son."

41. The Jews endeavor to evade this passage of the apostle by introducing wild interpretations. Unable to deny that the Psalm refers to a coming king and anointed one—or Christ, as "anointed" implies—they assert the allusion is to David, who was also a Christ. For they term all kings "messiahs" or "christs"—anointed ones. But their position will not hold. David never inherited the heathen, nor did his kingdom extend to the uttermost parts of the earth, as recorded of the king mentioned in the Psalm. Again, in no instance in the Scriptures is it said to any man, "Thou art my Son."

42. Even when the Jews do admit the Psalm's allusion to the Messiah they resort to two evasions. They maintain he is yet to come, that Jesus Christ is not the Messiah. Further, that despite being called the Son of God, he is not God. For, they say, it is written of the children of God in general (Ps 82, 6): "I said, Ye are gods, and all of you sons of the Most High"; and many times in the Scriptures the saints are called the children of God (Gen 6, 2; Ps 89, 27; Mt 5, 45; 1 Jn 3, 2); Paul, too, in various places calls us children of God, and we in return call him Father, as in the Lord's Prayer.

43. How shall we reply to them? Shall we leave the apostle unsustained, as if he had not given good, clear Scripture proof? To do so would be unjust. In the first place, we have the testimony of experience that Jesus is he of whom the Psalm speaks; in Christ the prophecy is fulfilled and become history. He was persecuted by kings and rulers. They sought to destroy him and only brought derision upon themselves in the attempt. They were themselves destroyed, as the Psalm says. Throughout the world Christ is recognized Lord. No king, before nor since, has ruled or can rule in equal extent. Now, if in Christ the Psalm is fulfilled, it cannot be made to refer to any other.

44. Admitting the saints are called "gods" and "the children of God," the apostle's reasoning based on the fact that nowhere is it said to any angel, much less to any man, "Thou art my Son," sufficiently proves that Christ is God. He must be peculiarly God's Son, having a relation unshared by men and angels. The fact that God does not include him among other sons but especially distinguishes him, indicates his superiority. He cannot be superior to angels without being true God, for angels are the highest order of beings.

45. Further, God begets all other children through some agency. For instance, James 1, 18: "Of his own will he brought us forth by the word of truth." Angels are not begotten, but are created. The Son, however, God did not

create; he begat him through himself. He says: "I, I myself—by myself I have begotten thee this day." Such language is not employed with reference to any other. This personal bringing forth of a single Being embraces a natural birth. True, God says of Solomon (1 Chron 22, 10), "He shall be my son;" but he does not make to him the personal declaration, "Thou art my Son, this day have I begotten thee." David begat Solomon, but the one referred to was begotten by God alone.

46. Again, God says "this day;" that is, in eternity. Natural birth cannot be effected in a day, as witness the human species as well as the animals. To specify concerning this particular birth, God adds "this day." He begets his Son instantaneously—eternally; begetting and bringing forth are simultaneous. God does not say, "I begat thee a year ago;" it is now—"Thou art my Son, I have begotten thee." Essentially, then, it is a transcendental birth, a birth of an exalted nature and incomprehensible to man.

47. According to Hosea 11, 1, God says he called his son out of Egypt. This verse, like the Psalm, implies the Son of God. The Jews assert the reference is to the people of Israel, but Matthew (ch 2, 15) applies it to Christ. But however this may be, nowhere in the Scriptures do we find it said to any man, not even to a renowned king, "Thou art my Son." Much less do we find where God says to any man, "I myself have begotten thee—this day have I begotten." Hence it is plainly evident from the Psalm that Jesus is the Christ and the true, natural Son of God.

48. Mark you, so much emphasis does the apostle lay upon Scriptural authority, we are under no obligation to accept anything the Bible does not assert. Were not this true, his argument, "Unto which of the angels said he at any time," etc., would not be conclusive. The Jews might say, "Notwithstanding God did not in the Scriptures make such assertion to the angels, he may have otherwise asserted it; for the Scriptures do not record everything." Now, if in the purpose of God we are under no obligation to

accept anything not presented in the Scriptures, we are also to reject all doctrines not taught therein.

49. This conclusion operates against the presumption of the Pope and his followers, who shamelessly assert we must accept more than the Scriptures present. They claim it is not conclusive reasoning to say of a certain thing, "It is not in the Scriptures, therefore it is not authentic." They oppose the apostle's teaching even to greater extent than do the Jews, introducing their councils, teachers and high schools. Beware of their error. Be certain you have full Scripture authority for all you accept. Of whatever is not in the Scriptures, ask as does the apostle here, "When did God ever assert it?"

"And again, I will be to him a Father, and he shall be to me a Son."

50. The Papists also impair the force of this passage. Apparently the purpose of their teaching is but to weaken the point of the Scriptures. They assert the verse has two meanings: first, it refers to Solomon as a figure of Christ; second, to Christ directly. But to admit the Scriptures to be of uncertain meaning would be immediately to make them not conclusive. The Jews might maintain that reference is to Solomon primarily. Then the apostle apparently would be overthrown and would establish nothing. So we should firmly hold that Christ alone is here spoken of, even as the preceding verse presents a Son peculiar and above all other sons. If the word was not spoken to angels, much less was it to Solomon. The apostle says this Son has obtained a more excellent name than the angels; therefore, by no means can the reference be to Solomon.

51. We are not to be content merely to accept the apostle's statement; we are under obligation to show how he clearly and conclusively establishes his position. Know, then, he cites Second Samuel 7, 14 and Psalm 89, 26. The books named are prophetic. In the passages adduced the reference is to Christ alone; not to Solomon. But in First Chronicles 22, 10, a historical book, reference is had to Sol-

omon alone: "He shall be my son, and I will be his father." Even the Jews admit the true Christ is alluded to in Psalm 89, 26-27: "He shall cry unto me, Thou art my Father, my God, and the rock of my salvation. I also will make him my first-born, the highest of the kings of the earth." Likewise is the reference to Christ in verse 6: "Who among the sons of the mighty is like unto Jehovah [the Lord]?" The meaning is: Among the sons of God is one who is God, and no one is like unto the Lord.

52. Though the passages in Second Samuel and First Chronicles are in harmony, yet such are the circumstances forming the setting in the first passage, the word cannot be understood to refer to Solomon. The two texts must be two different declarations to David, one concerning Christ and one concerning Solomon. In the first instance (2 Psalm 7, 12), God says to David: "When thy days are fulfilled, and thou shalt sleep with thy fathers, I will set up thy seed after thee, that shall proceed out of thy bowels."

53. Now, Solomon was not set up king subsequent to David's death, but while David yet lived. 1 Kings 1, 30ff. David well knew the declaration was made concerning Christ. It is for that reason he expressed heartfelt praise to God, saying (2 Sam 7, 19): "O Lord Jehovah, thou hast spoken also of thy servant's house for a great while to come." While he himself lived, David ordained Solomon his successor. He says (1 Chron 22, 8-10): "The word of Jehovah came to me saying . . . A son shall be born to thee, who shall be a man of rest . . . He shall build a house for my name;" not thou who "hast shed blood abundantly." In the passage from Samuel nothing is said about the shedding of blood. There God says he will build a house for David. Further argument for the idea advanced is found in the fact that in Second Samuel 7, 14-15 God freely unqualifiedly promises: "If he commit iniquity, I will chasten him with the rod of men, and with the stripes of the children of men; but my lovingkindness shall not depart from him." He freely promises his grace for the things so bitterly bewailed in Psalm 89.

54. As Psalm 132, 12 shows, the promise made concerning Solomon is made only upon the condition, "If thy children will keep my covenant," etc. This David indicates in First Kings 2, 4, and God makes it known to Solomon in the following chapter, verse 14. The passage from Samuel, then, should be understood particularly to refer to Christ, but not that from Chronicles. This is clearly and conclusively proven.

"And when he again bringeth in the firstborn into the world he saith, And let all the angels of God worship him."

55. Here we have cited a third passage from Psalm 97 (verse 7), which clearly speaks of the kingdom of God, whereof Christ in the Gospel teaches. In this kingdom Christ reigns; he is Lord. It had its beginning after his ascension and is completed through the preaching of the Gospel; for it plainly alludes to preaching. It reads:

"Jehovah reigneth; let the earth rejoice; let the multitude of isles be glad. Clouds and darkness are round about him [that is, he reigns in faith concealed]: righteousness and justice are the foundation of his throne. A fire goeth before him, and burneth up his adversaries round about. His lightnings lightened the world [these are his miracles]: the earth saw and trembled. The mountains [the great rulers, and the proud] melted like wax at the presence of Jehovah, at the presence of the Lord of the whole earth. The heavens [the apostles] declare his righteousness [faith], and all the peoples have seen his glory [for the Gospel is everywhere preached]. Let all them be put to shame that serve graven images, that boast themselves of idols: worship him, all ye gods. Zion heard and was glad and the daughters of Judah rejoiced, because of thy judgments," etc. [Edition A gives the whole of Psalm 97].

56. Experience and its fulfilment explain this Psalm. It was completely fulfilled in Christ. He is preached in all the world and reigns in the kingdom of God, which is not true of any other king. The apostle prefaces his quotation

with the words, "And again, when he bringeth in the first-begotten into the world," meaning that in the Psalm the Spirit speaks of the second coming of Christ into the world through the Gospel. He came first in bodily form. Through the instrumentality of his crucifiers he was driven out in death. But afterward, in his resurrection and in the Word, he re-entered the world and now reigns with authority. Nevermore will he die nor be driven out. It is of this second entrance the Psalm speaks.

57. The author of the epistle practically says. "I grant God has other sons, but it is the first-born son whom he brings into the world a king and whom the angels worship, which the angels would not do, nor would be commanded to do, were he not true God."

58. True, we read of David and many others being worshiped, but not by angels. No angel ever yet adored any but God. This passage proves that he whom angels reverence must be God. For since even men worship on earth only what is superior to themselves, and with angels only God is superior, that king whom ministers herald in the world and angels worship must be God. That the apostle does not cite the whole Psalm literally is of no significance. The language of the Psalm is: "Worship him, all ye gods," while the apostle says, "Let all the angels of God worship him." The meaning, however, is the same. The thought is of future action—the angels shall worship him. If so, he must be God. The angels are his, though he is himself man. Note, however, in the Hebrew the passage reads: "Worship him, all ye 'Elohim'; that is, all ye gods. The term is given to angels, and to saints in general, because they are the children of God.

> "And of the angels he saith, Who maketh his angels winds [spirits], and his ministers a flame of fire."

59. The apostle's intent here is to show that in the Scriptures the angels are not spoken of in terms that make possible a reference to them in the statements, "Thou art my Son," "He shall be my Son," "All the angels shall wor-

ship him." They are simply appointed messengers sent forth of God into the world. Although to them he has committed much, he does not constitute any among them Lord; they are characterized as wind and a flame of fire. He terms them "spirits," "winds" and "a flame of fire" because in such form do they execute his bidding, moving with the ease and swiftness of the wind, and having the brilliance of lightning or a flame of fire, as much Scriptural evidence testifies. Yet no one of them is withal Lord of the world and heralded everywhere in the manner the king here mentioned is proclaimed Lord over all things. Even the Jews must confess that.

> "But of the Son he saith, Thy throne, O God, is for ever and ever; and the sceptre of uprightness is the sceptre of thy kingdom. Thou hast loved righteousness, and hated iniquity; therefore God, thy God, hath anointed thee with the oil of gladness above thy fellows."

60. This fourth quotation is from Psalm 45, 6-7. To me it most clearly and forcibly proves Christ to be God. Even the Jews cannot oppose that interpretation. Let us consider: In the first place, it is universally acknowledged the Psalm refers to Christ, even were we to grant he is yet to come, as the Jews erroneously presume. In the second place, the first sentence, "Thy throne, O God, is for ever and ever," necessarily relates to the true God to whom throne and government belong. Though saints are sometimes termed "gods," as we learned from Psalm 82, 1, yet government and throne are the prerogative of none but the one true and actual God. Is not this indisputably plain? So, then, this God upon the throne who reigns eternally is our true God.

61. Then the succeeding sentence is spoken of the same God: "Thou hast loved uprightness . . . therefore God, even thy God, hath anointed thee . . . above thy fellows." What is implied? That the God upon the everlasting throne, who reigns eternally, is anointed by his God

above all his fellows. He who here anoints must certainly be the true God; and also the anointed must be actual God because of his throne and eternal reign. Now, God does not anoint himself; the anointed is subordinate to the one anointing. "To anoint" here implies, to infuse the Holy Spirit, with his graces; something to be exercised only upon a creature.

62. Note that indisputably the first part of the passage makes the king in question true God, and the latter part true man. In his humanity he has fellows, for he is the head of all believers, and they are partakers of the Spirit he possesses abundantly and above all others. But in his divinity he has no fellows; for there is only one God—one God but not one person. The passage forces the conclusion that there are two persons, one who reigns and another who anoints and whose divinity will not admit of his being himself anointed. Hence we must conclude the King is the Son of God; his title is ascribed because he is God. His eternal throne is the kingdom introduced after Christ's ascension. Yet he has fellows, is anointed, and deservedly anointed because he loves righteousness; things wholly characteristic of actual man.

63. The rod or scepter of the Son's kingdom is the Gospel. It is a scepter of uprightness because aggressive for the right and taking a straight course. This declaration stands opposed to human doctrines, which abound in intricacies and perplexities and yet contribute nothing to salvation. It is another reminder that we are to accept nothing in all Christendom but the scepter of Christ's kingdom. He would have his kingdom ruled by no other scepter than that righteous one, the Gospel.

64. It is necessary to use the word "God" twice in the latter part of the verse—"God, thy God"—because our language has but one word for that meaning. The Hebrew tongue has many, employing here these two, "Elohim" and "Elohe."

65. In the Old Testament are many similar passages,

mysteriously used but unquestionably conclusive upon this matter; for instance, Genesis 19, 24: "Jehovah rained upon Sodom and upon Gomorrah brimstone and fire from Jehovah out of heaven." What can it mean—"Jehovah," "from Jehovah,"—but that two persons are indicated, the Father and the Son? Again (Zech 3, 2), "Jehovah said unto Satan, Jehovah rebuke thee, O Satan." Observe here, God himself speaks of another God. And again, in Psalm 68, where frequent mention is made of God, it is stated (verse 18): "Thou hast ascended on high, thou hast led away captives." With respect to ascension, however, reference is only to the man Christ. Again, in the same Psalm (verse 28) we have, "Thy God hath commanded thy strength." Further, it says God commands the power of God. And there are many similar passages.

> "And, Thou, Lord, in the beginning didst lay the foundation of the earth, and the heavens are the works of thy hands; they shall perish; but thou continuest: and they all shall wax old as doth a garment; and as a mantle shalt thou roll them up, and they shall be changed: but thou art the same, and thy years shall not fail."

66. How this quotation testifies that Christ is God is not at once apparent. As written, it easily seems to refer to God as one person. But we must take into consideration the entire Psalm. The Psalm speaks of the future kingdom of God, direction of which the Scriptures assign to Christ. Among the various passages concerning Christ's kingdom is a portion of this last-cited Psalm (Ps 102, 12-16): "But thou, O Jehovah, wilt abide for ever; and thy memorial name unto all generations. Thou wilt arise, and have mercy upon Zion; for it is time to have pity upon her, yea, the set time is come. For thy servants [the apostles] take pleasure in her stones, and have pity upon her dust. [That is, through the Gospel. Reference is to Christ, whose servants the apostles are, bringing the stones of Zion—the elect—to grace, through their preaching. Such servants no earthly

king ever had.] So the nations shall fear the name of Jehovah, and all the kings of the earth thy glory. For Jehovah hath built up Zion; he hath appeared in his glory."

67. The Psalm concludes with, "And thou, Lord, in the beginning hast laid the foundation of the earth," etc. The psalmist's evident conclusion is: The King whose servants have favored the stones of Zion, who is proclaimed worldwide and commands the fear of the heathen and all the kings of the earth, is the God who created the earth and is in himself unchangeable. No earthly king has ever been proclaimed among all the heathen as Christ has been proclaimed. Christ, then, is true God and true man. What further comment the subject demands I leave for keener minds.

68. So we see this whole epistle lesson is simply armor to clearly maintain the article of faith that Christ is God, and Lord over all things even in his humanity. We note with amazement the perfect clearness of the Scripture teaching and that the defect is in ourselves, unperceived. Well does Luke speak (ch. 24, 32) of Christ's opening the understanding of the disciples to comprehend the Scriptures. It was not the Scriptures he opened, but their understanding; the former is plain, but our eyes are not fully open.

St. Stephen's Day

Epistle Text: Acts 6, 8-14, and 7, 54-60.

8 And Stephen, full of grace and power, wrought
great wonders and signs among the people. 9 But there
arose certain of them that were of the synagogue called
the synagogue of the Libertines, and of the Cyrenians,
and of the Alexandrians, and of them of Cilicia and Asia,
disputing with Stephen. 10 And they were not able to
withstand the wisdom and the Spirit by which he spake.
11 Then they suborned men, who said, We have heard
him speak blasphemous words against Moses, and
against God. 12 And they stirred up the people, and
the elders, and the scribes, and came upon him, and
seized him, and brought him into the council, 13 and
set up false witnesses, who said, This man ceaseth not
to speak words against this holy place, and the law:
14 for we have heard him say, that this Jesus of Naza-
reth shall destroy this place, and shall change the customs which Moses delivered unto us.

54 Now when they heard these things, they were cut
to the heart, and they gnashed on him with their teeth.
55 But he, being full of the Holy Spirit, looked up stedfastly into heaven, and saw the glory of God, and Jesus
standing on the right hand of God, 56 and said, Behold,
I see the heavens opened, and the Son of man standing
on the right hand of God. 57 But they cried out with
a loud voice, and stopped their ears, and rushed upon
him with one accord; 58 and they cast him out of the
city, and stoned him: and the witnesses laid down their
garments at the feet of a young man named Saul.
59 And they stoned Stephen, calling upon the Lord, and
saying, Lord Jesus, receive my spirit. 60 And he
kneeled down, and cried with a loud voice, Lord, lay
not this sin to their charge. And when he had said this,
he fell asleep.

STEPHEN'S EXAMPLE OF FAITH.

1. It is necessary to the understanding of this epistle lesson to introduce something of what is omitted and to present in connection with the narrative the things which gave rise to it. The dispute arose from Stephen's assertion that whatsoever proceeds not from faith does not profit, and that men cannot serve God by the erection of churches, or by works independent of faith in Jesus Christ. Faith alone renders us godly; faith alone builds the temple of God—the believing hearts. The Jews opposed the doctrine of faith, adducing the law of Moses and the temple at Jerusalem. For the Bible makes frequent mention of Jerusalem as God's chosen city, toward which his eyes are always directed, a city called the house of God. Such argument they presumed to be conclusive.

2. Stephen, however, opposes them by citing Isaiah 66, 1-2: "Heaven is my throne, and the earth is my footstool: what manner of house will ye build unto me? and what place shall be my rest? For all these things hath my hand made, and so all these things came to be, saith Jehovah." This statement is clear and forcible beyond gainsaying. It shows God does not dwell in houses made with hands, for the essential elements of these are, in the first place, of his own creating and belong to him. Further, if heaven nor earth can contain him—and he here asserts that heaven is not his house but his throne, and the earth not his habitation but his footstool—how can he be expected to dwell in a house made by men? Solomon speaks to the same purpose in First Kings 8, 27, referring to the house he has himself built.

3. Defeated by the power of this passage from Isaiah, and similar citations they could not gainsay, the Jews proceeded to misconstrue Stephen's words, making out that he declared Jesus would destroy the temple and change the customs of Moses. Yet Stephen had no intention of giving such impression. He simply asserted that we are saved not by the Law or the temple, but by faith in Jesus Christ;

and that having faith we may rightly observe the Law, whether there be temple or not. Stephen's purpose was merely to remove the Jews' false confidence in their own works and in the temple.

4. Similar to them, the Papists of today, when they hear it claimed that works are not effectual and that faith in Christ must precede and must be of sole efficacy, cry out that good works are prohibited, and God's commandments blasphemed. Were Stephen a preacher of today he might not, it is true, be stoned, but he would be burned, or dismembered with tongs, by the enraged Papists.

5. Stephen replies to the false accusation of the Jews. Beginning with Abraham, he goes on through the Scriptures, showing how, previous to the time of Solomon who built a house for God, neither Abraham nor any other of the patriarchs ever built a house for his service, but they were not for that reason the less regarded of God. Then Stephen adds the quotation from Isaiah. He says: "But Solomon built him a house. Howbeit the Most High dwelleth not in houses made with hands; as saith the prophet, The heaven is my throne, and the earth the footstool of my feet: what manner of house will ye build me? saith the Lord: or what is the place of my rest? Did not my hand make all these things?"

6. After these words he rebukes them, saying: "Ye stiffnecked and uncircumcised in heart and ears, ye do always resist the Holy Spirit: as your fathers did, so do ye. Which of the prophets did not your fathers persecute? and they killed them that showed before of the coming of the Righteous One; of whom ye have now become betrayers and murderers; ye who received the law as it was ordained by angels, and kept it not."

7. Now follows the latter part of our lesson, beginning, "Now when they heard these things, they were cut to the heart, and they gnashed on him with their teeth." Evidently, then, the dispute was in regard to faith and good works. But how is it with the Papists, who have not the

least semblance of grounds for their position other than their own human laws and doctrines? If they could produce for themselves a shadow of support such as the Jews had in adducing that God gave the law of Moses and chose the temple at Jerusalem, they would instantly raise a cry of, "By divine right" (de jure divino), as in fact did their forefathers the Jews.

BUILDING CHURCHES DOES NOT SECURE GOD'S FAVOR.

8. This epistle text seems to be not at all difficult; it is plain. It presents in Stephen an example of the faith of Christ. Little comment is necessary. We shall examine it briefly. The first principle it teaches is, we cannot secure the favor of God by erecting churches and other institutions. Stephen makes this fact plain in his citation from Isaiah.

9. But if we are to take this position and maintain it, we must incur the same risk Stephen did. Such position calls for the doing away with the bulls of the Pope, with innumerable indulgences, laws of the ecclesiasts and incessant preaching about churches, altars, institutions, cloisters, chalices, bells, tables, candles and apparel. Thus would the holiness of the Pope and his adherents be offended, and not without reason. For in consequence, luxuries of kitchen and cellar would be diminished, and all temporal possessions as well. In course of time idleness, voluptuousness and ease would have to give place to labor, poverty and unrest. The clerical order would be obliged to study and pray, or support themselves like other people do. Such a course would not be agreeable to them. The holy Christian Church would be despised, as were Christ and the apostles. Her officials could no longer live in royal pomp, waging war, plundering, and shedding blood, all under the pretext of honoring God and exalting the holy Church. For this have the most holy fathers in God done, and still do.

10. We must not, however, be led to conclude it is wrong to build and endow churches. But it is wrong to go to the extreme of forfeiting faith and love in the effort, pre-

suming thereby to do good works meriting God's favor. It results in abuses precluding all moderation. Every nook and corner is filled with churches and cloisters, regardless of the object of church-building.

11. There is no other reason for building churches than to afford a place where Christians may assemble to pray, to hear the Gospel and to receive the sacraments; if indeed there is a reason. When churches cease to be used for these purposes they should be pulled down, as other buildings are when no longer of use. As it is now, the desire of every individual in the world is to establish his own chapel or altar, even his own mass, with a view of securing salvation, of purchasing heaven.

12. Is it not a miserable, a deplorable, error and delusion to teach innocent people to depend on their works to the great disparagement of their Christian faith? Better to destroy all the churches and cathedrals in the world, to burn them to ashes—it is less sinful even when done through malice—than to allow one soul to be misled and lost by such error. God has given no special command in regard to the building of churches, but he has issued his commands in reference to our souls—his real and peculiar churches. Paul says concerning them (1 Cor 3, 16-17): "Ye are a temple [church] of God . . . If any man destroyeth the temple of God, him shall God destroy."

13. But observe the holiness of the Papists. The foundation of every soul is disturbed by their error, and the real Church of God is overthrown. This fact does not deter the Papists; indeed, they willingly contribute to the overthrow of the Church. By their doctrine of works they effect nothing else but the destruction everywhere of the true Church. Then they proceed to substitute for it church buildings, of wood and stone. They misuse the conscience until it believes the trivial defacement by knife of such wood and stone is a profanation of the whole church, and the expense and labor of reconsecration must be incurred. Are not the individuals who have no conscientious scruples

about the destruction of the actual Church, who even convert that great sin into eternal merit, and at the same time are extremely conscientious about the vain juggling of their own church building—are they not raving, raging, foolish and fanatical? yes, frantic, infuriated?

I continue to assert that for the sake of exterminating the error mentioned, it would be well to overthrow at once all the churches in the world, and to utilize ordinary dwellings or the open air for preaching, praying and baptizing, and for all Christian requirements.

14. Especially is there justification for so doing because of the worthless reason the Papists assign for building churches. Christ preached for over three years, but only three days in the temple at Jerusalem. The remainder of the time he spoke in the schools of the Jews, in the wilderness, on the mountains, in ships, at the feasts and otherwise in private dwellings. John the Baptist never entered the temple; he preached by the Jordan River and in all places. The apostles preached in the market-place and streets of Jerusalem on the day of Pentecost. Philip preached in a chariot to the eunuch. Paul preached to the people by the riverside; in the Philippian jail and in various private dwellings. In fact, Christ commanded the apostles (Mt 10, 12) to preach in private houses. I presume the preachers mentioned were equally good with those of today.

15. But it must be that costly buildings with magnificent arches are required for the false preachers and diabolical teachers of today, though the Word of God could find in all Bethlehem no inn wherein to be born. Should we not, then, with Stephen cry unto these unreasonable creatures: "Ye stiffnecked and uncircumcised in heart and ears, ye do always resist the Holy Spirit. Ye are betrayers and murderers of innocent, harmless Christian souls. Though having received the commandments from the apostles, ye have observed none of them"? I suppose, should we do so, their hearts would be ready to burst with rage and they would gnash their teeth, saying we had blasphemed against God

and spoken against the holy place; yes, had profaned all churches. O God, the blind leaders, and murderers of souls, who rule under the accursed popery!

16. You see now some reason why lightning strikes the costly Papist churches more frequently than it does other buildings. Apparently the wrath of God especially rests upon them because there greater sins are committed, more blasphemies uttered and greater destruction of souls and of churches wrought than take place in brothels and in thieves' dens. The keeper of a public brothel is less a sinner than the preacher who does not deliver the true Gospel, and the brothel is not so bad as the false preacher's Church. Even were the proprietor of the brothel daily to prostitute virgins, godly wives and nuns, awful and abominable as such action would be, he would not be any worse nor would he work more harm than those papistical preachers.

17. Does this astonish you? Remember, the false preacher's doctrine effects nothing but daily to lead astray and to violate souls newly born in baptism—young Christians, tender souls, the pure, consecrated virgin brides of Christ. Since the evil is wrought spiritually, not bodily, no one observes it; but God is beyond measure displeased. In his wrath he cries, through the prophets, in unmistakable terms, Thou harlot who invitest every passer-by! So little can God tolerate false preaching. Jeremiah in his prayer (Lam 5, 11) makes this complaint, "They ravished the women in Zion, the virgins in the cities of Judah." Now, spiritual virginity, the Christian faith, is immeasurably superior to bodily purity; for it alone can obtain heaven.

18. The false doctrines and works of the Papists are destructive not only of faith, but also of Christian love. The fool may always be known by his cap. Many a man passes by his poor neighbor who has a sick child or wife, or is otherwise in need of assistance, and makes no effort to minister to him, but instead contributes to endow some church. Or else while health remains he endeavors to heap up treasures, and when he comes at last to his deathbed makes a

will bequeathing his estate to some certain institution. He will be surrounded by priests and monks. They will extol his act, absolve the religious man, administer the Sacrament and bury him with honors. They will proclaim his name from the pulpit and during mass, and will cry: "Here is worthy conduct indeed! The man has made ample provision for his soul. Many blessings will hereafter be conferred upon him." Yes, hereafter but, alas, eternally too late.

19. But no one while he is living warns of the man's sins in not administering to the wants of his neighbor when it lies in his power to relieve; in passing him by, and ignoring him as the rich man did Lazarus in the Gospel. And he does not himself recognize his sins. Hence they must remain unconfessed, unrepented of and unabsolved, however many bulls, indulgences and spiritual fathers may have served. This neglect is the very sin concerning which Christ on the day of judgment will say: "I was . . . naked, and ye clothed me not." Mt 25, 43. The religious one will then reply, "I heaped up treasures to establish an institution for thee, in obedience to the Pope's decree, and hence he has absolved me from all my sins." What can individuals such as he expect to hear but the sentence: "Depart from me, ye cursed, into everlasting fire"? For by their works they destroy the Christian faith, and for the sake of mere wood and stone despise Christian love.

20. Let us, therefore, beloved friends, be wise; wisdom is essential. Let us truly learn we are saved through faith in Christ and that alone. This fact has been made sufficiently manifest. Then let no one rely upon his own works. Let us in our lifetime engage only in such works as shall profit our neighbors, being indifferent to testament and institution, and direct our efforts to bettering the full course of our neighbors' lives.

21. It is related of a pious woman, St. Elizabeth, that once upon entering a cloister and seeing on the wall a fine painting portraying the sufferings of our Lord, she ex-

claimed: "The cost of this painting should have been saved for the sustenance of the body; the sufferings of Christ are to be painted on your hearts." How forcibly this godly utterance is directed against the things generally regarded precious! Were St. Elizabeth so to speak today, the Papists assuredly would burn her for blaspheming against the sufferings of Christ and for condemning good works. She would be denounced as a heretic, though her merits were to surpass the combined merits of ten saints.

GOD'S COMMANDMENTS CANNOT BE FULFILLED BY MAN'S WORKS.

22. Stephen not only rejects the conceptions of the Jews in regard to churches and their erection, but also denounces all their works, saying they have received the Law by the disposition of angels and have not kept it. So the Jews in return reprove Stephen as if he had spoken against the temple and, further, blasphemed the law of Moses and would teach strange works. True, Stephen could not rightly have charged them with failure to observe the Law, so far as external works are considered. For they were circumcised, and observed the rules in regard to meats, apparel and festivals, and all Moses' commands. It was their consciousness of having observed the Law that led them to stone him.

23. But Stephen's words were prompted by the same spirit that moved Paul when he said (Rom 3, 20ff) that by the deeds of the Law no one is justified in the sight of God, faith alone being the justifier. Where the Holy Spirit is not present to grant grace, man's heart cannot favor the Law of God; it would prefer the Law did not exist. Every individual is conscious of his own apathy and disinclination toward what is good, and of his readiness to do evil. As Moses says (Gen 8, 21), "The imagination of man's heart is evil from his youth."

Man, then, being unwilling, he has no real delight in doing the works of the Law. Lacking right motive, he is constrained to works through fear of punishment, of shame and hell, or else through gainful motive and hope of salvation; not through love of God and desire to honor him. All works so wrought are sheer hypocrisy, and in God's sight are not good. But the Holy Spirit is promised to the believer in Christ, and through Christ's grace the Spirit produces in the heart a desire for good. Under its influence the individual voluntarily and without expectation of reward performs his good works for the honor of God. Through faith and the Spirit he is already justified and in a saved condition, a state he could never have attained by any works. In accordance with this principle, we may readily conclude that all who lack faith and grace fail to observe the Law, even though they torture themselves to death with its requirements.

24. When Stephen declares the Jews always resist the Holy Spirit, he means to imply that through their works they become presumptuous, are not inclined to accept the Spirit's aid and are unwilling their works be rejected as ineffectual. Ever working and working to satisfy the demands of the Law, but without fulfilling its least requirement, they remain hypocrites to the end. Unwilling to embrace the faith whereby they would be able to accomplish good works, and the grace of the Spirit that would create a love for the Law, they make impossible the free, spontaneous observance of it. But the voluntary observer of the Law, and no other, God accepts.

25. Stephen calls the Jews "stiffnecked, uncircumcised in heart and ears" because they refuse to listen and understand. They continually cry, "Good works, good works! Law, Law!" though not effecting the least thing themselves. Just so do our Papists. As their forefathers did, so do the descendants, the mass of this generation; they persecute the righteous and boast it is done for the sake of God and his Law. Now we have the substance of this lesson. But let us examine it a little further.

AN EXAMPLE OF GODLY ZEAL AND CHRISTIAN LOVE.

26. First, we see in Stephen's conduct love toward God and man. He manifests his love to God by earnestly and severely censuring the Jews, calling them betrayers, murderers and transgressors of the whole Law, yes stiffnecked, and saying they resist the fulfilment of the Law and resist also the Holy Spirit himself. More than that, he calls them "uncircumcised in heart and ears." How could he have censured them any more severely? So completely does he strip them of every creditable thing, it would seem as if he were moved by impatience and wrath.

27. But who today would the world tolerate were he to attempt such censure of the Papists? Stephen's love for God constrained him to his act. No one who possesses the same degree of love can be silent and calmly permit the rejection of God's commandments. He cannot dissemble. He must censure and rebuke every opposer of God. Such conduct he cannot permit even if he risks his life to rebuke it. Love of this kind the Scriptures term "zelum Dei," a holy indignation. For rejection of God's commands is a slight upon his love and intolerably disparages the honor and obedience due him, honor and obedience which the zealous individual ardently seeks to promote. We have an instance of such a one in the prophet Elijah, who was remarkable for his holy indignation against the false prophets.

28. We must infer from Stephen's example that he who silently ignores the transgression of God's commands, or any sin, has no love for him. Then how is it with the hypocrites who applaud transgression? and with calumniators and those who laugh and eagerly listen to and speak about the faults of others?

29. That the Pope in his absurd laws enjoins the Papists against censuring governors, is not sufficient reason for any man to refrain from administering proper reproof. Whom does Stephen censure here? Is it not the governors of

Jerusalem? Yet he was just an ordinary man; not ordained, not clothed with the priestly office. His example teaches the right of every Christian to justly censure the Pope and the governors. Indeed, he is under obligation to do so. Then let no one be content to think he has not such privilege. Especially should spiritual sins be rebuked. Stephen's reproof was not directed against gross sins, but against hypocrisy; for the Jews in unbelief resisted the Holy Spirit. Thus they wrought more harm than comes from gross sins. By their laws and their works they misled themselves and the multitude.

30. Similarly do the Pope, the bishops and all the Papists deserve public censure as stiffnecked and uncircumcised hypocrites, resisting the Holy Spirit and dishonoring all God's commandments, betraying and murdering Christian souls; thereby being betrayers and murderers of the Christ who bought them with his own blood.

31. We have just had occasion to state that Stephen was a layman, an ordinary Christian, not a priest. But the Papists sing his praises as a Levite, who read the epistle or the Gospel lesson at the altar. The Papists, however, pervert the truth entirely. It is necessary for us, therefore, to know what Luke says in Acts 4 and 5. He tells how the Christians in the inception of the Church, at Jerusalem, made all their possessions common property and the apostles distributed to each member of the congregation as he needed, But, as it happened, the widows of the Grecian Jews were not provided for as were the Hebrew widows; hence arose complaint. The apostles, seeing how the duty of providing for these things would be so burdensome as to interfere in a measure with their duties of praying and preaching, assembled the multitude of the disciples and said: "It is not fit that we should forsake the Word of God, and serve tables. Look ye out therefore, brethren, from among you seven men of good report, full of the Spirit and of wisdom, whom we may appoint over this business. But we will continue stedfastly in prayer, and in the ministry of the word."

Acts 6, 2-4. So Stephen, in connection with six others, was chosen to distribute the goods. Thence comes the word "deacon," servant or minister. For these men served the congregation, ministering to their temporal wants.

32. Plainly, then, Stephen was a steward, or an administrator and guardian of the temporal goods of the Christians; his duty was to administer them to those in need. In course of time his office was perverted into that of a priest who reads the epistle and Gospel lessons. The only trace left of Stephen's office is the slight resemblance found in the duty of the nuns' provosts, and in that of the administrators of hospitals and of the guardians of the poor. The readers of the epistle and Gospel selections should be, not the consecrated, the shorn, the bearers of dalmatics and brushers of flies at the altar, but ordinary godly laymen who keep a record of the needy and have charge of the common fund for distribution as necessity requires. Such was the actual office of Stephen. He never dreamed of reading epistles and Gospels, or of bald pates and dalmatics. Those are all human devices.

THE AUTHORITY OF LAYMEN TO PREACH.

33. As to the question that may arise whether an ordinary layman may be allowed to preach: Though Stephen was not appointed to preach—the apostles, as stated, reserved that office to themselves—but to perform the duties of a steward, yet when he went to the market-place and mingled among the people, he immediately created a stir by performing signs and wonders, as the epistle says, and he even censured the rulers. Had the Pope and his followers been present, they certainly would have inquired as to his credentials—his Church passport and his ecclesiastical character; and had he been lacking a bald pate and a prayer-book, undoubtedly he would have been committed to the flames as a heretic since he was not a priest nor a clergyman. These titles, which the Scriptures accord all Christians, the Papists have appropriated to themselves alone, terming all other men "the laity," and themselves "the

Church," as if the laity were not a part of the Church. At the same time these people of boasted refinement and nobility do not in a single instance fill the office or do the work of a priest, of a clergyman or of the Church. They but dupe the world with their human devices.

34. The precedent of Stephen holds good. His example gives all men authority to preach wherever they can find hearers, whether it be in a building or at the market-place. He does not confine the preaching of God's Word to bald pates and long gowns. At the same time he does not interfere with the preaching of the apostles. He attends to the duties of his own office and is readily silent where it is the place of the apostles to preach.

True, order must be observed. All cannot speak at once. Paul writes in the fourteenth chapter of First Corinthians that one or two are to be permitted to speak, and that if a revelation be made to a listener the speaker is to keep silence. That such was the practice of the apostles is evident from Acts 15, where we read how, after the discourses of certain Pharisees, Peter preached, and when he ceased Barnabas and Paul followed, and lastly James. Each spoke in his turn. To a very slight extent the custom still exists in the debates of colleges, but at present sermons are only idle talk about Dietrich of Bern or some dream of the speaker.

35. A sermon proper should be conducted as a dissertation upon any subject at the social board. Christ, therefore, instituted the Holy Supper as an occasion where we might treat of his Word as we sit at table. But now all is perverted and divine order is superseded by arrangements merely human. But let this suffice on this point.

36. In the second place, Stephen's conduct is a beautiful example of love for fellowmen in that he entertains no ill-will toward even his murderers. However severely he rebukes them in his zeal for the honor of God, such is the kindly feeling he has for them that in the very agonies of death, having made provision for himself by commending

his Spirit to God, he has no further thought about himself but is all concern for them. Under the influence of that love he yields up his spirit. Not undesignedly does Luke place Stephen's prayer for his murderers at the close of the narrative. Note also, when praying for himself and commending his spirit to God he stood, but he knelt to pray for his murderers. Further, he cried with a loud voice as he prayed for them, which he did not do for himself.

37. How much more fervently he prayed for his enemies than for himself! How his heart must have burned, his eyes have overflowed and his entire body been agitated and moved with compassion as he beheld the wretchedness of his enemies! It is the opinion of St. Augustine that Paul was saved by this prayer. And it is not unreasonable to believe that God truly heard it and that from eternity he foresaw a great result from this dispensation. The person of Paul is evidence of God's answer to Stephen's prayer. It could not be denied, though all may not have been saved.

38. Stephen aptly chooses his words, saying, "Lay not this sin to their charge;" that is, make not their sin unremovable, like a pillar or a foundation. By these words Stephen makes confession, repents and renders satisfaction for sin, in behalf of his murderers. His words imply: "Beloved Lord, truly they commit a sin, a wrong. This cannot be denied." Just as it is customary in repentance and confession simply to deplore and confess the guilt. Stephen then prays, offering himself up that abundant satisfaction may surely be made for sin.

39. Note how great an enemy and at the same time how great a friend true love can be; how severe its censures and how sweet its aid. It is like a nut with a hard shell and a sweet kernel. Bitter to our old Adam nature, it is exceedingly sweet to the new man in us.

EXAMPLE OF COMFORT AND ENCOURAGEMENT.

40. This epistle lesson, by the example given, inculcates the forcible doctrine of faith and love; and more, it affords comfort and encouragement. It not only teaches; it incites

and impels. Death, the terror of the world, it styles a sleep; Luke says, "He fell asleep." That is, Stephen's death was quiet and painless; he departed as one goes to sleep, unknowing how—unconsciously falls asleep.

41. The theory that the Christian's death is a sleep, a peaceful passing, has safe foundation in the declaration of the Spirit. The Spirit will not deceive us. Christ's grace and power make death peaceful. Its bitterness is far removed by Christ's death when we believe in him. He says (Jn 8, 51), "If a man keep my word, he shall never see death." Why shall he not see it? Because the soul, embraced in his living Word and filled with that life, cannot be sensible of death. The Word lives and knows no death; so the soul which believes in that Word and lives in it, likewise does not taste death. This is why Christ's words are called words of life. They are the words of life; he who hangs upon them, who believes in them, must live.

42. Comfort and encouragement are further increased by Stephen's assertion, "I see the heavens opened, and the Son of man standing on the right hand of God." Here we see how faithfully and lovingly Christ watches over us, and how ready he is to aid us if we but believe in him and will cheerfully risk our lives for his sake. The vision was not given solely on Stephen's account; it was not recorded for his profit. It was for our consolation, to remove all doubt of our privilege to enjoy the same happy results, provided we conduct ourselves as Stephen did.

43. The fact that the heavens are open affords us the greatest comfort and removes all terror of death. What should not stand open and ready for us when the heavens, the supreme work of creation, are waiting wide for us and rejoicing at our approach? It may be your desire to see them visibly open to you. But were everyone to behold, where would faith be? That the vision was once given to man is enough for the comfort of all Christians, for the comfort and strengthening of their faith and for the removal of all death's terrors. For as we believe, so shall we experience, even though we see not physically.

St. John's Day

Epistle Text: Ecclesiasticus (Sirach) 15, 1-8.

1. He that feareth the Lord will do good; and he that hath the knowledge of the law shall obtain her.

2. And as a mother shall she meet him, and receive him as a wife married of a virgin.

3. With the bread of understanding shall she feed him, and give him the water of wisdom to drink.

4. He shall be stayed upon her, and shall not be moved; and shall rely upon her, and shall not be confounded.

5. She shall exalt him above his neighbors, and in the midst of the congregation shall she open his mouth.

6. He shall find joy and a crown of gladness, and she shall cause him to inherit an everlasting name.

7. But foolish men shall not attain unto her, and sinners shall not see her.

8. For she is far from pride, and men that are liars cannot remember her.

EXHORTATION TO PIETY AND RIGHTEOUSNESS.

1. This lesson, apparently, is not designed to teach. Rather, its purpose is to present the advantages of right conduct. It does not enumerate certain works and the manner in which they are to be performed, but holds up the benefit accruing from right living. Its object is to admonish us and incite us to perform the duties we already recognize. Paul (Rom 12, 7-8) classifies all discourse under two heads, doctrine and exhortation. Doctrine present things we do not already know or possess. Exhortation incites and impels us to obey doctrine, and encourages to patience and

perseverance. While the latter feature of discourse is less difficult than the former, it is no less necessary and profitable.

2. He who would incite one to action, would arouse, encourage, admonish him, must present good reason for action. This may be accomplished by reference to the need and the advantages, the pleasures and honors, consequent upon a certain course, or to the disaster and disgrace following neglect of it. Such is the method employed in this lesson. It points out numerous advantages and honors coming to them who fear God and love righteousness. Its message we will now consider.

3. No definition of righteousness and the fear of God is given here. We have frequently stated, however, that to fear God is not to depend upon ourselves, upon any goodness within us, nor to rely upon our honor, our power, our wealth, strength, advantages or skill—no, not even upon our good works and piety. We must be careful not to sin in any of these things. We are to fear—yes, we know—that should God deal truly and justly with us, we should a thousand times be lost. Therefore, we must not in any way exalt ourselves above the most insignificant individual on earth. We must be humble and gentle in all our conduct and purposes. No arrogance may we show toward anyone; we must be gentle and affable. Humility will render our works good. Peter says (1 Pet 5, 5), "God resisteth the proud, but giveth grace to the humble." Whatsoever is done in that grace, then, is rightly done.

4. As we have heard, righteousness is simply faith. We experience faith in the following way: In the first place, being unable to stand before God's judgment, man is filled with fear in all his nature and actions. Fear impels him to seek something outside himself whereon he may confidently build and stand. He finds that to be nothing else but the pure mercy of God, promised in Christ and revealed in him. Such reliance, such confident faith, renders us just and righteous before God. As Paul says (Rom 1, 17), "The righteous shall live by faith."

5. In proportion as one distrusts himself, his own abilities, and feels he is in all things a sinner before a just God, will he find consolation outside himself, in the grace of God, and thus become righteous in all his works. The two must be kept together; where judgment is, fear must be; where grace exists, confidence is found. Judgment produces fear; grace begets trust and confidence. Through judgment, fear divests us of self with all its powers. But confidence invests us with God and his every attribute. Not our merits, then, but the blessings of God have praise. This teaching is endorsed by Psalm 147, 11: "Jehovah taketh pleasure in them that fear him, in those that hope in his lovingkindness."

6. If man's faith be right, he will conduct himself toward his neighbor in the way he believes God deals with himself. He will do all from pure grace, forgiving his neighbor, forbearing, endeavoring to alleviate his wretchedness, ministering to him, showing hospitality, denying him nothing, risking body, life, property and honor for his sake and conducting himself in all respects as God has done toward him. For faith tells him that God has dealt with him purely in grace, regardless of his demerits, and he is confident God will verify his faith in him. As God pours blessings upon him in disregard of his shortcomings, so will the individual pour all possible favor upon his neighbor, notwithstanding that neighbor may be an enemy and destitute of all merit. He is satisfied the favors he bestows will not impoverish him, for in proportion as he bestows will God pour out upon him; the more he does for his neighbor, the more will God bless him.

7. Such, you perceive, is the true faith, the faith that justifies before God. It is the Christian's righteousness, which receives blessings from above and delivers them below. We find a beautiful illustration of it in the piece of land Caleb, the holy father, gave to his daughter Achsah (Judges 1, 13-15), from which issued beautiful fountains of water. The land was watered by springs above and springs below; hence it was very fertile and very valuable. As already stated, we cannot say too much concerning this faith.

8. The word "Achsah" means ornaments, or jeweled shoes. The lovely Maggie in scarlet shoes, the little daughter of God, is the believing soul. The soul that trusts may be likened to the maiden who trips fearlessly along in her beautiful scarlet and golden shoes. Paul says (Eph 6, 15), "Having your feet shod"—with what? "With the preparation of the gospel of peace." Note that when the heart, through faith, enters the Gospel and lives in the Word, it is Achsah, Maggie in her beautiful shoes. Solomon also speaks concerning the bride (Song Sol 7, 1), "How beautiful are thy feet in sandals, O prince's daughter!"

MOTIVES TO FEAR GOD AND LOVE RIGHTEOUSNESS

Now, let us consider what is offered to incite and urge us to fear God and to love righteousness.

First: "He will do good."

9. All the world talks about doing good, but if you would know how, listen: Do not as the fools who consider various works with intent to choose such as are in their own conceptions good, and to reject such as they deem bad, thus making a distinction of the works themselves. Do not so. Let works be alike; regard one the same as another. Fear God and be just—as already advised—and then perform the duty that presents itself. Then all will be well done, it matters not if it be the duties of a hostler or a teamster.

10. The text is unalterable: "He that feareth the Lord will do good"—no matter what he may do. His works are good, not because of their character, but because of the fear that inspires them. Here, you see, is great comfort. Immediately you abound in good works, and your whole life is good, if you fear God. Whether it be eating or drinking, walking or standing, seeing or hearing, sleeping or waking—all your works are good. Who would not, by such advantage, be incited to fear God? Note, they who fear God are the lambs of God, for whom everything is useful, all their works are profitable.

11. But they who make distinction of works, the nice

saints with their choice, selected deeds, really perform no good works. Why? Because they do not fear God. Attaching great value to their own efforts, they do not trust in him. Consequently these same highly-prized works are evil. It is a fixed truth that his works are good who fears God, but the unbeliever's works are evil.

> "He that hath the knowledge of the law shall obtain her."

12. He who holds to righteousness will obtain her. The thought here is the same as in the first incentive, but differently expressed. To have a knowledge of the Law, to adhere to righteousness, is to persevere in faith. The individual of stedfast faith will apprehend righteousness—will make it his own. Having attained to the heritage of righteousness, being enabled to dwell in it, all his deeds, his whole life, will be right. Therefore, he who would do right and live in righteousness must believe; he must persevere in faith, and then perform, without distinction, such works as present themselves. Endowed with the prerogative faith, it is unnecessary for him to inquire how his works shall be good. They are good to begin with. They are performed without distinction. Righteousness is already apprehended. For he perseveres in faith.

13. But, whatever the works of the unbelieving, righteousness will flee from them because they neglect faith. They may catch at righteousness as a dog snaps at flies, still it will elude them. Paul says of the Jews (Rom 9, 31), "Israel, following after a law of righteousness, did not arrive at that law." Like the Jews are those unbelieving ones who pursue their shadows, chasing after righteousness with their works. It flees from them. They cannot apprehend it for they did not first permit themselves to be made righteous in faith and then adhere to that righteousness. So doing, they would have been righteous in all works; the shadow would have followed of itself.

Third: "As a mother shall she meet him."

14. What is meant here? It is a Hebrew expression.

The Hebrews are wont to speak of a child of wisdom, child of wickedness, child of wrath, child of condemnation; so here the thought, child of righteousness. The child of sin, of unrighteousness, must have a disgraceful mother, of whom he must be ashamed and in whom he cannot rejoice. But the child of righteousness has an honorable mother. Of her he may boast and in her he can rejoice. A human mother, if she be a reputable woman, is an honor, a glory and comfort to her child. On the other hand, if she be disreputable, she is a disgrace to the child. One can hardly suffer a more stinging reproach than to be reminded of a mother's disgrace or to be accused of illegitimate birth or ill-breeding.

15. Now, the wise man intends to say that Righteousness deals affectionately with her own, as a mother meets the wants of her child. The mother is always ready to do for her child to the full extent of her knowledge and power. Solomon designs thus to illustrate the security, comfort, peace, joy and glory the heart experiences before God, through faith. The human mother caresses and kisses her child; she supports and carries it, always ready to meet its wants and grant its desires. The kindness of a mother toward her child is unsurpassed anywhere. Similarly, Righteousness embraces and supports man, meeting his wants in every way and purposing to have him rest in peace and security of heart. Man is entitled to this great privilege of confidence and may boast of it before God, for he has an honorable mother.

Fourth: "And receive him as a wife married of a virgin."

16. What do these words imply? The meaning is similar to that of the preceding phrase. The object is to illustrate the anxious care Righteousness manifests for her child. Solomon represents Righteousness as having affections like those of a new bride, one never before a wife. He means to say, "Precisely as a virgin in her new wifehood feels toward her bridegroom, so is the attitude of Righteousness toward her child." I shall leave the description of the bride's affections to those who have experienced them. It is well

known, however, that nothing surpasses the desire, love and concern of a young bride for her bridegroom. The Scriptures abound with references to the love of brides. Sirach says "a wife married of a virgin," meaning one just married and for the first time knowing love for a husband. A widow becoming again a wife has not such feeling toward her second bridegroom.

17. Note how carefully and thoughtfully the wise man makes his admonition. Does he not present a vivid picture, a burning incentive to faith and godliness? What simile could he have introduced more expressive of affection than these of a virtuous mother's love for her child and a new bride's love for her bridegroom? Woman is naturally more affectionate than man. Now, we cannot by works obtain such favor, affection and care on the part of Righteousness for us. We must conceive it in the heart. Faith enables the conscience to feel in Righteousness all the security, desire and love that a child finds in its mother or a husband in his new bride.

> Fifth: "With the bread of [life and] understanding shall she feed him."

18. Or, "She shall feed him with life and understanding." To explain the process: Just as natural bread sustains the body and also nourishes and increases it in growth until it becomes hale, robust and strong to labor; so, too, righteousness nourishes man, making him daily increase in the Spirit and grow in the knowledge of things divine and human. We know this from experience. Without experience the passage would not be intelligible. He who is nourished by righteousness improves his mind with everything coming under his observation. He grows in knowledge and increases in life and wisdom, especially when contemplating the Scriptures.

19. Solomon had learned much, as his Proverbs and Canticles show. He puts the word "life" before the word "understanding," for without life understanding would be of no significance. It is not that knowledge which is the product of the heathen and of natural reason, knowledge of tem-

poral things—not this sort would Solomon have us regard; but the knowledge faith gives, concerning spiritual and divine things, knowledge making the soul alive before God. This sentence contains all necessary teaching in regard to salvation.

Sixth: "And give him the water of wisdom to drink."

20. The import of this clause is similar to the foregoing sentence. It refers to the increase of the Spirit. Particularly does it present saving knowledge and exclude worldly knowledge, the knowledge of men, which is not profitable. This figure of drinking is to be understood similarly to the figure of eating. Man draws wisdom from everything he observes. All things in heaven and earth afford him pasture, but particularly the Scriptures. From them alone he derives meat and drink in a real, saving knowledge.

Seventh: "He shall be stayed upon her."

21. Hitherto Solomon has been enumerating the blessings and advantages righteousness gives us to enjoy in ourselves and in times of peace. Now he enumerates its blessings in times of conflict, in contentions with enemies. He says, "He shall be stayed upon her." That is, righteousness will throw about us protections enabling us not only to receive blessings but to guard them against all attempts to wrest them away. At the same time, he recognizes here that he who fears God and would be godly must encounter labor, conflict and many misfortunes. Crosses are bound to come. As Paul tells us (Acts 14, 22), "Through many tribulations we must enter into the kingdom of God.'

22. Thus Solomon meets the timid and faint-hearted who would readily be won by the great inducements presented, and would accept the benefits offered, were it not for their fear of having to risk property, honor, bodies, lives and all they have. Solomon does not deny the condition; he does not make any effort to relieve their minds on that point nor to offer flimsy comfort. But he strengthens them, admonishes them against viewing the matter from that standpoint and affords them the consolation that if they cleave to righteousness it will give courage and stability to endure all ills.

Eighth: "And shall not be moved."

23. Another expression of the thought in "He shall be stayed upon her." With ability to overcome all things, what more is to be desired? The self-righteous have not that ability. They do not stand securely—have no firmness. They only yield and vacillate, for they rely upon their own efforts. Their achievements may be easily taken away and themselves with them. But the believing righteousness of the Christian hangs upon the immovable lovingkindness of God. They who rely upon that lovingkindness cannot be moved even though they be deprived of everything else.

Ninth: "And shall rely upon her."

24. That is, righteousness will sustain man's honor. Solomon here acknowledges the pious believer must suffer many evils, and also endure shame and scandal. It is a peculiarity of the Christian's sufferings that he not only has to endure the evils common to all men, but shame and scandal as the worst of evil-doers, just as Christ suffered. Such unmerited sufferings are called sufferings of Christ, or crosses. It is not so much temporal dishonor, but spiritual dishonor, disgrace of the conscience before God. All the martyrs were put to death, not for committing crime against the State, but as being extreme enemies and blasphemers of God. Lest anyone be deterred from Christianity by fear of spiritual dishonor, Solomon makes this declaration for the comfort and encouragement of all believers, an assurance of preservation, and of their ability to maintain their honor before God and the world.

Tenth: "And shall not be confounded."

25. This is the same as the last clause only more clearly expressed. Righteousness may, it is true, permit her child to be overtaken by shame and disgrace, but merely to test her power. [But she never leaves him helpless and prostrate, if he only cleaves to her. Editions A, B, C.] As the Wisdom of Solomon 10, 12 says: "In a sore conflict she gave him the victory; that he might know that godliness is stronger than all." The heart must be continually tempted. As sure as existence, it must experience disgrace. So sensi-

ble of shame will it be, it will tremble and waver as if God were to leave it in disgrace. But in this promise it finds help to maintain a firm confidence. So sustained, it overrides shame; all this the self-righteous can by no means do.

Eleventh: "She shall exalt him above his neighbors."

26. The Christian's temptations and conflicts only give him distinction and elevate him in the minds of the people. Paul (1 Cor 11, 19) says that by heresies the approved Christians are made manifest. Conflicts serve to distinguish the Christian, to raise him in the estimation of men unto great eminence and honor. In contrast with him, the selfrighteous go on unnoticed, without experience, untried, dwelling in their own element and uninformed of the blessings and workings of God.

Twelfth: "And in the midst of the congregation shall she open his mouth."

27 So the Christian's experience makes him a good preacher and teacher. Faith helps him to a right understanding of all things, and conflict gives him the personal experience which brings perfect assurance. Therefore, he may speak with the utmost confidence and may instruct all men. Well may Tauler say the experienced Christian is able to judge and to teach the world. Without trials no one can ever become a successful preacher. He must remain a mere babbler, unknowing what to say or to what end to speak. As Paul has it (1 Tim 1, 7): "Desiring to be teachers of the law, though they understand neither what they say, nor whereof they confidently affirm." He calls them useless babblers.

Thirteenth: "And shall fill him with the Spirit of wisdom and understanding."

28. Solomon previously, in the third verse said, "With the bread of understanding shall she feed him, and give him the water of wisdom to drink." The reference there is simply to receiving the gifts of God, while not yet exposed to temptations and trials. But after the Christian has experienced temptations, has been tried and proven, he shall have something more than the gifts of wisdom and under-

standing; the Giver of these gifts, the Holy Spirit himself, will fill him and render him wholly perfect.

Not that the Holy Spirit did not before exist in the individual; assuredly where the gifts of the Spirit are, there he surely is. But while the individual is not exposed to temptations, he has not yet come to experience the presence of the Holy Spirit. He will not reach that position until he is tried and proven. Then, though previously endowed with gifts, he will be filled with the Spirit. His gifts will not, as before temptation, serve only himself; from the period of his trial they will render him useful to others, enabling him to bring to men the same grace he possesses. Formerly he was chiefly useful in a temporal way, in distributing favors to his neighbors, as mentioned. He was prompted by faith and the gifts received. His was not, however, a spiritual usefulness, but a temporal one.

After his experience in temptation, the Spirit enters and effects something more than his being fed with the bread of wisdom and understanding as before; he enables him to open his mouth—to feed others with that bread, thus rendering them spiritual service. Before Christ's sufferings the apostles were merely the Lord's guests, eating of his understanding and drinking of his wisdom, and leading pious lives. But no one was affected but themselves. After his resurrection, however, they became hosts; they fed others and rendered them godly through the Spirit of wisdom and understanding that filled them after their temptation.

> Fourteenth: "With a garment of honor shall she clothe him."

28. Righteousness will give the Christian an eminent reputation and a great name, far and wide; as God said to David: "I have made thy name great." Righteousness will adorn the Christian until the world shall honor him for his wisdom and knowledge. "Honor" here means "glory," which is a great and glorious name and distinction among men. Such honor Solomon terms a garment, for it adorns more than do ornaments and jewels.

Fifteenth: "He shall find joy and a crown of gladness."

30. Up to this time Solomon has spoken of the blessings the Christian shall enjoy in this life. Now he concludes with the blessings reserved to the future life—eternal joy and gladness. Here is the treasure Righteousness reserves for the Christian, an everlasting treasure.

Sixteenth: "And she shall cause him to inherit an everlasting name."

31. Not merely during life, but after death, will the Christian's name be prepetuated in honor. After such remembrance the self-righteous vainly strive. For they do not fear God and rely upon the righteousness of faith.

32. Note these precious fruits, these great blessings, so well calculated to give comfort and to constrain us to persevere in faith and in the fear of God. I have gone over this subject hastily, giving it the briefest consideration. An extended sermon might have been preached on each point, if one wished to develop it with the aid of Scripture passages.

33. We must not, however, infer from what has been presented that we are to fear God—believe in him—simply to secure the blessings named. That idea is deceptive. The passage is not written to induce us to seek these blessings; it is merely an assurance that such blessings await the believer. They alone shall receive them who do not seek them; that is, who fear God without seeking their own honor, and who constantly rely upon the grace of God. To them the blessings come unsought. The self-righteous with all their pretense cannot obtain them.

34. This epistle lesson harmonizes beautifully with the Gospel selection. Here Righteousness receives the individual as a virtuous mother receives her child, or the bride her bridegroom. Thus, too, Christ took John to his breast as the beloved disciple. In both selections the nature of faith is commended and illustrated.

Sunday After Christmas

Epistle Text: Galatians 4, 1-7.

1 But I say that so long as the heir is a child, he differ-
eth nothing from a bondservant though he is lord of all;
2 but is under guardians and stewards until the day appointed of the father. 3 So we also, when we were children, were held in bondage under the rudiments of the
world: 4 but when the fulness of the time came, God sent
forth his Son, born of a woman, born under the
law, 5 that he might redeem them that were under the
law, that we might receive the adoption of sons. 6 And
because ye are sons, God sent forth the Spirit of his Son
into our hearts, crying, Abba, Father. 7 So that thou
art no longer a bondservant, but a son; and if a son, then
an heir through God.

THE PEOPLE OF LAW AND OF GRACE.

1. This text is very characteristic of the apostle Paul. It is not generally understood. Not because of any obscurity in itself, but because the doctrine of faith, a doctrine it is very necessary to understand if we are to comprehend Paul, for his energetic and zealous mind is, in all his epistles, occupied with the subject of faith—because, I say, this doctrine is almost obsolete in the world today. A lengthy exposition is necessary to make it plain. To gain space to treat the subject clearly, we will let this suffice for the introduction.

MAN'S JUSTIFICATION.

2. We must know it is one thing to handle the subject of good works and another that of justification; just as the nature or personality of an individual is one thing and his

actions or works another. Justification has reference to the person and not to the works. It is the former, not the latter, which is justified and saved, or is sentenced and punished.

3. Therefore, it is settled that no one is justified by works; he must first be justified by other means. Moses says (Gen 4, 4-5), "Jehovah had respect unto Abel and to his offering." First, he had respect to Abel the person, and then to his offering. Abel being godly, just and acceptable in person, his offering was acceptable. The sacrifice was accepted because of the person, and not the person because of the sacrifice. "But unto Cain and to his offering he had not respect." In the first place, God had not respect unto Cain the person; hence later he respected not his offering. From this quotation we may conclude it is impossible for any work to be good in God's sight unless the worker first be good and acceptable. Conversely, it is impossible for any work to be evil before God unless the worker first be evil and not acceptable.

4. Now, let it be sufficiently proven for the present that there are two kinds of good works; some precede and others follow justification. The former merely appear to be good and effectual; the latter are really good.

5. Now, this is the point of contention between presumptuous saints and God. Right here carnal nature contends, even rages, against the Holy Spirit. The Scriptures everywhere treat of this contention. Therein God concludes all man's works, previous to his justification, evil and ineffectual; he requires justification and goodness on the part of the individual first. Again, he concludes that all persons in the state of nature and of the first birth are unjust and evil. As said in Psalms 116, 11, "All men are liars." And in Genesis 6, 5, "Every imagination of the thoughts of man's heart was only evil continually." Hence the natural man can perform no good work, and all his attempts will be no better than Cain's.

6. Here Madam Huldah with her scornful nose—human nature—steps in and dares to contradict her God and to

charge him with falsehood. She hangs upon herself her old frippery, her straw armor—natural light, reason, free-will and human powers. She introduces the heathenish books and doctrines of men, and proceeds to harp upon these, saying: "Good works do precede justification. And they are not, as God says, the works of Cain. They are good to the extent of justifying. For Aristotle taught that he who does much good will thereby become good." To this doctrine Madam firmly cleaves, perverting the Sriptures and presuming that God must first respect the works and then the doer. This satanic doctrine universally reigns at present in all the high schools and other institutions, and in the cloisters. Its advocates are but Cain-like saints, disregarded of God.

7. In the second place, Madam Huldah, basing her position simply on works and attaching very little importance to the justified individual, proceeds still further and attributes all merit and supreme righteousness to the works following justification. She quotes James 2, 26, "Faith apart from works is dead." Not understanding this statement, she undervalues faith. Consequently she continues to hold to good works, presuming to require of God acceptance of the doer for the sake of the works. So the two continually strive against one another. God respects the individual, Cain the works. God rewards the works for the sake of the doer; Cain would have the doer crowned because of his works. God will not yield his just and righteous position, and the young nobleman Cain will never while the world stands allow himself to be convinced of his error. We must not reject his works, slight his reason or look unto his free-will as powerless; for so he will become angry with God and slay his brother Abel, a fact to which all history gives abundant testimony.

8. Do you ask: "What then am I to do? How shall I make myself good and acceptable in person to begin with? how secure that justification? The Gospel replies: "Hear Christ and believe in him, utterly despairing of yourself and resting assured you will be changed from a Cain to an

Abel and then present your offerings." Just as faith is proclaimed without merit or work on your part, it is also bestowed regardless of your works, without any of your merits. It is given of pure grace. Note, faith justifies the individual; faith is justification. Because of faith God remits all sins, and forgives the old Adam and the Cain in our nature, for the sake of Christ his beloved Son, whose name faith represents. More, he bestows his Holy Spirit. The Holy Spirit changes the individual into a new creature, one with different reason and different will, and inclined to the good. Such a one, wherever he is, performs wholly good works, and all his works are good; as taught in the preceding epistle lesson.

9. Then nothing else is necessary to justification but to hear and believe in Jesus Christ as our Saviour. But that is not a work of the natural man; it is a work of grace. He who presumes to attain justification by works, only obstructs the way of the Gospel, of faith, grace, Christ, God and all good. On the other hand, nothing but justification is necessary to render works good. The justified man and none other does good; all he does, being justified, is good, without distinction of works. Therefore, the order of man's salvation, the beginning and the sequel, is first to hear and then believe God's Word as supreme, and then to act. Thus shall man be saved. He who perverts this order and acts accordingly is certainly not of God.

10. Paul prescribes this order where he says (Rom 10, 13-15): "Whosoever shall call upon the name of the Lord shall be saved. How then shall they call on him in whom they have not believed? and how shall they believe in him whom they have not heard? and how shall they hear without a preacher? and how shall they preach, except they be sent?" Christ teaches us to pray the Lord of the harvest to send laborers into his harvest; that is, faithful preachers. When they come they preach the true Word of God. Hearing it, we are enabled to believe, and such faith justifies us and renders us godly; then we call upon God and do only good. Thus are we saved. So then, the believer shall

be saved, but he who works without faith shall be damned. Christ says (Mk 16, 16), "He that disbelieveth shall be condemned;" here works avail nothing.

11. Now, observe what people commonly do and say. "Yes," they tell you, "I expect to become godly. Yes, we must be godly." But if they are asked what we are to do to accomplish it, they go on to say, "Indeed, we must pray, fast, attend Church, abstain from sin, and so on." One will enter a monastery, another some order. One will become a priest, another will don a hair-garment. One will punish himself in a certain way, and another in another way. They are like Cain and do the works of Cain. Personally they are as at first—without justification. They but assume an external change, an alteration of works, clothing, condition and habits. They are really apes, assuming the habits of saints but remaining unholy. Unmindful of faith, they rush along with their good works toward heaven—as they imagine—torturing themselves.

Relative to them, Christ in the Gospel (Lk 13, 24) says: "Strive to enter in by the narrow door: for many, I say unto you, shall seek to enter in, and shall not be able." And why not? Because they do not recognize the narrow door. It is faith. Faith humbles one, reduces him to nothing, until he must despair of all his good works and cleave only to God's grace; for that he must forsake all else. But the Cain-like saints imagine good works to be the narrow door. Hence they do not humble themselves. Nor do they despair of their good works; no, lading themselves with the cumbersome bundles of their collected deeds, they strive to pass throuh the door. They will pass as the camel with his great hump passes through the eye of the needle.

12. Mention faith to them and they scoff and laugh, saying: "Are we Turks or heathen that we must first learn what faith is? Is it possible that our multitude of monks, nuns and priests do not know? Who can be ignorant of what believing is when even they who openly sin know its meaning?" As if having finished with faith, they imagine they must henceforth devote themselves to works. As

before said, they regard faith of slight importance; for they do not understand that it is our sole justifier. To accept as true the record of Christ—this they call faith. The devils have the same sort of faith, but it does not make them godly. Such belief is not Christian faith; no, it is rather deception.

13. In the preceding epistles we have heard that to be a Christian it is not enough simply to believe the story of Christ true—the Cain-like saints possess such faith—but the Christian must without any hesitancy believe himself one to whom grace and mercy are given, and that he has really secured them through baptism or through the Holy Supper. When he so believes, he is free to say of himself: "I am holy, godly and just. I am a child of God, perfectly assured of salvation. Not because of anything in me, not because of my merits or works, am I saved; it is of the pure mercy of God in Christ, poured out upon me." To such extent will he appreciate God's precious mercy, he cannot doubt that it renders him holy and constitutes him a child of God. But he who doubts, disparages to the utmost his baptism and the Holy Supper, and censures as false God's Word and his grace in the sacraments.

14. The Christian should entertain no fear—he should not doubt—that he is righteous and a child of God through grace. Rather he needs to entertain anxiety as to how he shall endure steadfast to the end. There is where all fear and anxiety are due. For while he assuredly is given to possess full salvation, it may be somewhat doubtful whether or no he will steadfastly retain it. Here we must walk in fear. True faith does not hang upon works nor rely upon itself; it relies only upon God and his grace. Grace cannot forsake the individual so long as reliance continues. But he knows not how long it will continue. Should temptation force him to lose his confidence, grace also will fail. Solomon (Ecc 9, 1) says: "The righteous, and the wise, and their works, are in the hand of God; whether it be love or hatred, man knoweth it not; all is before them." He does not say it is uncertain at present, but in the future,

because man knows not whether he will withstand the attacks or temptation.

15. When the Cain-like saints hear the doctrine of faith, they cross themselves, both with hands and feet, and exclaim: "God forbid! How could I call myself holy and righteous? How could I be so egotistical and presumptuous? No, no; I am a poor sinner." You see how they make faith of no value to themselves, and so must regard as heresy all doctrine based upon it. Thus they do away with the whole Gospel. These are they who deny the Christian faith and exterminate it from the world. Paul prophesied concerning them when he said (1. Tim 4, 1): "In later times some shall fall away from the faith." The voice of faith is now silenced all over the world. Indeed, faith is condemned and banished as the worst heresy, and all who teach and endorse it are condemned with it. The Pope, the bishops, charitable institutions, cloisters, high schools, unanimously opposed it for nearly four hundred years, and simply drove the world violently into hell. Their conduct is the real persecution by Antichrist, in the last times.

16. Tell them what the prophet says in Psalm 86, 2: "Preserve my soul; for I am godly"; and Paul's words in Romans 8, 16: "The Spirit himself beareth witness with our spirit, that we are children of God;" and they reply: "Yes, but the prophet and the apostle did not mean by these statements to establish a doctrine or leave an example of what others may claim. They were enlightened and their holiness was revealed to them." Similarly, they construe every passage relating to the subject as not doctrinal in design, but exhibiting a remarkable miracle, a special prerogative of certain individuals not to be possessed by every believer. This explanation is a mere invention of their own minds. Themselves unbelievers, tasting not the Spirit, they think no one else should so believe or taste. By such conduct—their own fruits—they may be clearly identified as thorns and thistles; not as Christians, but as enemies and destroyers of Christians, and persecutors of the Christian faith.

17. Such, however, is the character of their own faith, they are led to believe they are made godly and holy through their works, and that therefore God must save them. Note, in their opinion, to become godly through works is Christianity; but to become godly through divine grace is heresy. Apparently their works are of greater importance and value than the grace of God. Their faith can rely upon works, but not upon God's grace. Since they reject the rock and build upon the sand, they but get their deserts when they fall into the error of their own works and torture themselves to death, to the devil's advantage. It is all because they will not rely upon the grace of God and render him reasonable service.

18. They who possess the Christian faith must in consequence of it be confidently happy in God and his grace. They will even delight in good works. The prayers the Cain-like ones offer, and the costume they affect, are not good works. Only such works as minister to the profit of a neighbor are good, as we said in the last Gospel lesson. Yes, Christians will readily suffer everything, for they doubt not God's presence with them, and his favor. These are they who honor God and are useful to man.

19. But the Cain-like people profit not God, the world nor themselves. They are mere useless burdens to the earth, harmful to themselves and everyone else. Lacking faith, they do not serve nor honor God. They do no work that contributes in any way to the benefit of their neighbor's bodly or property, his honor or his soul. Their works exclusively their own, consisting in certain gestures, apparel and meats and performed in honor of certain places and times.

Tell me, how does it benefit me for you to affect a large bald pate or to wear a gray cowl? Who profits by your fasting on a certain day and observing a certain other day as holy? by your abstaining from particular meats, and secluding yourself in a certain place, to read and mutter so much every day? So doing, you simply murder yourself to please the devil, leaving a pernicious example, that others may follow in the same life and conduct as if it were good, and consistent with the principles of Christianity. Having not a Christian belief, you cannot pray in a Christian manner. Hence your fasting is not, as it should be, a mortification of the body; it is performed as a good work. Such a life is nothing else than the idolatry of Baal and of Moloch formerly practiced among the Jews, who tortured, burned and otherwise murdered their children for the devil's honor.

THE USE AND NECESSITY OF THE LAW.

20. Perhaps you ask, "If it is true that we are justified not by works, but by hearing of Christ and believing in him as ours personally, what is the need and use of the commandments? Why has God so urgently taught them? I answer: We come now to this our epistle lesson. It tells us the object of the commandments. The Galatians first learned the Christian faith from Paul. Afterward, being perverted by certain false teachers, they turned back to their works, imagining they must become righteous through the deeds of the Law. In our lesson Paul recalls them from their works unto faith, and with multiplied terms points out to them the two kinds of works of the Law. His conclusion is: the works preceding justification—or faith—are unprofitable and merely constitute us servants; but faith makes us children of God—his sons—whereupon really good works must follow.

21. But we must acquaint ourselves with Paul's language, his distinction between the servant and the child. The self-righteous he terms a servant. Concerning that individual much has been said heretofore. The believer in Christ he calls a child. The believer is and will be justified by faith alone—without works. This distinction is based upon the fact that the self-righteous one does not serve in the same spirit that actuates the child and heir conscious of his own inheritance. He renders his service in the spirit of a day-laborer upon another's property. Although the works of the two may be precisely of the same character, the spirit that moves them—the conscience, and faith—makes a difference. The child confidently expects

to remain heir to the estate. The servant, recognizing his ultimate dismissal, does not await inheritance. As Christ declares (Jn 8, 35): "The bondservant abideth not in the house for ever: the son abideth for ever."

22. Now, the Cain-like saints have not, as they themselves confess, the Christian faith which would assure them of being the children of God. They protect themselves from that awful heretical presumption by making the sign of the cross. So they continue to hang in doubt. As they believe, so is it with them. They are not children of God and never will become his happy children in the way they are going, notwithstanding they may perform the requirements of the Law, may faithfully put it into practice. Observance of the Law will constitute them servants, and servants will they continue to be securing no more than a temporal reward—a competence on earth, and rest, honor and pleasure. We see this in the spiritual orders, where all the wealth, power, pleasure, honor and favors of the world are enjoyed. Here is the reward of the self-righteous. They are servants and not children; therefore in the hour of death they will all be cast out from the eternal inheritance which they refused in this life to believe in and to receive through faith. You see, so far as the works are concerned, there is scarcely a difference between the child and the servant. Faith, however—the spirit of service—makes the distinction.

23. The apostle's design is to make plain the fact that, lacking faith, the Law, with all its works, constitutes us simply servants. Only faith can make us children. Not the Law, nor the works of the Law, nor human nature can create faith within us; the Gospel alone brings it. It is present when we give ear to the Gospel, the Word of grace, which Word is accompanied by the Holy Spirit when preached and heard in quiet sincerity. Witness the example of Cornelius and his family (Acts 10, 44), who received the Holy Spirit simply upon hearing Peter preach.

24. The Law was given merely to reveal to man his graceless and servile condition and his lack of filial affection;

to show him how he serves God without faith and confidence, and a free, spontaneous spirit. The self-righteous saints confess to their utter want of confidence; and, if they would but make further confession, they must admit that they prefer to have no Law, and do not submit to it from choice. Destitute of faith as they are, their whole conduct is regulated by restraints. They must acknowledge the Law powerless to yield them any higher perfection. Let them learn from the Law their condition as servants and not as children, and be led to come out of their servitude into the prerogative of the child, regarding their own efforts ineffectual. Thus through faith and the grace of God they may attain their rightful place in life.

25. Such is the right way to view the Law; such is the use we are to make of it. It is calculated simply to convict and vanquish all who presume to fulfil it without faith. For these, being servants, undertake its requirements with no free, spontaneous spirit and with no reliance on grace. The Law is designed to try men, to teach them by defeat in the conflict with it how unwilling, how faithless, they are, and thus lead them to seek help elsewhere and not to presume by their own strength to meet its demands. A voluntary spirit is necessary, and only the child of God can fulfil the Law. The Law is an enemy to the unwilling and to servants.

26. But the self-righteous go so far as to acknowledge their utter lack of faith, yes, they reject the faith which would constitute them children; they are sensible of their unwillingness, and really prefer freedom from the Law; yet they presume by their own works to render themselves godly; they desire to remain servants instead of children, but at the same time to cleave to the inheritance, so perverting all order. Though, as we said, the purpose of the Law is to bring them into conflict and teach that they are servants lacking a voluntary spirit, and to lead them to despair of their own efforts and cleave to faith, which would afford grace and constitute them children—notwithstanding all this, they pervert the Law to the extent of undertaking to

fulfil its demands by their works. Thus they frustrate the end of the Law and its true meaning, striving against faith and grace, to which the Law points, even urges, them. So they remain forever a blind, perverse, laboring and servile people. Such is the teaching of Paul where he fearlessly says (Rom 3, 20), "By the works of the Law shall no flesh be justified in his sight." Why not? He answers (Rom 7, 7), Because the Law effects only the knowledge or experience of sin.

27. Beloved, how does the Law do this? Study a Cain-like individual and you will see. In the first place, only with great pains and labor does he perform all his works in obedience to the Law. Yet, as he readily confesses, he does not believe himself a child of God and holy. Indeed, as before said, he condemns such faith as the most abominable presumption and heresy. He continues in doubt, expecting to become a child through his own works.

28. You see plainly, that individual is not good nor righteous, for he is destitute of faith, in fact is an enemy to faith. Being an enemy to faith, he is an enemy to righteousness. Consequently his works are not meritorious, no matter how admirable they may appear judged by the standard of the Law. So you see Paul is right when he says, "By the works of the law shall no flesh be justified in his sight." In God's sight the doer must be good before his works are good. True, his works may justify him before men, who judge according to the deeds performed and not according to the doer's spirit—the state of his heart. While men judge individuals by their works, God judges the works by the individual.

The first commandment of the Law demands that we have one God and honor him, that is, trust and confide in him, build upon him. This is true faith, whereby we are made children of God. Thus the Law clearly reveals the sin of the Cain-like—their unbelief. In like manner you experience whether you believe or not. Without such a law no one could experience or know this. Note, this is what Paul calls a knowledge of sin by the Law.

29. You cannot extricate yourself from unbelief, nor can the Law do it for you. All your works in intended fulfilment of the Law must remain works of the Law and powerless to justify in the sight of God, who regards as just only believing children. For only these fulfil the first commandment and hold him true God. Though you torture yourself to death with works, yet they will not afford your heart the faith this commandment requires. Indeed, as before stated, works neither know nor tolerate faith. They do not recognize that the Law requires faith. Therefore, he who puts his trust in works must continue the devil's martyr and a persecutor of faith and the Law through those very works wherein he trusts, until he comes to himself, knows himself and, despairing of himself and his works, gives honor to God; until, perceiving his own worthlessness, he ardently desires pure grace, driven to it by God, through the Law. Then faith and grace come to fill the empty heart, to feed the hungry soul. Then follow really good works. These works are not of the Law; they are works of the Spirit of grace, in the Scriptures styled the works of God—works he produces in us. All not produced in us by God through grace, all that we perform of ourselves without grace, is really wrought of the Law and avails nothing to justification. Rather it is evil and opposed to God, because of the unbelief in which it is wrought.

30. In the second place, one like Cain never performs his duty willingly and voluntarily unless he is hired and is permitted to exercise his own pleasure, to have his own desires. He is precisely like the servant who will not do his duty unless he is driven, or is given his own way. Now, servants that have to be driven or coaxed or flattered are very disagreeable. Likewise the Cain-like are displeasing, and by no means acceptable in the sight of God. For they perform no work of the Law unless driven by fear of punishment and of hell; or only after being coaxed and given their own way; or again, unless they do it to secure from God a competence to use as they desire.

You see they are not actuated by hearfelt love for the

Law, but by the expectation of reward or fear of punishment. Being with all their hearts enemies to the Law, evidently they would prefer that the Law did not exist. If the doer be evil, the work is also evil. It is merely extorted by fear, or secured by conceding the doer his own pleasure in the matter; just as entreaty and persuasion move one to action.

31. The Law teaches us to recognize the unwillingness and perversity of our minds. They are wholly sinful before God. Where is the holiness in performing with the hands required duties when our hearts are unkindly disposed toward the Law and the Law-giver? Indeed, ill-will toward the Law is very sinful.

Note, what Paul calls knowing sin by the Law, is coming into conflict with it, feeling and experiencing the perversity of our hearts and in consequence shuddering, despairing of ourselves, and eagerly striving after grace. Grace removes disinclination and generates a willing, cheerful spirit, a spirit giving us sincere good-will for the Law and enabling us to perform our duties voluntarily, without constraint, our only motive being pure delight in righteousness and the Law, while we are uninfluenced by expectation of reward or by fear of punishment. Thus, of the slave, the child is made; of the bond-servant, an heir. The faith of Christ alone can create such a spirit, as sufficiently stated before. Now let us consider the epistle.

> "So long as the heir is a child, he differeth nothing from a bond-servant, though he is lord of all."

32. Paul introduces a figure from material life. As we know, a minor, a child, who is heir to an estate left from parents or bequeathed by will, is reared in restraint like a servant so far as control of the estate is concerned. He is powerless to exercise his own pleasure in regard to it. He is kept under restraint and discipline, being permitted to derive from the estate only enough for food and raiment, notwithstanding the property is really his own. In the matter of his own possessions, he is but as a stranger and a servant.

33. Similarly, in spiritual matters God made a testament when he gave Abraham the promise (Gen 22, 18) that in his seed, Christ, should all the nations of the earth be blessed. This testament was afterward established by the death of Christ; and after his resurrection it was published through the Gospel. The Gospel is merely a revelation, a manifestation, of this testament wherein it is declared to the world that in Christ, the seed of Abraham, grace and blessing are willed and given to all men, and may be received by every one if only he believes it.

34. Before this testament was opened and published, children of God were under the Law, burdened and constrained by its works. Nevertheless, their works did not justify; rather they were servile and unprofitable. But because God's children were predestined to a future faith which should constitute them children, they were unquestionably heirs of the grace and blessing conveyed in the testament; though not then in possession of it and able to appropriate it, but, like others without faith, servile and occupied with works. Just so, it is the case now, and always has been, that many believe, and acknowledge faith, after having been previously overwhelmed with works and in ignorance of faith; after having been, with hypocrites, occupied in works. From the fact of their now apprehending faith and receiving the inheritance, they certainly must have been all the time heirs and predestined of God, though in ignorance of the fact, and though servants, self-righteous and Cain-like.

35. So some who are now occupied with works and whose holiness is like Cain's, who are servants as he was, are nevertheless future heirs and children, because they will yet believe. Faith will enable them to lay aside their servility, to surrender their works and to obtain the great blessing, the vast inheritance, of justification. And being justified, righteousness and salvation are theirs without works. Then will they voluntarily do all their works to the honor of God and the benefit of their neighbors, without expectation of reward or intent to secure righteousness or a re-

ward. For they are in possession of the inheritance and blessing; they have what Christ has bequeathed to them in his testament and caused to be opened, proclaimed and distributed through the Gospel, all of pure grace and mercy.

36. Abraham and every other patriarch, you will observe, recognized God's testament or covenant. It was delivered to them just as much as to us, although not at that time read and proclaimed to the world as after Christ's ascension. They obtained the very same thing that we and all God's children obtain, and through the very same faith. The grace, the blessing, the testament, the faith—all are the same; the Father is one and the same God of us all.

37. Note, Paul everywhere teaches justification, not by works, but solely by faith; and not as a process, but instantaneous. The testament includes in itself everything—justification, salvation, the inheritance and great blessing. Through faith it is instantaneously enjoyed, not in part, but all. Truly is it plain, then, that faith alone affords such blessings of God, justification and salvation—immediately and not in process as must be the case with works—and constitutes us children and heirs who voluntarily discharge their duties, not presuming to become godly and worthy by a servile spirit. No merit is needed; faith secures all gratuitously—more than anyone can merit. The believer performs his works gratuitously, being already in possession of all the Cain-like saints vainly seek through works and never find—justification and divine inheritance, or grace.

> "But is under guardians and stewards until the day appointed of the father."

38. These guardians and stewards are they who bring up the heir on his father's estate, restraining him from a wild and vagabond life. Though they withhold from him control of the inheritance, they are necessary and benefit the heir in various ways. In the first place, as stated before, they keep him at home on the estate, to better fit him for enjoyment of it. Secondly, the fact of his being carefully and closely restrained will inspire in him stronger desire for control of the inheritance; when he arrives at the age of

discretion he will yearn for freedom and be unwilling to continue under others' control.

39. The same is necessarily true of everyone still occupied with works under the Law, and a servant. The Law is his guardian, his steward. He is under its control as one in constraint of another. The Law is designed, in the first place, to train him and keep him in bounds; to restrain him externally, through fear of punishment, from committing evil works; to save him from becoming wholly dissolute, from risking everything and altogether shutting himself out from God and his salvation, as do the profligate.

The Law is intended, in the second place, to teach man to know himself; to bring him to reason, where he may recognize his unwilling allegiance to the Law, how he performs no work willingly as a child, but by constraint as a bond-servant. The Law gives him experience as to his shortcomings; it shows him his lack of a free, new and ever-willing spirit—a spirit the Law and its works cannot give. Indeed, the more he works, the more unwillingly is it done; and the harder is it to work, for he is influenced by a grudging spirit.

40. Being made aware of his unwilling attitude, he sees that his works are only an external observance of the Law, while in his heart he is an enemy and opposer of the Law, so far as cheerful obedience is concerned. Hence he truly is constantly at heart a sinner against the Law, and externally a saint according to the Law; in other words, a real Cain, an egregious hypocrite. Manifestly to himself, his works are works of the Law, but his heart is a heart of sin. His heart being not disposed to the Law, it is disposed to sin, while merely his hands are constrained to observe the Law's requirements.

41. Very aptly has Paul styled works without faith "works of the Law." For the Law forces them; they are simply compulsory works. Now, the Law demands the heart also. It desires a willing obedience. A willing obedience may be said to be not only "a work of the Law," but "a heart of the Law"; not only "hands of the Law," but

"will, spirit and all the powers of the Law." As Psalm 1, 1-2 declares: "Blessed is the man whose delight is in the law of Jehovah; and on his law doth he meditate day and night." Such a spirit the Law demands, but it does not create it; nor is human nature able of itself to produce it. Hence the Law oppresses the soul and condemns it to hell as disobedient to God's commandments. Anguish and distress of conscience follow, but there is no help.

This is the time appointed of the Father. Now the child of God will crave grace and help. He will confess his wretchedness, weakness and guilt. He will let go his claim to security in works, and despise himself. For he recognizes that between himself and public sinners there is no difference except as to external conduct. In his heart he is as much opposed to the Law as any other sinner; in fact, his heart may be even more embittered toward it. For the sinner of actual practice may find less desire to sin and may become somewhat inimical to sin, in consequence of the resulting unpleasantness and injury he must meet. The child of God, hindered and restrained by its tutor the Law, may really burn and rage in his desires and lusts for sin, though he dare not commit the deed. Thus, in expression he may be more righteous than the public sinner, but in heart more wicked.

42. Now, it is easily apparent to everyone that to give our hands to the Law and our whole hearts to sin, is a very unequal division of service; for the whole heart means vastly more than the works of the hands. What is such a proceeding but giving the chaff to the Law and the grain to sin, or the shell to God and the kernel to the devil? This explains how, as taught in the Gospel, the sin of the public transgressor is but a mote, while that of the secret offender is a great beam.

43. Now, where circumstances are such that Cain does not see this beam and does not learn to know himself in this sense of the Law, but continues obdurate and blind in his works, disregarding his inner wickedness—where such is the case, he proceeds very inconsistently to judge with

malice the world in general, despising sinners as did the Pharisee in the Gospel—presuming to regard himself godly in contrast with others. If any attempt to rebuke him, and justly to condemn his conduct, he rages and raves, kills Abel and persecutes all men, claiming that he does it for the sake of good works and righteousness, to the praise of God. He expects to merit much as a persecutor of blasphemers, heretics, offenders and wicked ones who would lead him astray and lure him from good works. Right here all Scripture denunciations of these venomous spirits come in. Christ calls them serpents and a generation of vipers. Mt 23, 33. They are like Cain, and will continue like him. Servants are they, and will remain servants.

44. But the prospective Abels and future children learn to recognize themselves by the Law, to discover how little heartfelt delight they have for that Law. Ceasing to rely upon their own presumption, they let go their hold and with this knowledge are completely helpless in their own eyes. Just here the Gospel comes in. Here is where God gives grace to the humble. These children of God lay hold of the testament and believe. With and in this faith they receive the Holy Spirit. He gives to them a new heart, a heart delighting in the Law and hating sin, and doing right voluntarily and cheerfully. Works of the Law are now superseded by hearts of the Law. This is the time appointed of the father for the heir to come into his own—no longer to be a servant nor under a guardian. Now we understand what Paul means by the words:

> "So we also, when we were children, were held in bondage under the rudiments [elements] of the world."

45. The apostle uses a word familiar to us—"rudiments." But we are not to understand here the four rudiments or elements of nature—fire, water, air and earth. That is not its Scriptural meaning. That use of the term originated in heathen philosophy, and in such sense it would be entirely inadmissible in the Scriptures. The apostle means by "rudiments" the literal characters—the letters—

of the Law. In both the Latin and the Greek languages, letters are terms the "rudiments" of the language.

Similarly, Paul says (Heb 5, 12), "When by reason of the time ye ought to be teachers, ye have need again that some one teach you the rudiments of the first principles of the oracles of God." And (Col 2, 8): "Take heed lest there shall be any one that maketh spoil of you through his philosophy and vain deceit, after the tradition of men, after the rudiments of the world, and not after Christ." Again (Gal 4, 9-10), "How turn ye back again to the weak and beggarly rudiments, whereunto ye desire to be in bondage over again? Ye observe days, and months, and seasons, and years."

46. It is in a rather contemptuous sense that Paul terms the Law "rudiments," or letters; it is "weak and beggarly" because it can afford no relief. It renders us likewise weak and beggarly, for it demands service of the heart and mind; and the heart and mind are not present. Hence the conscience grows weak and beggarly, confessing it has not and can not have what it should have. As the apostle expresses it (2 Cor. 3, 6), "The letter killeth, but the spirit giveth life."

47. Some understand by "rudiments" not the letter of the law, but the ceremonials and outward forms of worship incident to the religious life, and which we early teach children. In that connection, "rudiments" implies the first crude, childish forms of worship.

48. Paul qualifies "rudiments" by the phrase "of the world," because the self-righteous, while boasting obedience to the Law, observe it only in external and worldly things, such as days, meats, apparel, places, persons, vessels and the like. These are all creatures of this world, and such, practically, is the extent of the works of the Law. [Therefore we rendered the meaning in German by "Aeuszerliche Satzung," outward or worldly laws. Editions of 1540 and 1543.]

49. But faith, independent of the world, hangs upon God, his Word and his mercy; and justifies us, not by works or

any other wordly thing, but by the eternal, invisible grace of God. To the Christian, one day is like another; and meats, places, apparel and all worldly things are alike. They neither help nor hinder his salvation and justification, as they do in the case of Cain and the self-righteous. Therefore, the Christian gives no heed to the rudiments of this world, but regards the fullness of the eternal blessings.

So, though the Christian has to do with external, temporal affairs, yet he is indifferent to worldly things. He is free to disregard them. All are alike to him—persons, places, days, meats, apparel, etc. He makes no particular choice. Doing the duty that presents, he is unconcerned about what does not. His external conduct does not represent something select and peculiar.

50. The Cain-like take a different course. They must make some distinction—must be recognized by some peculiarity. They eat no meat, wear nothing black, pray not in houses, observe days. One is bound to one custom, another to another. Yet these are all temporal and transitory things. The observers are servants of the rudiments of this world. Nevertheless, their practices are styled holy orders, good morals and real ways to salvation.

Upon this point Paul says (Col 2, 20-23): "If ye died with Christ from the rudiments of the world, why, as though living in the world, do ye subject yourselves to ordinances, Handle not, nor taste, nor touch (all which things are to perish with the using), after the precepts and doctrines of men? Which things have indeed a show of wisdom in will-worship, and humility."

51. From this quotation and from our foregoing arguments, clearly all orders, institutions and cloisters, now styled ecclesiastical positions, are directly opposed to the Gospel and to the freedom of Christian life; and they who are bound by them are in greater danger than are actual worldlings. The things they devise are mere rudiments of this world. They pertain only to apparel, persons, conditions, times, forms, meats and vessels—solely worldly and temporal things. Adhering to these as having power to

make them pious and spiritual, faith is excluded and they are not Christians. Their whole life is but sin and corruption.

52. These ecclesiasts have more need than anyone else to guard against such dazzling devices. They have especial need to adhere stedfastly to faith, the righteousness of which is beyond the world and worldly things. The glitter and show of works tear away from faith with greater violence than do gross, open sins, and place the doers in the condition to which Paul here refers when he says, "So we also, when we were children, were held in bondage under the rudiments of the world." When we were ignorant of faith and occupied with the works of the Law, we performed—yet unwillingly and as servants—works relating to temporal things, presuming thereby to become righteous and saved. It was a false idea, and made of us children and servants. The mere works would have been harmless had it not been for the idea that excluded faith and the doctrine of godliness only through grace, and had all temporal things been left optional.

> "But when the fulness of the time came, God sent forth his Son, born of a woman, born under the law, that he might redeem them that were under the law, that we might receive the adoption of sons."

53. Now, since the law cannot effect justification nor faith, and human nature with all its works cannot merit them, Paul introduces him who merited faith in our stead, and who is master of justification—and justification was not secured without price; it cost much, even the Son of God himself. Him Paul introduces, saying: "When the fulness of the time was come"; that is, at the expiration of the time when we were children and servants. The apostle follows a usage of the Scriptures in speaking of the expiration of the time as its "fulfilment." For instance, Acts 2, 1: "When the day of Pentecost was [fulfilled] fully come"; that is, when it was completed. And Exodus 23,26, "The number of thy days I will fulfil," meaning, "I will not shorten them; I will give their full measure." Also Luke 1,

57: Now Elizabeth's time was fulfilled that she should be delivered; and she brought forth a son."

54. Hence the learned doctors erred in interpreting this passage by Paul to mean that the time of fulfilment was the time of grace following Christ's birth. This is directly contrary to the apostle, who does not say, "the time of the fulfilment," but "the fulfilment of the time," meaning the previous time appointed of the Father for the heir,—the period of his guardianship.

55. Like as the time of the bondservant was fulfilled for the Jews by the bodily advent of Christ, so is it still daily fulfilled for the individual when he is enlightened by faith, and his period of servitude in legal works terminates. Christ's bodily advent would have been to no purpose had it not effected a spiritual advent, the advent of faith. The purpose of the former appearance was the establishment of the latter one. Christ came spiritually to all who, whether previously or subsequently, believed in his bodily advent. Hence, because of their faith, he was always present with the ancient fathers; but he has not yet come to the Jews of today because of their unbelief.

Everything, from the beginning of the world to the end, depends on that bodily advent. Faith therein terminates the state of servitude whenever, wherever and in whomsoever it exists. Therefore, the time is fulfilled for each individual when he begins to believe in Christ as the promised one now come.

WHAT WE ARE TO BELIEVE CONCERNING CHRIST.

56. So rich in meaning is this verse, I am not sure I shall be able to do it justice in my explanation. It is not enough merely to believe that Christ is come; we must believe also what Paul here states: that he is sent of God and is the Son of God; that he is true man; that his mother was a virgin; that he alone has fulfilled the Law, and not for his own sake but for our good—to secure grace for us. These points we will examine in order.

On the first point John's entire Gospel insists, as we said

on the selection for Christmas. John continually proves Christ the Son of God and sent of the Father. He who does not believe that Christ is true God is lost; witness John 8:24: "Except ye believe that I am he, ye shall die in your sins." And (Jn 1, 4): "In him was life; and the life was the light of men." And again (Jn 14, 6): "I am the way, and the truth, and the life." And the reason that we must believe if we would be saved, is this:

57. The soul cannot, and should not, be content with anything but the Highest Good—its Creator and the fountain of its life and salvation. Now, God chose to be himself that one on whom the soul should rely and believe. No one but God deserves the creature's confidence. Therefore, he himself came to earth as man, gave himself for man, and draws man unto himself, inviting him to believe in him. No necessity on God's part demanded that he come to earth as man; the necessity was ours—it was for our benefit. Now, if we were not to cleave by faith unto Christ as true God, God would be robbed of the honor due him, and we of life and salvation. It is our duty to believe in God only, who is the Truth; without him we cannot live or be saved.

58. The apostle says, "God sent his son." The fact of sending necessitates previous existence of the Son. Christ must have existed before he manifested himself on earth in human form. Again, if he is a Son, he must be greater than an angel. Being more than man and more than angels, the highest creatures, he must be true God. To be the Son of God is to be superior to an angel, as said in the Epistle for Christmas day. Further, Christ being sent by God, and being God's Son, he must be a distinct person from him who sends. Thus Paul teaches here the existence of one God in two persons, Father and Son. We shall speak later of the Holy Spirit.

59. For the second point: We are also to believe Christ to be true, natural man, and the Son of man. Paul says he was born of a woman, or made of a woman. Now, he who is born of a woman must be truly a natural man. A woman

can bear only according to her nature—bear true man. In John 6, 53, Christ says: "Except ye eat the flesh of the Son of man and drink his blood, ye have not life in yourselves." Eating and drinking here means simply believing that Christ, the Son of God, had a true flesh-and-blood nature, like other men.

This is also the testament or covenant of God to Abraham (Gen 22, 18), "In thy seed shall all the nations of the earth be blessed." To be the seed of Abraham, Christ must surely have Abraham's flesh and blood—must be his natural child.

60. No one, then, must presume by his own devotion, his own efforts, to institute a way of approach to God. It is futile to call on God in the manner of the Jews and the Turks. We must approach him through the seed of Abraham, and be blessed through that seed, according to God's covenant. God will not make a special way for you. He will not, because of your service, annul his covenant. You must abandon your own efforts and cleave to the seed he mentions, to that flesh and blood; otherwise you will be lost with all the spiritual skill and wisdom you may have gained from God. Christ says (Jn 14, 6), "No one cometh unto the Father, but by me."

61. Because of the exalted and incomprehensible character of the divine nature, God has for our good manifested himself in the most familiar form—in our own nature. In this character he awaits us. Here, and nowhere else, he may be found. Whosoever calls upon him in this relation will be heard at once. Here is the throne of grace, where no one who comes is excluded. But they who permit Christ to dwell here in vain, and presume in some other way than through his humanity to serve and call upon God, the Creator of heaven and earth, may see their sentence already pronounced in Psalm 18, 41, where it is said of such: "They cried, but there was none to save; even unto Jehovah, but he answered them not."

62. In the third place, we must believe that Christ's mother was a virgin. The apostle makes this plain when he declares the Son of God was made of a woman—not of man

like other children. He alone among men is born of woman only. The apostle is not disposed to say "born of a virgin," because "virgin" is not naturally consistent here. But "woman" represents a state in nature—the natural instrumentality for bearing fruit, for bringing forth children. The mother of Christ is truly woman by nature, who brought forth the divine fruit; yet from herself alone, not by man. Therefore she is a virgin woman—not simply a virgin.

63. Paul attaches more importance to the birth of Christ than to Mary's virginity. He passes over in silence her virginity, merely a peculiar personal grace that benefited none but herself, and points out her womanhood, advantageous not only to herself but to her fruit. Her virginity ministers not so much to Christ as does her womanhood. She was selected in her virginity not for her own sake, but for Christ's sake. He chose to be born of a virgin that he might be born without sin. A sinless birth was impossible except through the instrumentality of a virgin woman who was able to conceive and bring forth without the aid of man.

64. Such seems to be included in God's covenant, declaring that all the nations of the earth shall be blessed in the seed of Abraham. From the fact of a blessing being promised, it is evident that men must be under a curse because of their physical birth in sin resulting from Adam. Should this seed of Abraham be a blessing to all, it could not itself be under a curse; therefore, the Saviour could not come of Adam's birth, which is altogether under the curse.

65. Further, to verify the testament or covenant of God who cannot lie, Christ must be the natural child of Abraham—his flesh and blood. But to what is such reasoning leading us? Christ is to be a natural child, born of flesh and blood, and yet not to be a child of carnal birth. The inconsistency of the reasoning is removed by the fact that a woman alone, independent of man, was chosen to effect the birth. Thus it was possible for a real, natural child, one truly the seed of Abraham, to be born sinless, of a woman, and productive of abundant blessings. In him, then, mankind, under the curse in consequence of its own sinful birth,

may be blessed. Thus the requirements of God's covenant are fully met; the carnal birth of Adam with its inordinate desire is avoided, and a physical birth in spiritual manner really effected.

66. If to Mary, the holy virgin, is due great honor for her virginity, infinitely greater honor is due her for her womanhood. For her procreative powers were instrumental in the fulfilment of God's covenant, and in making the blessed seed of Abraham the blessed fruit of her womanhood. Her mere virginity would have been insufficient to accomplish it; in fact, entirely futile.

67. In the fourth place, we must believe that none but Christ has fulfilled the law. He says (Mt 5, 17), "Think not that I came to destroy the law . . . but to fulfil." Such, too, is the meaning of the covenant that says the whole world is condemned, and shall be blessed in Abraham's seed. Gen 22, 18. Now, if all men are condemned and unblessed, the individual cannot be good; he is only Cain-like. Consequently his works cannot be good, as said before. God does not regard the works, but the persons—Abel and Cain. And the works of the law render no one righteous.

68. The fact that Christ rejects all works of the Law and demands that the person first be good and blessed, may seem to teach that he rejects good works and designs to destroy the Law altogether. But in reality Christ teaches us to perform good works. For the very purpose of correcting error on this point, he says (Mt 5, 17): "Think not that I came to destroy the Law" because I reject the works of the Law. Rather I design its fulfilment through men's faith in me, which first renders the individual good and then enables him to do really good works.

Similarly Paul says, rejecting all works of the Law and exalting faith alone: "Do we then make the law of none effect through faith? God forbid: nay, we establish the law." Rom 3, 31.

Of us at the present day also it is said that we forbid good works when we condemn the practices of the cathedrals and cloisters in the matter of works. Nevertheless, our actual desire for the people is that they first embrace true faith whereby they may become personally good, and be blessed in Christ the seed of Abraham, and thus be enabled to do good works contributing to the mortification of the body and to the good of mankind. To this end the things wrought in cathedrals and cloisters contribute nothing, as already fully stated.

69. Observe, no one is able to fulfil the Law until he first is liberated from it. We must become accustomed to Paul's peculiar phraseology in his reference to some being "under the Law" if we would know who is really under it and who is free. All who perform good works simply because commanded, and from fear of punishment or expectation of reward, are under the Law. Their piety and good deeds result from constraint, and not from a willing spirit. The Law is their master, their driver, and they its bondservants and captives. Such is the attitude of all men without Christ the blessed seed of Abraham. Our own experience and the voice of everyone's conscience teach this. Were it not for the restraint of Law—the fear of punishment or the expectation of reward—were each individual left to his own inclinations and there were no punishment or reward, he would do evil and neglect good, particularly under the influence of temptation and allurements. But when the Law with its threats and its promises interposes, man abstains from evil and endeavors to do good; not from love of good and hatred of evil, but through fear of punishment or hope of reward. Thus the Cain-like saints are under the Law, controlled by it, like servants.

70. But they who are liberated from the Law do good and avoid evil, regardless of the threats and promises of the Law—not from fear of punishment or expectation of reward. They act voluntarily, from love for the good and hatred of the evil, because they delight in the Law of God. Even were there no Law, they would not have it otherwise, and be prompted by the same spirit to do good and abstain from evil. Such are really children. Human nature cannot create that spirit; it has origin with the seed of Abraham. The

blessing of Christ gives the willing disposition. Willingness is the result of his grace and of the influence of the Holy Spirit.

Therefore, "not under the Law" does not mean liberty to do evil and to neglect good as we feel inclined. It means doing good and avoiding evil, not in consequence of fear, not from the restraints and requirements of the Law, but from pure love and a willing spirit. Freedom from the Law involves a spirit which would voluntarily do only good, as if the Law did not exist and our nature were prone to do good. It is a freedom paralleled by that of the body, which willingly eats, drinks, assimilates, sleeps, moves and performs all natural functions. No law, no compulsion, is necessary. It acts voluntarily and seasonably, without fear of punishment or expectation of reward. It may truly be said that the body is under no law, still it performs its functions; it acts spontaneously.

71. Mark you, we must have within ourselves a ready, natural willingness that will incline to good and recoil from evil. This is spiritual liberation, or redemption from the Law. Thus is explained Paul's words (1 Tim 1, 9): "Law is not made for a righteous man." From his own impulse the righteous man inclines to good and abstains from evil; it is with no fear of penalty or hope of recompense. Again, we read (Rom 6, 15), "We are not under law, but under grace." That is, we are children, not bondservants; we incline to good readily, without constraint. Again (Rom 8, 15), "Ye received not the spirit of bondage again unto fear; but ye received the spirit of adoption, whereby we cry, Abba, Father." The Law produces a spirit of fear; a servile, Cain-like spirit. But grace produces a free, filial, Abel-like disposition, through Christ the seed of Abraham. To that spirit, Psalm 51, 10, has reference: "Create in me a clean heart, O God; and renew a right spirit within me." Again, in Psalm 110, 3, it is said concerning the people of Christ: "Thy people offer themselves willingly . . . in holy array."

72. Thus Christ fulfilled the Law and did all, of his own

free will; not because of the compelling or restraining power of the Law. No other has ever fulfilled it, nor will any fulfil it, except in and through him. So Paul here says that Christ was "born under the law, that he might redeem them that were under the law."

73. In the fifth place, we are to believe that Christ's motive was to benefit us. He desired to make children of us servants. What is meant by the phrase "that he might redeem them that were under the law"? Unquestionably, that he might redeem us from under the Law. But how does Christ effect that? As said before, not by the threats or the rewards of the Law, but by bestowing a voluntary spirit; a spirit prompted neither by compulsion nor restraint; a spirit that regards not the terrors nor the rewards of the Law, but proceeds as if no Law existed and all action were voluntary, as was the case with Adam and Eve before the fall.

74. But what is the process whereby Christ gives us such a spirit and redeems us from under the Law? The work is effected solely by faith. He who believes that Christ came to redeem us, and that he has accomplished it, is really redeemed. As he believes, so is it with him. Faith carries with it the child-making spirit. The apostle here explains by saying that Christ has redeemed us from under the Law that we might receive the adoption of sons. As before stated, all must be effected through faith. Now we have discussed the five points of the verse.

HOW CHRIST WAS UNDER THE LAW.

75. The question, however, still arises: How can Christ be under the Law if to be "under the Law" is to be prompted to obedience only by its restraints and compulsion, and if no one under the Law can fulfil it since God requires a voluntary conformity to its demands? I answer: The apostle seems to make a distinction when he says that Christ was put, or made under the Law; that is, he voluntarily placed himself under the Law. Again, with his voluntary consent, the Father placed him under the Law, though properly he was not subject. We, however, were made subject against our desires. We, as Paul says, were naturally and essen-

tially in forced subjection. While Christ was voluntarily, not by nature, under the Law, we were by nature, not voluntarily, in subjection.

76. There is a marked difference between being placed under the Law and being of choice under the Law; just the difference there is between volition and the compulsion of nature. Acting according to the pleasures of the will differs materially from obeying the impulses of nature. What is performed by pleasure of the will may be omitted; it is not compulsory. But what is wrought in obedience to the impulses of nature is of necessity; it is not optional. One may go to the Rhine or not, as he pleases; but he must eat, drink, assimilate, sleep, grow and advance in years regardless of his will. Christ put himself under the Law voluntarily, when he had power to refrain. But we were by nature under it; there was no alternative. We could not voluntarily obey and suffer the Law as if under no constraint, as before stated. But Christ, independent of any obligation to obey the Law, observed it voluntarily; he acted as if there were no law for him.

77. To illustrate: Peter, the apostle (Acts 12, 6-7), lay captive in the prison of Herod, bound with chains to two soldiers, while the keepers stood guard at the door. The angel of God entered the prison in a brilliant light, awoke Peter and led him past all the keepers and out the door, leaving the chains in the prison. This event is an illustration of how Christ liberates us from the Law. Let us analyze it.

Peter was an inmate of the prison not willingly; he was kept there by force. He knew not how to deliver himself. The angel also entered the prison, but willingly. He was not compelled to be there. He was not there for his own sake, but for the sake of Peter. And he knew how to deliver himself. Now, Peter, when he followed the angel obediently, was liberated.

The prison represents the Law, in which our consciences are unwillingly held captive. For no one voluntarily effects the good required by the Law or omits the evil it forbids.

Man acts through fear of punishment or hope of reward. The fear or threat and the reward, or rather the expectation of reward, are the two chains that hold us in prison under the Law. The keepers are the teachers of the Law, who explain it to us. Thus we remain—yes, unwillingly lie—in the Law. Christ is the angel who voluntarily approaches us in prison—approaches us under the Law; he does willingly the works we unwillingly perform. His motive is to benefit us; he would attach us to himself and liberate us. Christ well knows how to liberate, for he is himself independent of will. Then, mark you, if we cleave to him and follow him, we too shall be liberated.

78. But how is this done? We cleave to Christ and follow him when we believe that he effects all for our benefit. Such faith introduces the Spirit. Having faith, we too shall perform the requirements of the Law voluntarily, unfettered and liberated from the prison of the Law. The two chains, fear of punishment and hope of reward, will no longer restrain us. All our acts will be spontaneous, prompted by pure love and a cheerful spirit.

79. To further understand how Christ was put under the Law: Observe, he placed himself in subjection in a twofold manner. In the first place, he put himself under the works of the Law. He permitted himself to be circumcised and to be presented and purified in the temple. He was submissive to his father and mother, and all those things, when no obligation required. For he was Lord over all laws. He acted voluntarily in this respect, unprompted by fear of punishment or expectation of reward as far as he was himself concerned. When we consider the question of mere external works, we can perceive no difference between his conduct and that of individuals actuated by compulsion and restraint. His liberty and free will were concealed from men, just as the imprisonment and unwillingness of others were not apparent. Thus Christ acts under the Law, though properly not under the Law. He conducts himself like those in bondage to it, but he is himself free. His will being free, he is not under the Law. In the matter of

works, which he voluntarily performs, he is subject. But we, both as to our wills and to our works, are under the Law; for we effect works by constraint of will.

80. In the second place, Christ willingly put himself under the penalty of the Law. He did more than perform the works of the Law to which he was not obligated; he willingly and innocently suffered the penalty threatened and inflicted of the Law upon all who fail of observance. Now, the Law adjudges to death, condemnation and eternal punishment every transgressor of its commands. Paul, quoting from Deuteronomy 27, 26, says: "Cursed is every one who continueth not in all things that are written in the book of the law, to do them." Gal 3, 10.

81. We have now made sufficiently plain the fact that no individual out of Christ is able to keep the Law; all of that class are under the Law, like servants, and fettered and constrained. Consequently, the disregarder of the Law deserves its judgment and penalties. He who is under the Law in the first respect—in the matter of works—must also be subject in the second respect—the matter of punishment. Now, first, all our works are sinful because not performed from a willing spirit but rather in opposition to our will. And second, we are adjudged to death and condemnation.

Christ Redeems Us.

But Christ intervenes before sentence is executed upon us. He interposes, approaching us as we are under sentence. He suffers the penalty—death, curse and condemnation; just as if he had himself violated the entire Law, and deserved the full penalty resting upon the transgressor. At the same time he has not broken the Law; he has fulfilled it, and that without obligation. He is doubly innocent. First, even had he observed no Law—and such was his privilege—he was under no obligation to suffer. Second, he observed the Law from superabundant willingness and was liable to no penalty. In contrast, our guilt is also of twofold character. First, we, under obligation to keep the Law, failed so to do; consequently we should justly suffer its calamities. Second, even had we observed it, it would be right that we should suffer whatever God designs.

82. Note, the Son of God is put under the Law in that he redeemed us who were under it. For us, for our good, he effected all; not for himself. He purposed to manifest toward us only love, goodness and mercy. As Paul has it (Gal 3, 13), "Christ redeemed us from the curse of the law, having become a curse for us." In other words: For us, Christ put himself under the law and complied with its demands, designing every believer of this fact to be redeemed from under the Law with its curse.

83. Mark you, then, the priceless blessing for the believing Christian: To him are attributed as his own all the works and sufferings of Christ. He may rely upon them as if they were his—wrought by himself. For, to repeat, Christ effected all, not for himself, but for us. Christ needed not any of the things he wrought. He accumulated the treasure that on it we might confidently rest. Further, such faith will be accompanied by the Holy Spirit.

84. What more should God do? How can the heart avoid being free, joyous and cheerfully obedient in God and Christ? What work can it encounter or what suffering endure to which it will not respond singing and leaping in love and praise for God? When such is not the case, there is certainly some defect in our faith. For the greater our faith, the greater our freedom and happiness; the less our faith, the less our joy. Note, this is the Christian redemption, the Christian freedom from the Law and its curse—sin and death. Not that the Law and death shall be removed, but they shall become as if they were not. The Law shall not lead us to sin, nor death to shame. But faith shall guide us into righteousness and eternal life.

85. This is an occasion to admonish the poor Cain-like saints, the ecclesiasts, if that is possible in their condition. Were they to observe their orders, laws, ceremonies, prayers, masses, clothing and meats as Christ observed the Law, these might be retained. For example, if they assigned the Christian faith its true place and allowed it to control the

heart; if they confessed that they did not become pious and were not saved through their orders, stations and works, but alone through faith in Christ; and if then they considered their works and laws optional, needed only for the mortification of the body and the benefit of the neighbor; then these ordinances might be retained. But the impression at present is that such practices are essential to piety and eternal salvation. This is nothing but a delusion and very sinful. It drives people to perdition by severe martyrdom, and it merits eternal martyrdom; because full, child-like faith is opposed by servile and compulsory works. Faith cannot tolerate such stupid works; it alone makes us pious and forever happy. With the believer all works are optional; he cheerfully suffers all that God sends and does as his neighbor's need requires. These are the works of faith, these and no other. Faith inquires not about masses, appointed fasts, particular clothing, special meats, rare positions, persons or works; nay, faith rejects all these as hindrances to its liberty.

86. Let this suffice on that verse. We were compelled to treat the subject at length because so little is known concerning the doctrine of faith, a knowledge of which is necessary to a right understanding of Paul. Now follows:

> "And because ye are sons [children], God sent forth the Spirit of his Son into your hearts, crying, Abba, Father."

87. Here we see that the Holy Spirit is communicated, not through works, but through faith; for as it reads, the Spirit is given to men because they are children and not servants. Children believe; servants only work. Children are free from the Law; servants are under it. The foregoing explanations make all this plain. It may be necessary, however, for us to consider in some measure the sense in which Paul uses the words "child" and "servant," "free" and "bond." Works performed under compulsion are the works of servants, and works wrought of free will are the works of children.

88. Why does Paul tell the Galatians the Holy Spirit

was given them because they were children, when the fact is, the Holy Spirit creates children from servants, and must be essentially present before they can become children? I reply: He speaks in the same future sense characteristic of verses three and four, where we read that before the time was fulfilled we were under the rudiments. Here the reference is to children prospectively, in the sight of God. The Holy Spirit was sent to transform the servants into the children they were designed to be.

89. Paul speaks of the Spirit as the Spirit of the Son of God. Why not the Spirit of God? Because he would emphasize the point he is making. Being children of God, God sends them the Spirit of Christ, himself a child, giving them the right to cry, with him, "Abba, Father." In other words, God sends you his Spirit, who dwells in his Son, that you may be brethren and heirs with him, crying as he cries, "Abba, Father." The unspeakable goodness and grace of God are extolled in the fact that through faith we share with Christ the full blessings, having all he has, and all he is —also his Spirit.

90. These words also establish the doctrine of a third person—the Holy Spirit—in the Trinity. For not only does the Spirit dwell in Christ as he does in men, but he also is Christ's, deriving his divine substance from him just as he does from the Father. Otherwise the language of Paul—"the Spirit of his Son"—would be false. No creature can claim the Holy Spirit as his own spirit; he is the Spirit of God alone. Creatures are the property of the Holy Spirit; though one might, it is true, say "my Holy Spirit" in the sense in which we say "my God," "my Lord." The Son is God, then, because the Spirit of God is his Spirit.

91. But let everyone be certain that he feels the Holy Spirit's presence in himself and hears his voice. Paul says: When the Holy Spirit is in the heart he cries, "Abba, Father." Again (Rom 8, 15), "Ye received the spirit of adoption, whereby we cry, Abba, Father." We recognize that voice when the conscience, without doubt or wavering, is firmly persuaded, fully satisfied, that our sins are for-

given and that we are children of God; and when, having such assurance of salvation, we may with joyous and confident heart approach God and call him our beloved Father. But we must be as certain as we are that we live, and must prefer death in any form, yes, hell with all its pangs, to being deprived of the Spirit or to distrusting him. It would be unreasonable doubt of the unbounded achievements of Christ and of his unlimited sufferings were we not to believe that he freely wrought all for us, and not to let this fact incite us to confidence and strength in him equal to the force wherewith sin or temptation terrifies or dissuades us.

92. True, conflict may arise here. The individual may have a fearful feeling that he is not a child of God. He may imagine God to be a judge over him, angry and austere. Such was the case with Job, and many others. In such conflict, filial confidence must gain the victory, however it may tremble and quake; otherwise all will be lost.

93. Now, the Cain-like individual, hearing this doctrine, blesses himself, and crossing his hands and his feet, and affecting great humility, he exclaims: "Guard me, O God, against such abominable heresy and presumption! Shall I, a poor sinner, be so bold as to say, I am a child of God? No, no; I humbly confess myself a poor sinner"; and so on. Ignore such a one. Guard against him as the worst enemy to Christian faith and to your salvation.

We, too, know full well what poor sinners we are. But it does no good to contemplate what we are and what we do. Rather we are to consider what Christ is and what he has accomplished and still accomplishes for us. The point is not our nature, but the grace of God, which is as high above us as the heaven is above the earth, or as far removed as the east is from the west. Ps 103, 11-12. If you regard it a wonderful thing to be a child of God, think it not a small thing that the Son of God came to earth, was born of a woman and was subject to the Law, for the very purpose of enabling you to be a child of God.

94. All the works of God are wonderful and of mighty import. Hence they fill us with joy and courage, giving us

fearlessness and ability to endure anything that may befall us. But the principles of the Cain-like are narrow, productive only of quaking hearts, which are wholly incapable of endurance and action, hearts that tremble at the sound of a driven leaf, as Leviticus 26, 36 has it.

95. Let us, then, heed closely the text. We must perceive the cry of the Spirit in our hearts. It is truly the cry of our own hearts; why, then, should we not recognize it? Paul uses the term "crying" when he might as easily have referred to the Spirit as "whispering," "speaking" or "singing." But the first word is more forcible. The Spirit calls, or cries, with power; that is from our full heart, a heart that always lives and moves in true, child-like confidence. As said in Romans 8, 26, "The Spirit himself maketh intercession for us with groanings which cannot be uttered." Again (Rom 8, 16), "The Spirit himself beareth witness with our spirit, that we are children of God." Then why should not our hearts perceive that crying, intercession and witness-bearing?

96. How preciously effective temptations and afflictions are in this direction! They drive us to cry; they rouse the Spirit. But we fear and flee at sight of the cross. Consequently we never feel the Spirit, and we continue Cain's subjects. If we do not recognize the Spirit's cry, we must reflect, and must not cease to pray until God hears us; for we are like Cain and our condition is perilous. We are not to expect, however, that no voice but the Spirit's will cry within us. The voice of murder will cry, to impel us to desire the Spirit's voice and to exercise ourselves to hear it. So has it ever been with men.

Our sins will also cry: they will produce in our conscience strong tendencies to despair. But the Spirit of Christ must, and shall, outvoice that cry. He will create in us a confidence stronger than the tendency to despair. John says (1 Jn 3, 19-22): "Hereby shall we know that we are of the truth, and shall assure our heart before him: because if our heart condemn us, God is greater than our heart, and knoweth all things. Beloved, if our heart condemn us not, we have boldness toward God; and whatsoever we ask we receive of him, because we keep his commandments and do the things that are pleasing in his sight."

97. The Spirit calling and crying within us is simply a powerful assurance, a perfect confidence, from the depths of the hearts of loving children toward God their beloved Father.

98. Note how far above mere human nature is the life of the Christian. Human nature is not capable of such a cry, of such confidence in God. It only fears and cries murder upon itself. It exclaims, "O wo, wo, is me! Thou austere and intolerable judge!" Just as Cain cried to God (Gen 4, 13-14): "My punishment is greater than I can bear. Behold, thou hast driven me out this day from the face of the ground; and from thy face shall I be hid; and I shall be a fugitive and a wanderer in the earth; and it will come to pass that whosoever findeth me shall slay me." Such exclamations are necessarily characteristic of Cain-like saints. Why? Because they rely upon themselves and their works, and not upon God's Son, who was sent to earth, was born of a woman and put under the Law. They do not believe that salvation through him was designed for them; nor are they concerned about it. They are occupied merely with their own works, endeavoring by such means to help themselves and to secure the grace of God.

99. In persecuting faith and defaming and condemning it as heresy and presumption, the unbelievers conduct themselves as their father Cain did to his brother Abel. Thus in themselves they slay Christ their brother. His innocent blood will not cease to cry toward heaven against them, as the blood of Abel cried against Cain. God will inquire after Abel; he will demand of each of them, "Where is Christ your brother?" Then the disordered Cain will go on to dissemble, saying: "What do I know about him? am I my brother's keeper?" For it is the same thing to say: "Shall I be presumptuous enough to regard myself righteous and holy and a child of God merely through Christ? No, no; I

will work until I become righteous myself, without his aid." Mark you, thus the crying blood of Abel continued to be upon Cain; and the crying blood of Christ will continue upon all believers, still demanding vengeance and wrath. But as for the believers, the blood will, through the Spirit of Christ, cry for pure grace and reconciliation.

100. The apostle places a Hebrew word in apposition with a Greek word; he says Abba, Pater (Father). In the Hebrew, Abba means "father"; hence the prelates in certain cloisters are called "abbots." In former times the holy hermits gave their chiefs the name Abba, Father. These terms were introduced also into the Latin and German. Abba, Pater is equivalent to "Father, Father." In full German, Mein Vater, Mein Vater; or Lieber Vater, Lieber Vater—My Father, My Father, or Dear Father, Dear Father.

101. But why does Paul duplicate the word to express the cry of the Spirit? Permit my opinion. In the first place, for the sake of emphasizing the cry. The earnest suppliant frequently makes repetition of his cry. So strenuous must be our appeal and so great our confidence that sin, the cry of Cain, has not power to suppress them.

102. In the second place, it seems to be Scripture usage to indicate certainty and assurance by duplicating words and phrases. Joseph tells King Pharaoh (Gen 41, 32) that by repetition God indicates it is assured and done even as the words teach. So here the Spirit twice cries "Father" to give us the assurance that God is and will be our Father; to make us not only hopeful of great things, but certainly confident.

103. In the third place, the apostle may have purposed to show the Spirit's persistence. The first word, Abba, marks the beginning of the Spirit's cry. But at that point great conflict will arise. The devil will assail us unceasingly and we must persevere. The addition of the word Father so teaches. We must not cease to cry; as we have begun, we are to continue. So doing, we will come to know what confidence is; the utmost assurance will possess us. Paul may also have designed by employing the word Abba, a somewhat unfamiliar Hebrew word, and supplementing

it with Father, a native and familiar Greek term (he was addressing the Greeks and wrote in their own language)—he may also have designed to teach that we hardly know the meaning of confidence at the first. But confidence grows with exercise. In time, seemingly it becomes a part of the believer's nature and he feels at home with God his Father.

"So that thou art no more a bondservant, but a son; and if a son, then an heir through Christ."

104. Christ having come and having been recognized, Pauls says, you are no more a bondservant. As before stated, there is a remarkable difference between a child and a servant. Their dispositions are altogether unlike. The child has freedom and is willing; the servant is constrained and is unwilling. The child is ruled by faith; the servant, by works.

105. Plainly, then, in the sight of God no one by works can accomplish anything toward his salvation. Salvation must be obtained and enjoyed before works are begun. Having salvation, works will follow spontaneously, to the honor of God and to the benefit of our neighbor. They will not be in any wise prompted by fear of punishment or expectation of reward. This is implied in the words: "If a son, then an heir through Christ."

106. Now we have made it sufficiently plain that faith alone, faith before any works are done and without them, constitutes us children. If it makes us children, it makes us heirs; a child is an heir. When the inheritance is already possessed, can it be first secured through works? It is an inconsistent conclusion that the inheritance bequeathed through grace is already possessed, and at the same time is still to be sought and obtained first through works and merits, as if it were not present or not given. The inheritance is simply eternal salvation. We have frequently asserted that through baptism and faith the Christian instantaneously possesses all, but does not yet behold it visibly. He possesses it only in faith, for in this life he could not bear the open manifestation of such blessings. As Paul

says (Rom 8, 24-25), we are already saved, but in hope; we do not yet see our salvation, but we wait for it. And Peter tells us (1 Pet 1, 4-5) that our salvation is reserved in heaven ready to be revealed in the last time.

107. For this reason, the Christian ought not to be influenced, like a servant, by a desire to secure advantage for himself, but by a longing to benefit others in their need. Truly, he must live and act, not for himself, but for his neighbor here on earth. So doing, he will most assuredly live and work for God. Through faith he has sufficient for himself; he is rich, well filled and happy for ever.

108. Paul adds "through Christ" to avoid the implication that the inheritance is bestowed upon us without any merit or cost whatever. Although it costs us nothing, and although it is bestowed without merit on our part, yet Christ was placed under great obligations. For the sake of that inheritance he was put under the Law for us; he paid the cost to secure, or to merit, the inheritance for all who believe in him. When we confer an unmerited favor upon a neighbor, it costs him nothing. But what we bestow on him freely, of our pure goodness, as Christ bestows blessings upon us, costs us labor and substance.

109. The unlearned may be somewhat confused by Paul's assertion that men are no longer servants, but children, and when the fact is, there are few believers in Christ, few children, while the world is filled with heretics and Cain-like people. But we must remember he speaks in a doctrinal connection. His meaning is: Before Christ came, and before the preaching of the Gospel whereby children are made, only the Law was preached—the Law which can make only servants with its work. The Gospel being preached at the present time, we have no need for the servant-maker, the Law. All who aforetime were, through the Law and its works, servants like Cain, now may become, through faith, righteous and saved without works. Therefore, to say there are no more servants, but children, is practically saying that now no servile doctrine is to be taught; now we become children, not servants. Only faith

and the Gospel are to be preached. Only they are to be our doctrine. This doctrine imparts the Spirit and teaches us to confide in God and to serve only our neighbor. Thus the whole Law is fulfilled.

110. In this manner Paul calls the Galatians again from the teachers who had led them back to the Law and its works. Similarly, the Pope with his foolish laws has for a long time misled the people through his bishops, priests and monks, and has exterminated the Christian faith—conduct foretold in the Scriptures concerning Antichrist. Then let him who would be saved, shun the Pope and his adherents, and all church orders, as he would Lucifer's own servants and apostles.

New Year's Day

Epistle Text: Galatians 3, 23-29.

23 But before faith came, we were kept in ward under the law, shut up unto the faith which should afterwards be revealed. 24 So that the law is become our tutor to bring us unto Christ, that we might be justified by faith. 25 But now that faith is come, we are no longer under a tutor. 26 For ye are all sons of God, through faith in Christ Jesus. 27 For as many of you as were baptized into Christ did put on Christ. 28 There can be neither Jew nor Greek, there can be neither bond nor free, there can be no male and female; for ye all are one man in Christ Jesus. 29 And if ye are Christ's, then are ye Abraham's seed, heirs according to promise.

THE LAW AND ITS WORKS.

1. This, too, is really a Pauline Epistle lesson concerning faith as opposed to works, and taken in connection with the preceding lesson is easily understood. What is said there concerning the servant is true here concerning the pupil. Paul employs the two figures to teach us the office of the Law and what it profits. We must, therefore, again refer to the Law and its works, to the fact that works are of twofold origin. Some are extorted by fear of punishment or prompted by expectation of pleasure and gain; others are spontaneous, cheerful and gratuitous, not performed to escape punishment nor to gain reward, but inspired by pure kindness and a desire for what is good. The first class are the works of servants and pupils; the second class, of children and free heirs.

2. The youth under a tutor follows not his own will;

but, from fear of the rod, his master's will. While under control of his master, his real character cannot be detected. Were he free, his true self would be apparent, for he would manifest his natural disposition and his works would be his own. The works he performs under restraint and coercion are not really his own, but those of the tutor who forces them. Were he not under control of the tutor, he would do none of them, but rather things quite the reverse.

3. In this homely but apt illustration Paul presents at once the province of the Law and the limitation of free will, or human nature, with a clearness not to be surpassed. It plainly teaches the meaning, operation and end of the Law, and the extent of human nature's power.

We note that constraint has a twofold effect upon the youth: First, fear of his tutor preserves him from many evils into which he would otherwise fall; he is withheld from indulging in a wicked, licentious life, in becoming utterly dissolute. Second, his heart is filled with hatred toward the tutor who curbs his will. This is the situation with him: the greater his external restraint from evil, the greater his inward hatred of him who restrains. His character is in the scales; when one side goes up, the other goes down. While outward sin decreases, inward sin increases. We know from experience that those youths most strictly reared are, when given liberty, more wicked than young men less rigidly brought up. So impossible is it to improve human nature with commandments and punishments; something else is necessary.

4. Likewise, so long as man is in his natural state and destitute of grace, he does not what he would, but what his tutor the Law obliges him to do. It must be confessed by all that were it not for hell and the Law's penalties, no one would do good. Now, man's works being not wrought of free will, they are not his own; they are the works of the coercive and restraining Law. Well may the apostle declare them not our works, but the "works of the Law," because what we do against our will is not our achievement, but that of the constraining power.

5. For instance, should one forcibly make my hand the instrument to slay another, or to bestow alms upon a destitute individual, it would not be my deed, though performed by my hand, but the deed of him who forced the action. Consequently, I would be neither injured nor benefited in the least by the act. Likewise, the works of the Law render no one righteous, notwithstanding man performs them. For, so far as our will is concerned, we do them merely from fear of the Law's penalty. The will would much prefer to do otherwise and would if not constrained by the coercive and menacing Law. Such works are not our own, then. Notwithstanding, everyone must be saved through his own act.

6. Further, one may not, or may think he does not, do works through fear of punishment; he is, however, inspired by the promises and inducements of the Law. And that motive is as wrong, if not more so, than the other. Such a position implies that if heaven were not promised, if they knew there were no reward, no effort would be made. The deeds wrought from this latter motive are, therefore, likewise not our own; they are the works of the Law with its inducements in the nature of favors and rewards. They are more dangerous and less easily recognized than the former kind, being more subtile and bearing greater resemblance to true, spontaneous works.

7. But tribulation will prove them. They will appear in their true character when they are rejected as to merit, when gratuitous service is required, service uninfluenced by hope of reward, service rendered only for the honor of God and for the benefit of one's neighbor. Then human nature utterly fails—is powerless. Then is evident the fact that it does no good work of its own, nothing but the extraneous works of the Law; just as the irrational animal obeys in fear of the lash, or labors for the sake of its food. How many righteous individuals, men of honorable character, think you, would there be today if neither heaven nor shame, punishment and hell were before them? Not one. Order is preserved through fear of punishment or expecta-

but, from fear of the rod, his master's will. While under control of his master, his real character cannot be detected. Were he free, his true self would be apparent, for he would manifest his natural disposition and his works would be his own. The works he performs under restraint and coercion are not really his own, but those of the tutor who forces them. Were he not under control of the tutor, he would do none of them, but rather things quite the reverse.

3. In this homely but apt illustration Paul presents at once the province of the Law and the limitation of free will, or human nature, with a clearness not to be surpassed. It plainly teaches the meaning, operation and end of the Law, and the extent of human nature's power.

We note that constraint has a twofold effect upon the youth: First, fear of his tutor preserves him from many evils into which he would otherwise fall; he is withheld from indulging in a wicked, licentious life, in becoming utterly dissolute. Second, his heart is filled with hatred toward the tutor who curbs his will. This is the situation with him: the greater his external restraint from evil, the greater his inward hatred of him who restrains. His character is in the scales; when one side goes up, the other goes down. While outward sin decreases, inward sin increases. We know from experience that those youths most strictly reared are, when given liberty, more wicked than young men less rigidly brought up. So impossible is it to improve human nature with commandments and punishments; something else is necessary.

4. Likewise, so long as man is in his natural state and destitute of grace, he does not what he would, but what his tutor the Law obliges him to do. It must be confessed by all that were it not for hell and the Law's penalties, no one would do good. Now, man's works being not wrought of free will, they are not his own; they are the works of the coercive and restraining Law. Well may the apostle declare them not our works, but the "works of the Law," because what we do against our will is not our achievement, but that of the constraining power.

5. For instance, should one forcibly make my hand the instrument to slay another, or to bestow alms upon a destitute individual, it would not be my deed, though performed by my hand, but the deed of him who forced the action. Consequently, I would be neither injured nor benefited in the least by the act. Likewise, the works of the Law render no one righteous, notwithstanding man performs them. For, so far as our will is concerned, we do them merely from fear of the Law's penalty. The will would much prefer to do otherwise and would if not constrained by the coercive and menacing Law. Such works are not our own, then. Notwithstanding, everyone must be saved through his own act.

6. Further, one may not, or may think he does not, do works through fear of punishment; he is, however, inspired by the promises and inducements of the Law. And that motive is as wrong, if not more so, than the other. Such a position implies that if heaven were not promised, if they knew there were no reward, no effort would be made. The deeds wrought from this latter motive are, therefore, likewise not our own; they are the works of the Law with its inducements in the nature of favors and rewards. They are more dangerous and less easily recognized than the former kind, being more subtile and bearing greater resemblance to true, spontaneous works.

7. But tribulation will prove them. They will appear in their true character when they are rejected as to merit, when gratuitous service is required, service uninfluenced by hope of reward, service rendered only for the honor of God and for the benefit of one's neighbor. Then human nature utterly fails—is powerless. Then is evident the fact that it does no good work of its own, nothing but the extraneous works of the Law; just as the irrational animal obeys in fear of the lash, or labors for the sake of its food. How many righteous individuals, men of honorable character, think you, would there be today if neither heaven nor shame, punishment and hell were before them? Not one. Order is preserved through fear of punishment or expecta-

tion of gain. The works of the Law, then, are all deceptive. As the Scriptures declare: "All men are liars." Ps 116, 11. "Surely every man at his best estate is altogether vanity." Ps 39, 5.

The Office of the Law.

8. Thus, too, we find with all men two effects of the Law: First, by that tutor they are secured against shameful, dissolute conduct. Under the discipline of the works of the Law, they maintain an honorable outward life. Secondly, in their hearts they really become enemies to the Law with its penalties; and the more severe the chastisement, the greater their hatred. Who is not an enemy to death and hell? And what is that but being an enemy to the Law that imposes such punishment? And what is enmity to the Law but enmity to righteousness? But is not the enemy of righteousness an enemy of God himself? Then do we not arrive at the ultimate conclusion that we are not only unjustified, but we also hate righteousness, love sin and are enemies to God with all our hearts, however beautiful and honorable our outward conduct—our works—may appear?

9. Now, unquestionably God desires to be loved with the whole heart. The commandment (Deut 6, 5) reads, "Thou shalt love Jehovah thy God with all thy heart." God wills that our good works should be really our own, not those of our tutor the Law, or of death, hell or heaven. That is, we are not to act from a fear of death or hell, or for the sake of enjoying heaven, but from a willing spirit, a desire and love for righteousness. He who does a good deed through fear of death and hell, does it not to the honor of God. It is a work of death and hell, for they have extorted it. Because of these, he has wrought; otherwise he would not have done the deed. Therefore, he remains a servant, a slave, of death and hell, so long as these inspire his works. Now, if he remains their servant, he must die and be condemned. To him apply the proverbs, "He that fears hell, enters it" and "Trembling will not deliver from death."

10. But you say, "What must be your conclusion, for who then can be saved? who does not tremble and fear

death and hell? who executes his works, or leads an honorable life, without fear?" I reply: Yes, but who, being filled with such fear and with a hatred of God's Law and his righteousness, loves God? Where is human nature here? Where is free will? Still you refuse to believe in the absolute necessity of God's grace; still you will not admit the conduct of all men sinful, and false; still you cannot be persuaded that works do not make one righteous.

11. Here, indeed, is evident the necessity for the Law, and the purpose it serves—God's design in it—its office being twofold: First, to preserve discipline among us; to impel us to an honorable outward life, a life in which we can dwell together without devouring one another as we would were Law, fear and punishment lacking, and as formerly was the case with certain heathen. This is why God did not, in the New Testament dispensation, abolish the secular sword. He established its place, though he did not make use of it. And it is not necessary for his followers to employ it otherwise than to restrain bold and dissolute conduct; and to enable men to live together in peace, to maintain themselves and to rear their families. Without it, all countries would be demoralized, and overrun with murderers and robbers. No woman or child would escape violence. The sword and the Law preserve men and impel them to a quiet, peaceful and honorable life. But they do not through these restraints become righteous; their hearts are not made better. Their hands are restrained and bound, that is all. Their works, their apparent righteousness, is not their own; it is of the sword, which extorts it by inspiring the fear of punishment.

12. Similarly, God's Law impels us, through fear of death and hell, to forsake many evils. Like a tutor, it holds us to an honorable outward life. But by the Law no one becomes righteous before God. The heart remains an enemy to its tutor, hates his chastisements and would prefer freedom.

13. Second, God's design in the Law is to enable man to know himself; to perceive the false and unjustified state of

his heart; to discover how far he is from God and how utterly impotent his own nature is; to disdain his own goodness and to recognize it as nothing in comparison to what is necessary to the fulfilment of the Law; to be humbled in consequence of such knowledge and come to the cross, yearning for Christ, longing for his grace, despairing of himself and placing all his hope in Christ. Christ will then give him a different spirit and change his heart. No longer will he fear death and hell, no longer look for life and heaven. For, being voluntarily and unselfishly devoted to the fulfilment of the Law, he will maintain a clear and confident conscience toward it during his whole life and even in the hour of death. He will be equally uninfluenced by fear of death, hope of heaven or any other motive. We read in the Epistle to the Hebrews (ch 2, 15) how Christ made atonement that he "might deliver all them who through fear of death were all their lifetime subject to bondage." These words make it evident enough that we must have no fear of death, and that they who live in fear of it are servants, nor will they be saved. Now, neither our own nature nor the Law can liberate us from that fear. Indeed, they but increase it. Christ alone has freed us from it. If we believe in him, he will give us that free, undaunted spirit which fears neither death nor hell, which seeks neither life nor heaven, but voluntarily and joyfully serves God.

14. Therefore, we see, first, how dangerous are the doctrines which urge the attainment of righteousness only through commandments and laws. These things but separate man farther from God, from Christ; yes, from the Law and all righteousness. The effect of the inculcation of such doctrines is simply to render man's conscience continually more fearful, timid, dejected and wretched, and to teach him ever to fear death and hell, and only them; until eventually his heart is filled with naught but despair, and he must become, in any aspect, a martyr of the devil.

15. Secondly, we see three attitudes toward the Law; that is, mankind conducts itself in three ways with reference to it. Some disregard it utterly, and boldly oppose

it by a dissolute life. To them it is practically no Law. Others because of the Law refrain from such a course and are preserved to an honorable life. But while outwardly they live within the Law's prohibitions, inwardly they are enemies of this their tutor. The motive of all their conduct is the fear of death and hell. They keep the Law only externally; rather, it keeps them externally. Inwardly they neither keep it nor are kept by it. The third class observe it both externally and with the heart. This class are the tables of Moses, written upon outwardly and inwardly by the finger of God himself.

16. The first class are righteous neither without nor within; the second are only outwardly pious and not in heart; but the third are thoroughly righteous. Upon this point Paul says (1 Tim 1, 8), "But we know that the Law is good, if a man use it lawfully." But in what way is it lawfully used? I answer, "Law is not made for a righteous man, but for the lawless" (verse 9). And what are we to understand by that? Simply that he who would preach the Law aright must be governed by these three classes. He must not by any means preach the Law to the third class as an instrument of righteousness; this were perversion. But to the first class such preaching is in order. For them is the Law instituted. Its object is that they may forsake their dissolute life and yield themselves to the preserving power of their tutor. However, it is not enough for them to be guarded and kept by the Law; they must learn also to keep it. So, in addition to the Law, and beyond it, the Gospel must be preached, through which is given the grace of Christ to keep the former. There is a considerable difference between observing the Law and being preserved by it; between keeping and being kept. The first class neither keep it nor are kept; the second are kept; and the third keep it.

17. These three attitudes of mankind toward the Law are prefigured in certain acts of Moses. First, where he broke the tables when the Jews worshiped the golden calf. Ex 32, 19. The breaking of the tables, and the people's con-

sequent failure to receive them, suggest the first class, who do not receive the Law at all, but break it. Second, Moses brought other tables, which were received by the people and the skin of his face shone, but Aaron and the Israelites could not endure the shining of Moses' face, and he was compelled to cover it with a veil when he would speak to them. Ex 34, 30-33. Here is suggested the second class, who receive the Law but only for outward observance. With them it is too bright for inward obedience; they are afraid of it.

18. Hypocrites make for themselves a veil, as Paul explains (2 Cor 3, 13-15)—the arrogance of their works, of their external righteousness. They will not look the Law squarely in the face and see how futile is their righteousness. As Paul says, to this very day the veil is upon their hearts.

Then, too, Moses leads the people no farther than to the Jordan, slays only two kings—Sihon and Og—and gives only two and a half tribes of Israel their portion of the land. Here is illustrated half-hearted righteousness; insignificant, outward righteousness. Then, there in the wilderness of Moab, Moses dies; the Law can go no farther.

19. Now, third: Joshua succeeds Moses and leads the whole multitude dry-shod through the Jordan, into all parts of the promised land. There is now no Moses, no Law; only Joshua, Christ, who leads by faith and fulfils all Moses' commandments. Thus is suggested the class to whom no Law is given, as Paul says, and who become righteous, not through works, but through grace; that is, their good works are not performed through constraint of the Law. Moses is not in evidence with them. With all this explanation, Paul should, I think, be easily understood in this lesson. Let us now consider it.

> "But before faith came, we were kept in ward under the law, shut up unto the faith which should afterwards be revealed."

20. Paul does not say, Before faith came we were righteous and kept the Law. On the contrary, he says that the Law kept us. Under it we were locked up—preserved—

that we might not boldly and independently rush into wickedness. At the same time, the restraint did not render us really and inwardly righteous. Nor was it designed to be permanent. It led to the faith to be revealed in the future, a faith which was to set us free; not free to do the evil from which the Law shut us up, but free to do the good to which the Law impelled us. The "shutting up," the confinement, of the Law should teach us to desire faith and to recognize the evil tendencies of our nature; for faith is a spiritual freedom, liberating only the heart.

21. To illustrate: Suppose you were confined in a prison, where you were very reluctant to remain. Your captor might release you in either of two ways: First, he might give you physical freedom by destroying the prison and letting you go where you desire. Secondly, he might make you mentally free by bestowing many blessings upon you in this prison—illuminating and enlarging it, making it pleasant in the extreme, adorning it richly and to an extent rendering it more desirable than any royal palace, more to be desired even than a kingdom; and by so reconciling you to your surroundings, so altering your mind, that you would not, for all earthly possessions, be removed from that prison, but would pray for its preservation that you might continue therein, it being to you no longer a prison, having become a paradise. Tell me, which form of freedom would be the better? Would not the latter be preferable? The former liberation would leave you but a beggar, as before. But in the latter case, your mind being free, you would possess all you might desire.

22. Thus, mark you, has Christ given us spiritual freedom from the Law. He did not abrogate, did not destroy, the Law. But he changed the heart which before was unwillingly under the Law. He so benefited it and made the Law so desirable that the heart has no greater delight and joy than in the Law. The heart would not willingly have the Law fail in one tittle. Again, as the prisoner makes his prison narrow and oppressive for himself by his unwillingness, so, too, are we enemies to the Law and make it dis-

agreeable to ourselves because unwillingly we are shut up from evil and impelled to good.

23. Thus, in this verse the apostle beautifully presents both the fruit and the office of the Law. To the inquiry, Wherein is the Law good? he answers: Though it truly does not make us righteous, but rather increases our sinfulness and provokes our human nature by its commands and prohibitions, yet it has a twofold office. First, it locks us up, secures us, against breaking out violently into an openly shameless life, as do the class who will not permit themselves to be thus restrained. For this reason it is much better that the Law should exist. Without it, who could withstand the encroachments of his fellows? According to Paul (Rom 13, 4), the secular sword is borne for a terror, not to the righteous, but to the evil-doers.

24. Second, constraint of the Law leads to a future faith by revealing to man his wickedness and his dislike for what is good; by teaching him to know himself, to humbly confess his evil nature, to acknowledge its guilt and to desire the grace of God—grace that does not abrogate the Law, which he now recognizes as right, good and holy, but produces another heart in him, a heart to love that right, good and holy Law. Note, this is the true meaning and best office of the Law. It is truly necessary that the Law should exist, to bring man thus to know himself and to implore the grace of God.

25. Over this office of the Law, however, a contention arises between the true and the false saints. False saints will receive the Law only so far as its first office goes. They presume that in submitting to its restraint and preservation they are become righteous. They will not learn from it to perceive their wicked nature, but deem human nature inherently good and truly capable of loving the Law. The true saints deny this doctrine; and indeed it is false. The Word of God and the universal experience of men declare otherwise. And he who does not falsify nor dissemble will confess himself naturally without delight in the Law of

God; much more without delight in the punishment of sins, in death and hell, which the Law presents.

The intensely abominable filth of their hearts, great and deep, the self-justifiers palliate by covering it with the fig-leaves of their own works in the Law, as Adam and Eve covered their shame. But the sin in the heart of Adam and Eve was not made less by the covering; so, too, by works of the Law, by self-justification, no one is made better, but rather is made worse. It was because of this very filth that Christ rejected and dispersed the congregations of the synagogues.

26. It is now plain to whom Paul addresses the words of this verse—the work-righteous, who would become godly through the Law and its work, who consider the first office of the Law sufficiently effective to make them righteous. This doctrine gives rise to a class who might be styled "Absalomites." For as Absalom remained hanging by his head, in an oak tree, suspended between heaven and earth (2 Sam 18, 9), so this class hang between heaven and earth. Shut up by the Law, they do not touch the earth; they are restrained from the things their evil nature ardently desires. On the other hand, since the Law, powerless to improve their nature, only irritates and provokes it, making them enemies to the Law, they are not godly and so do not reach heaven.

27. Zechariah (ch 5, 9) saw two women, between heaven and earth, carrying an ephah to Babylon, while in the vessel sat a woman called "Impietas"—unbelief, or ungodliness. This vessel, the ephah, represents the self-justifiers, vacillating between open vice and true piety. Unbelief sits within. The two women bearing it are Fear and Reward; from fear of punishment or in quest of reward are all their works performed. These two carry and maintain the unbelievers in their self-righteousness; such is the significance of the wings like a stork, or vulture, which the prophet mentions. Wings, in the Scriptures, signify oral preaching, because speech is swift. The false saints preach only of fear and reward. They would make men righteous merely by terror

and allurements, but they only increase men's sin. Men become greater enemies to the Law because of its terrors, and for the sake of its allurements are only the more desirous to accomplish their own designs. Therefore, these false saints are simply wings for the stork, the vulture, that devours the chickens—that murders souls.

28. But the true saints do not remain midway between heaven and earth. They, too, hear of the terrors and the persuasions of the Law; but they recognize their own proneness to regard the threats and enticements rather than the purpose of the Law, and so are made aware that truly they are not pure nor righteous. They fall down in confession, crying, "Grace, grace, O Lord God!" To them Christ comes, bringing true liberty through his Spirit. Thus they become altogether of heaven.

29. This, mark you, is what is meant by being "kept in ward under the Law and shut up unto the faith, which should afterwards be revealed." Not only were the Jews thus shut up before the revelation of faith, but they are still shut up, as are all who attempt to become righteous through the works of the Law and because of fear of its threats or hope of its rewards, and like reasons. If they be not directed to the faith, if they fail of faith, it being not made known to them, the works of the Law must but render them more wicked, and they will ultimately fall into despair or obdurate presumption, and so pass beyond the reach of help. So perilous is it to fail of making a right use of the Law and of thus arriving at faith.

> "So that the Law is become our tutor [schoolmaster] to bring us unto Christ, that we might be justified by faith."

30. Observe the import of these words: no one is justified by the Law and its works. If we could be justified by the Law, faith would be unnecessary, and Paul's statement here—we are justified by faith—would be false. In this matter of justification, faith and works utterly exclude each other. If justification be ascribed to faith, it must not be attributed to works, to the Law, to human nature. If it

be ascribed to works, it must not be attributed to faith. If one theory be true, the other must be false. They cannot both be true. The power and virtue of the Law cannot consist in anything but the making of sinners or the permitting men to remain sinners. Whatever does not justify, certainly makes sinners or permits them so to remain. But since the purpose of the Law is to deal with sins and sinners, it must do something more than permit sinners to remain as they are. What kind of an agency would that be which has no effect upon the object of its operation?

31. What, then, can the Law accomplish if it does not justify us, and neither makes us better nor leaves us as we are? Wonderful indeed must be its province to help, when it neither justifies nor leaves the sinner as it finds him. Necessarily it must increase sin. Paul says (Rom 5, 20), "The law came in besides, that the trespass might abound." As before said, this result is in consequence of the Law's shutting up the sinner, restraining his hands from committing open wickedness and awakening in his heart only increased hatred for and opposition to the Law; just as a pupil's indignation arises in proportion as he is chastised, or his will is crossed, by his tutor. His hatred or unwillingness is simply an increased development of his restrained evil will, and it never would have been called forth had not that will been opposed.

32. Before the introduction of the Law, man sins voluntarily, of his own evil nature, with no thought of the Law. But the advent of the Law with its threats and constraint irritates his human nature and excites his aversion; he begins not only to love sin but to hate righteousness. Note, this is the province of the Law concerning the sinner and his sins. Paul says the Law increases sin; so far is it from justifying any man. Blessed is he who recognizes this truth. The self-righteous do not at all perceive it. They assign to human nature no such wickedness and no enmity toward the Law; they find much to commend in human nature. Hence they understand not a syllable of the words of Paul, who never speaks of the Law otherwise than as

arousing sin; and, if we would but confess it, such is the testimony of our own hearts.

33. The apostle says "unto Christ." That is, until Christ, the Law is our tutor. No leave is given to embrace any other faith than the faith in Christ. The Law directs us only to Abraham's seed, Christ, on whom all saints from the beginning have believed, as stated in the preceding epistle lesson.

34. Therefore, it is of no benefit to the Jews and the Turks to believe in God the Creator of heaven and earth; he who does not believe in Christ, neither believes in God. Even were Christ truly not God—a thing impossible—still they who should fail of belief in him would not be believers in God; for God has promised his grace in Abraham's seed. Abraham's seed being Christ, as the Jews, the Turks and all the world acknowledge, he who disbelieves in Christ, also disbelieves the promises of God. Hence he is not a believer in the God who created heaven and earth, for no other God is the author of the promise to Abraham, and in the name of no seed of Abraham except Christ has the blessing gone forth, and the faith been preached, in all the world.

35. Outside of Christ, then, no Law, no belief, can secure blessing and justification. God will keep his promise made to Abraham, the promise to bless all the world in his seed, and in no other. God will not establish a new and peculiar faith for each person and neglect or recall his promise. So then, faith in Christ justifies, as Paul says (Rom 10, 4): "For Christ is the end of the Law unto righteousness to every one that believeth." What is implied? Simply that all believers in Christ are justified and receive his Spirit and his grace, through faith. Here the Law ends for them because they are no longer under it. This is the final meaning of the Law; for it follows:

> "But now that faith is come, we are no longer under a tutor."

36. The preceding verses make plain enough what is meant by being under the Law, or under a tutor; yet, the doctrine of faith and the expression "under a tutor or under

the Law" having become obsolete, enough cannot be said in explanation. To be under a tutor, to be subject to the Law, is, briefly, to be a dissembler; to do many good works and yet not be pious; to lead a good life without ever being righteous; always to teach without learning, and to preach without understanding. The reason for such deficiency is, the character of those under the Law does not permit them to do good voluntarily and through love, without fear of punishment or hope of reward. Therefore are they servants, driven by the Law. And since it ever continues to rule and to drive, they remain always its debtors and subjects.

The Law demands a joyous, free and ready will. This its subjects have not, nor can they have it of themselves. Faith in Christ alone produces it. Where such a spirit exists, the Law ceases its demands. It is satisfied—fulfilled. The pupil then being able to accomplish the requirements of his tutor, the tutor dismisses him, demanding no more. He is no longer his tutor, but his good friend and companion.

Faith Liberates From the Law.

37. Similarly, faith liberates us from the Law. Not a physical liberation, effected by separating us from the Law, by removing us forever from its jurisdiction: but freedom in the sense that we satisfy the demands of the Law; we satisfy it by knowing and possessing the Holy Spirit, who brings us to love the Law. The Law did not desire works. Works could not appease it. It desired love. Only our love could satisfy it. Without love it would not release us —would not be remunerated. Destitute of love, we must, even with all our works, remain its debtors and our consciences know no peace. The Law continually chastises us as sinners and transgressors, and threatens us with death and hell, until Christ comes and bestows his Spirit and his love, through the faith preached in the Gospel. Then we are freed from the Law. No longer it demands, no longer chastises, but lets the conscience rest. No more it terrifies with death and hell. It has become our kind friend and companion.

38. The tutor's release of the pupil does not mean the death or departure of the tutor, but spiritually, that the child has been changed, and can do what the father wished the tutor to teach him. Likewise the Law releases us, not by its passing, not by being abrogated, but spiritually; and because a change has been effected in us and we have the experience God designed us to have through the Law.

39. Hence I have called the figure of the pupil and tutor a beautiful and striking illustration whereby we may rightly understand the Law, and the work of grace in ourselves. The first office of the Law, that of shutting us up and producing outward piety, is so well established, so emphasized by all teachers and books, and besides so closely approaches human nature, that it is difficult for us to recognize its second office, of magnifying inward sin. I may well liken the two offices to a pair of scales, one empty and the other full.

So the Law, when producing external piety, increases inward sin. It imposes as much sin inwardly, by arousing hatred and rebellion, as it corrects externally by works; and much more. According to Paul (Rom 7, 13), through the Law sin becomes exceeding sinful, sinful beyond measure. And the experience of every man must lead him so to confess.

"For ye are all sons of God, through faith, in Christ Jesus."

40. He who is under the Law, and works unwillingly, is a servant, as the preceding sermon declares. But whosoever has faith and cheerfully works, is a child; for he has received the Spirit of God, through Christ. Now, the apostle names Christ, referring to the faith that believes and abides in Jesus Christ. No other faith is effective, no other faith is the right faith, let one believe in God as he will.

41. Some there are, particularly among our modern high school men, who say: "Forgiveness of sins and justification depend altogether on the divine imputation of grace; God's imputation is sufficient. He to whom God does not reckon sin, is justified; to whom God reckons sin, is not justified."

They imagine their position is verified in the testimony of Psalm 32, 2, quoted in Romans 4, 8, "Blessed is the man to whom the Lord will not reckon sin."

Were their theory true, the entire New Testament would be of no significance. Christ would have labored foolishly and to no purpose in suffering for sin. God would have unnecessarily wrought mere mockery and deception; for he might easily, without Christ's sufferings, have forgiven sins —have not imputed them. Then, too, a faith other than faith in Christ might have justified and saved—a faith relying on God's gracious mercy not to impute sin.

42. In contrast to this deplorable theory, this abominable error, it is the holy apostle's practice to speak always of faith in Jesus Christ, and he makes mention of Jesus Christ with a frequency surprising to one unacquainted with the important doctrine of faith in him. In fact, it is said that every second word in Paul's epistles is "Jesus Christ." But these pagan doctors of divinity have maliciously rooted it out, have silenced it for us, by their abominable and hellish dreams of such perversion.

43. Hence our learned university doctors no longer know Christ. They do not recognize the need of him and his benefits, nor understand the character of the Gospel and the New Testament. They imagine Christ to be a mere Moses—a teacher who institutes laws and commandments showing how men may be righteous and lead a faultless life. Then they proceed with free will and the workings of human nature, designing therewith to fit themselves for grace, thus basely storming heaven.

44. Now, if God confers his grace because of their works, their careful preparation, Christ must be without significance. What need have they of Christ if they can obtain grace in their own name and by their works? And this doctrine they teach openly; indeed, they defend it with their utmost power and with the Pope's bulls, condemning a contrary teaching as the very worst heresy. Therefore I have warned, and still warn, all men that the Pope and the universities have cast Christ and the New Testament farther

out of the world than ever did the Jews or Turks. Hence the Pope is the true Antichrist, and his high schools are the devil's own taverns and brothels. What does Christ signify if by effort of my own human nature I can obtain God's grace? Or, having grace, what more will I desire?

45. Let us, therefore, guard against the hellish poison of this false doctrine and not lose Christ, the consoling Saviour. He must be retained above all things. True, Psalm 32, 2 and Romans 4, 8 do say, "Blessed is the man to whom the Lord will not reckon sin." But Paul introduces the statement as testimony to the fact that it is only believers to whom Christ does not reckon sin; free will and the works of human nature are not considered. He cites Abraham, whose faith in the divine promise concerning his seed was counted to him for righteousness. Although it is of pure grace that God reckons not to us our sins, yet he would not so forgive were not his Law and his standard of righteousness already completely satisfied. The gracious reckoning had first to be bought for us from the divine righteousness.

It being impossible for us to purchase forgiveness, God ordained in our stead one who took upon himself all our deserved punishment and fulfilled the Law for us, thus averting from us God's judgment and appeasing his wrath. So it is true that grace is given us gratuitously—without cost to ourselves—and yet the gift to us cost another much, and was obtained with a priceless, an infinite, treasure—the Son of God himself. It is supremely essential, therefore, to possess him who has accomplished the purchase for us. Nor is it possible to obtain grace otherwise than through him.

46. Note, from the time of Adam to Abraham's day, no one was saved except through faith in the woman's seed, who should bruise the serpent's head. And after Abraham no one was saved except through faith in his seed. And now no one can be saved otherwise than through faith in the seed of Abraham now come. Oh, you are not sufficient of yourself to come to God; you may not attempt to come without this Mediator—through yourself and of your own energy, as the Jews, the Turks and the Papists teach you

may. Who will reconcile you with God in the first place? Christ says (Jn 14, 6), "No one cometh unto the Father, but by me."

In the time of the famine the Egyptians desired to make their complaints to Pharaoh, the king himself, but he referred them to Joseph, saying (Gen 41, 55): "Go unto Joseph; what he saith to you, do." Similarly, God hears, and aids to salvation, no one of us; we must all come to Christ, who is made Lord over all things, and with whom is the throne of grace. He has obtained salvation for us. Consequently it is in vain to seek it elsewhere. Yes, if we were devoid of sin, as was Adam before the fall, we would have no need of Christ; we might come before God in our own merits. But in the time of famine—since the fall—we must have a Joseph, one who is without sin and who yet will receive us needy sinners when we come to him in earnest.

Error of the Papists.

47. Consequently the Papists do not believe and teach otherwise of human nature than that it is still undefiled as it was before the fall of Adam. They do not believe it is wholly corrupted in sin, and the enemy of God. God is an enemy to sin; so is sin an enemy to God, as Paul teaches in the fifth and eighth chapters of Romans. The Papists, then, certainly do not believe what Moses writes concerning the fall of Adam (Gen 3), or else they regard the fall merely a passing disgrace, not affecting our nature, not making it sinful nor subjecting it to God's wrath. Because they do not believe Moses and have no need of Christ, and in thus rejecting the Old Testament and the New condemn the entire living Scriptures, God has justly permitted them to become disciples of Aristotle, that dead and condemned heathen; permitted them to be a retreat for the devil. Through the laws of the Pope and the doctrines of men, the devil fills them with his pollution to constant overflowing, wherewith they contaminate the whole world. But they ever remain in darkness, attempting, while lacking faith in Christ, to force acceptance with God by their prayers and fasts, their masses, study and preaching.

48. Even if they do name and confess Christ, they simply mean that God has superfluously made him Lord, a Lord who requires us to obey God in that we regard himself as Lord; that, independent of Christ's dominion, free will may, by its natural powers, obtain the grace of God; that for them Christ's kingdom is not an essential, but is the mere wantonness of God in desiring Christ to be Lord after the fashion of earthly kingdoms; and that they confess him, not because confession is necessary to their salvation, since man may be saved otherwise than through his kingdom, but because God wills and commands obedience to the King.

Consequently, with the Papists Christ is really no Saviour. In the depths of their hearts he is a tyrant and a taskmaster, and unnecessary to human nature in its effort to obtain grace; rather, he is to human nature an added burden, for it must then obey not only God as heretofore, but Christ with his commandments.

49. Of olden time, many prophesied that in Antichrist's day all heretics would unite in the extermination of the whole world. And today, under the rule of the Pope and the Turk, heresy has full sway. In the rejection and condemnation of Christ and the entire Scriptures, a rejection leaving nothing but the name, is easily proven that all heresies, errors and darkness existing from the beginning of the world, now reign. I often have fears for the condemnation of all men of the present age except those who die in their cradles. Yet no one sees and deplores the awful wrath of God overhanging us.

50. Mark you, Paul's essential reason for always emphasizing faith in Christ is the fact that he clearly foresaw this virulent doctrine, the doctrine presuming to treat with God independently of Christ, as if God and human nature were harmonious, as if righteousness might love sin and grant its desires.

Let us, therefore, beloved friends, be wise and learn Christ aright, namely: Of first importance, we must hear the Gospel and believe in Christ; believe in him not merely as a Lord to whom honor is due, but as that one who offered himself in place of our sinful nature, who took upon himself all the wrath of God merited by ourselves with our works, and overcame; believe that the fruit of that conquest he did not reserve unto himself, but assigned it to us, for our own; and that all who believe in him as such a conqueror shall thereby surely be redeemed from God's wrath and received into his favor.

So we see how great the need and benefit of Christ is to us, and recognize the fallacy of the position that one may by his own natural powers earn God's grace; yes, recognize it as a device of Satan himself. For if human nature can obtain grace, Christ is unnecessary as an intercessor, a mediator. But, he being essential, human nature can obtain only disgrace; the two are inconsistent—man his own mediator, and Christ the mediator for man.

> "For as many of you as were baptized into Christ did put on Christ."

51. Note the beautiful order in Paul's reasoning. "But after that faith is come we are no longer under a tutor." Why not? "For ye are all sons of God, through faith, in Christ Jesus." But how are we become the children of God? "For as many of you as were baptized into Christ did put on Christ." Christ is the child of God; therefore, he who clothes himself in Christ, God's son, must be the child of God. He is clothed with divine adoption, which unquestionably must constitute him a child. Now, if a child, he is no longer under the Law, where are none but servants. For the child himself, while under the Law, like a pupil under a tutor, is but as a servant. Such is the word of Paul, as stated in the following and the preceding epistle lessons.

52. But what is meant by "putting on Christ?" The faithless will readily reply, "It means to follow Christ, imitating his example." But in the same way I might put on Peter, or Paul, or any saint, and thus nothing special would be said of Christ. We will let faith speak here; it is faith which Paul so beautifully suggests in the words "put on."

Naturally, until baptism the individual has never followed Christ. In baptism he begins to follow. Therefore, Christ must be "put on" before he can be followed. And essentially there is a marked difference between putting on Christ and following his example.

Reference is to a spiritual putting on—in the conscience. This is effected by the soul receiving as its own Christ and all his righteousness, and confidently relying on these as if it had itself earned them; just as one ordinarily receives his apparel. This spiritual reception is the putting on; such is the nature and character of true faith.

53. Unquestionably Christ is given to us in a way that makes his righteousness, all he is and all he has, stand as our surety; he becomes our own. The believer in this doctrine will enjoy the blessing, as Paul teaches (Rom 8, 32): "He that spared not his own Son, but delivered him up for us all, how shall he not also with him freely give us all things?" Again (1 Cor 1, 30), "Christ Jesus, who was made unto us wisdom from God, and righteousness and sanctification, and redemption."

Note, he who thus believes in Christ puts on Christ. Faith, then, is something great enough to justify and save man. It affords him all the blessings in Christ, giving the conscience comfort and security. Thus man rejoices in Christ and is inclined to work all good and avoid all evil; he no longer fears death or hell, or any evil, richly clothed as he is in Christ. This is satisfying the Law and being no more under it. In connection with Christ as the garment, the Holy Spirit is in the soul, and the individual is a wholly different person. The soul is clothed in the adoption of God. It must, therefore, be a child.

54. Now, no saint can in God's sight be thus put on. It is necessary for every soul to put on Christ for himself. Man has nothing to give to another to put on. After receiving Christ, after putting on the garment of his righteousness, there follows imitation of Christ's example. Man treats his neighbor as Christ has treated him. He gives and helps his neighbor with all the good he has and can com-

mand; he permits himself to be put on—clothes his neighbor with what he possesses. But the garment of Christ's righteousness wherein he is himself clothed, he cannot give to his neighbor. No man can confer his faith upon another; he cannot give another man faith like his own. True, man may pray for his neighbor to be clothed with Christ as he is. But everyone must believe for himself. Christ alone must clothe us all with himself.

55. He who has not this faith, to believe that Christ with all his blessings is his—he does not yet rightly believe. He is not a Christian and is not in heart cheerful and happy. Only faith renders Christians willing, joyous, secure, saved and children of God. Where faith is, the Holy Spirit must dwell. What a beautiful, rainbow-hued and priceless garment is this Christ's righteousness, which combines in its magnificent and profuse decorations, its jewels and ornaments, all virtue, grace, wisdom, truth, righteousness and every blessing in Christ! Well may Paul exclaim (2 Cor 9, 15), "Thanks be to God for his unspeakable gift." And well may Peter say (2 Pet 1, 4) that through Christ great and precious gifts are given to us. Christ is the coat of many colors which Jacob made for Joseph, thus favoring him above his other children (Gen 37, 3); for Christ alone is full of grace and truth. Again, Christ is the precious garment of Aaron the high priest wherein he served God; concerning that figure much might be said. Paul's words here suggest these historical things.

56. Further, while we put on Christ—receive him—he also puts on or receives us and all we have as if his own. Now, he finds in us nothing good; he finds naught but sins. These he assumes. He removes them from us as disfigurements from his glorious garment. More, he intercedes for us before God, bearing our sins and saving us from eternal punishment. Paul says in Romans 8, 34 that Christ maketh intercession for us before God. Psalm 41, 4 testifies: "I said, O Jehovah, have mercy upon me: heal my soul; for I have sinned against thee." And Psalm 69, 5: "O God, thou knowest my foolishness; and my sins are not hid

from thee." All this testimony has reference to us personally. Paul so construes it in Romans 15, 3, where, quoting from Psalm 69, he speaks of how Christ bore our sins and neither rejected us nor regarded his holiness too good for us. He says, "But, as it is written, The reproaches of them that reproached thee fell upon me."

57. Now, we are pleased with the message that Christ is a garment for us, and that he intercedes for us as his garment; but with great reluctance do we suffer him to purify us. However, if we would be his garment, we certainly must suffer him to purify us. He cannot and will not appear in impurity. In the days of the martyrs, when he had but lately clothed himself with us, he began with zeal to purify the garment with death and various forms of suffering. Then he sat, as Malachi 3, 3 says, and purified the sons of Levi, as a fuller purifies garments. When Christ effects much suffering, indications are favorable for good. Wherever his garment is in evidence, he unceasingly purifies with various forms of suffering. Where suffering is not present, there his garment is not.

> "There can be neither Jew nor Greek, there can be neither bond nor free, there can be no male and female; for ye all are one man in Christ Jesus."

58. Of course Paul does not mean that physically there is no Jew and Greek, no man and woman. He means, as related to the subject he is handling. But of what is he speaking? Not of the natural body, but of faith, justification and Christ—how, through faith, we become children of God in Christ, a change effected in the soul, in man's conscience; not in his flesh and blood, not through his members, but through the Word of the Gospel.

In this sense there is no difference in persons, whether they be Jews or Greeks, bond or free, male or female. According to the customs of men, physically the Jew is bound by a different law and a different manner of life from the Greek; the bond from the free; the male from the female. The Jew is circumcised, the Greek is not; the male covers not his hair, but the female wears a veil. Then, too, every man serves God in his own way; hence the saying, Many countries, many customs. These customs, however, as well as all things external and not of faith, are powerless to render one righteous and pious before God. Neither do they hinder justification. Faith may exist equally well with all classes of persons, differing not with any custom and distinctions.

59. The trouble is, one falls into certain habits, adopts certain customs, and adheres to them in the endeavor to become righteous and just; in the attempt to aid the soul in putting off its sins and securing salvation. In such case all is perverted. Christ is denied, God is lost, faith and the Gospel are abandoned, works and the Law rule again, and the conscience is misled into thinking that to fail of observing customs means manifestly to be lost, while observance might effect salvation. This is the most pernicious error existing among men. Against it the apostle vehemently warns. It is impossible for Christian faith to live in connection with such a misguided conscience. The individual will never—he cannot—be justified and saved by anything in heaven or earth except Christ. All temporal manners, laws, labors, customs, and all persons but Christ, are fitted to serve the earthly life and to profit mankind.

Works Cannot Save.

60. What defect of the Jews, then, prevents their being saved? According to Paul (Rom 9, 32), they seek salvation by works and not by faith. They would have none but Jews admitted to heaven. But God designs that none but Christians, whether Jews or Greeks, male or female, shall enter there. The Jews think observance of the Law will save them, and failure to observe it will condemn them. God, however, intends that he who believes in Christ shall be saved, and he who believes not shall be damned. Mark 16, 16. Moreover, without faith no one can keep the Law, as stated above, and as Paul testifies again in the sixth chapter and thirteenth verse: "Not even they who receive circumcision do themselves keep the Law." Why not? Because they do not observe the Law willingly, but merely

through fear of its threats and hope of its rewards. Since the Jews think it necessary for them to be Jews, to undertake observance of the Law strictly according to the manner of their sect, thus cleaving to Judaism with its laws, while the conscience is fettered, they must eternally perish. For, according to Paul, the conclusion is, there is no Jew nor Greek; but only Christ and Christians.

61. Now, were they first to believe in Christ and then, if they feel so disposed, to remain Jews in custom, following or omitting the practice of circumcision and observing such laws as they see fit, not presuming thereby to become righteous and to be saved, but to be saved only through the grace of Christ, as were their fathers and the patriarchs, according to Peter's statement (Acts 15, 11)—were the Jews so to proceed, observance of the Law would be no detriment to them. But they will not do thus. So firmly do they cleave to the works, the terrors and the allurements of the Law, they even condemn and persecute all who teach otherwise, who preach faith. Their predecessors, upon this same point of Law-observance, persecuted and killed the prophets under the plea of exterminating, for the sake of God and his Law, deceivers of the people and blasphemers of the Law and of the service of God as commanded by Moses.

62. But note, the Jews of our day are yet more rude and arbitrary. The ancient Jews had at least the plausible excuse that they were bound by the Law of God. But our Jews—the Pope and his followers—drive us to observe things of their own invention, to laws merely human and even forbidden of God. They make a great cry about the noble virtue of obedience, teaching that without it salvation is impossible to any, but with it everyone may be saved; obedience, however, not of God's Law, but of their own laws and inventions.

If we but notice their conduct, we see plainly that their expectation of attaining righteousness and salvation is based, not upon Christian faith, but upon their works, upon the observance of their own laws, as Carthusians, Franciscans, Augustinians, Benedictines, preachers, prebendaries, vicars and so on. They even acknowledge that they regard their orders and positions as the proper medium for attaining righteousness and salvation. Plainly enough, then, their consciences cleave to works and not to the grace of Christ. Reading the words of Paul, "There is neither Jew nor Greek," they yet say, "There is, nevertheless, Carthusians, Franciscans, Benedictines, Augustinians, preachers of this and that order.

63. At the mention of faith in Christ, the Papists exclaim: "We know, indeed, that faith in Christ is essential, but that only through him can we become righteous and be saved, we do not believe." And they demand: "What would be the use of good works at all then? Our orders and positions would be vain. You would abolish good works and the service of God. Away with such a cursed heretic! Fire here! Fire! Heretic! Heretic! Shall it be that St. Francis, St. Dominic, St. Benedict, St. Augustine, St. Bernard, St. Anthony, have all so erred? What are you thinking about? Where did you get that diabolical faith?" Now, is not that the manner of our saintly Jews? What, then, shall we do with them? We must take the attitude of Paul when he said to the Galatians, and repeated the statement (Gal 1, 8-9): "Though we, or an angel from heaven, should preach unto you any gospel other than that which we preached unto you, let him be anathema."

64. So we also say: "Our preaching and the foundation of our faith, is that by faith alone, independently of the Law and of works, justification and salvation stand. And were the whole world Carthusians and taught otherwise, let it be accursed. Were the entire world barefooted friars, preachers, Augustines, Benedicts, and taught otherwise, let it be accursed. Or, again, if there were one whole world of holy Augustines, another of holy Francises, a third of holy Dominics, a fourth of holy Benedicts, a fifth of holy Anthonys, a sixth of St. Pauls, a seventh of angelic Gabriels —what then? If they teach otherwise, let them be accursed. The Word of God must stand, and emphatically Christ alone must remain. What more do you want?

65. Christ said of such sects as the Papists (Mt 24, 24) that many false Christs and prophets should arise who would say, "Lo, here is the Christ," or "here," and these were not to be believed. They would perform signs, he said, calculated to deceive even the elect, if that were possible. Two things for a long time prevented my understanding this passage as having reference to these sects and orders. The first thing was the fact that they are so numerous; they fill the world. Had their numbers been less, I would not have hesitated to believe that the words were spoken of them. But I imagined God would not permit so many to err. I did not perceive the plain import of the text, that many shall err; for even the elect, the minority, will err with the majority. The other reason why I understood not was, there are holy persons among the sects; such as Benedict, Bernard, Augustine, Francis, Dominic and many of their followers. I thought no error could exist in their case. I failed to perceive Christ's meaning, that the elect should stumble, should be tempted by error, though they should not continue therein.

66. Gideon was a man strong in faith, and by faith wrought great things. Yet he was misled when he made an ephod (Judges 8, 27)—when he instituted a special form of divine service and a peculiar form of apparel. Many evils later resulted from that act. According to the Scriptures, his whole race was exterminated. Why, then, should it be surprising that St. Benedict, St. Francis, St. Dominic, should err? Who can with certainty say they did not?

67. It is possible that in their case, as is generally true in the legends of saints, the people overlooked the worthiest practices and true order of the beloved saints and seized upon the things wherein the saints as men stumbled. Their infirmities are exalted for their strength, and their strength is suppressed. Everyone is disposed to follow what is weakest and most insignificant; the worst rather than the best.

68. Yet, if the Papists would make use of these orders and positions as things optional, not as a means of attaining righteousness and salvation, but merely as a medium of

bodily exercise, of service to their neighbors and of honor to God; and if they would leave their righteousness and salvation to be secured by faith alone—if they would so do, their orders and positions would not be an intolerable injury to them. However, these things would not even then be without offense to the illiterate mass, who are led to think them the true way, to the disparagement, if not the destruction, of their faith. For faith is sensitive and precious. It is easily injured, especially by hypocritical works and practices so showy as these of the Papists.

69. No doubt the holy fathers, in their relation to their disciples, made free and proper use of the orders; yes, with intent to increase the faith of their disciples. Otherwise the fathers would not have been really holy. But the blind Papists only mimic them. In following, they lose sight of the kernel and retain the shell; they do the works of the fathers, but forget their faith. They boastfully desire the appearance of observing the position and the orders of these holy men, and of following their example, when in reality they observe but the shadow of the fathers' religion. They are true apes, mimicing everything they see and yet remaining apes. They do not practice anything like Christian liberty. This is evident from their protest: "Shall we not become righteous and be saved through our positions, our orders, our works? If salvation depends on faith alone, something all men have, what sought we in the cloisters? Why did we become monks? Why are we priests? What avail the masses we hold and the prayers we offer? We might as well have continued laymen."

You see, their own words prove them unbelievers and not Christians, and show their unwillingness to unite with all Christians; a unity to which Paul here refers, saying that all the baptized have put on Christ and are one in him. The Papists seek ways peculiar to themselves and superior to the ways of Christians. Christ is not good enough for them to put on; he is not sufficient to justify and to save them.

70. They pervert Paul's statement and say, "All the bap-

tized are not one in Christ. Not only are there Jews and Greeks, but also Carthusians, barefooted friars, preachers, priests and similar orders. And these orders are true means of salvation." Thus they seek to find first in their own works the salvation and righteousness which should have been already theirs through baptism—in faith—as other Christians enjoy. Forgetting their Christian duties and Christian name, they assume instead human works and human names. No longer are they called Christians, but Carthusians, Benedictines, barefooted friars, and so on.

71. Paul's reference here to the bond and the free is derived from the ancient custom—formerly common in Germany, but no longer so—making of servants bondmen whom their masters had the right to sell, and the right to deal with as they would with their beasts. They who are not such bondmen spiritually, are here called by the apostle "free." Well might the occupants of the cloisters be called servants and bondmen, for they give themselves into the possession of men. Would God they might take some thought for themselves and let their spiritual existence be a willing incarceration; not to obtain righteousness and salvation by their bondage, but to use it as a medium for exercising these things already received through faith.

72. As little as the fact that you are a man or a woman contributes to or impedes your salvation, just so little is your salvation affected by your being a Carthusian or a priest, your performing certain external works and various duties, or your assuming different orders or ranks. Again, to be a woman renders you neither righteous nor wicked, even if you do all the works appropriate to a woman. Faith in Christ, independently of your womanhood and its duties and works, renders you righteous.

Being a nun does not make you spiritual nor pious. It does not save you, even though you observe most minutely all the regulations and laws, and perform all the works, pertaining to the order of nuns; indeed, not though you alone were to fulfil the combined works, the united duties, of all nuns. Faith in Christ secures to you the blessings of righteousness and salvation—faith which knows neither nuns nor monks, laymen nor priests, shoemakers nor tailors, fasts nor prayers, any more than it knows Jews and Greeks, male and female, bond and free. Faith is in all and above all, without distinction of orders and ranks, of persons and works, of gestures, customs and meats, of days, places and occupations. In short, upon none of these things depend righteousness and salvation.

Unity in Christ.

73. But Christians may indeed cleave to righteousness and eternal life—may believe in Christ and unite in him—no matter how different their external pursuits. Paul says, "Ye all are one man in Christ Jesus." And Psalm 133, 1 reads, "Behold, how good and how pleasant it is for brethren to dwell together in unity." Again: "God setteth the solitary in families.' Ps 68, 6. Faith is the same experience in all, and renders all alike righteous. Such is not the case with sects and orders. There each individual adopts his own way; consequently he follows a by-path.

Where cloisters have no prelate to teach the true faith they would better be destroyed. They are only gates to perdition. It were better to leave them and learn faith elsewhere than to remain in them an hour. Continence is possible without them. Oh, the numberless snares and scandals! How many noble souls who could be easily helped must be unmercifully strangled and stifled. Wo, wo, wo to you pontiffs, bishops and all who are intrusted with the oversight of these multitudes. Here the words of Christ apply (Mt 24, 19): "Woe unto them that are with child and to them that give suck in those days."

74. Paul says, "Ye all are one"—just the same as one man. He would not give the idea of multitude; his meaning is: "Ye are not many, but one. Notwithstanding your number and differences externally, notwithstanding your differences of position and occupation, things upon which righteousness and salvation do not depend; inwardly, in the matter of salvation and righteousness, ye are one. True, in the eyes of men the layman differs somewhat from the

priest, the monk from the nun, the man from the woman; but before God there is neither layman nor priest, monk nor nun, man nor woman. One is like another in faith." A proverb of Scripture, one generally employed by the apostles, reads, "There is no respect of persons."

75. The teaching of this passage fulfils the figures in Exodus 16, 18, relative to the gathering of the manna by the children of Israel. One gathered more, another less, yet afterward when they measured it by the omer, which contained the amount one was permitted to eat daily, they received an equal share, each his omer. According to the text, "He that gathered much had nothing over, and he that gathered little had no lack." So should it be with us. In the matter of faith we receive alike one Christ in one omer of faith, even though one individual may hear more of the Gospel than another; so should we share in love. The advantages and blessings of all Christians ought to be common. Thus does the apostle (2 Cor 8, 15) explain this same figure, that he who gathered much should help him who had little or nothing, and the one having little was to be supplied by the possessor of much. In such case burdens would be equal, as they were in the beginning, with the apostles.

76. As Christ treats us in the matter of faith—manifesting his love, pouring out his blessing upon us, making us all like himself and himself like us—so must we follow him in sharing our possessions with our neighbor—if we would be Christians. Is our faith right, we certainly will so act, with willing hearts. So then, all blessings are one, and all Christians one person; and the Law is wholly fulfilled. But if we are unwilling to conduct ourselves in this Christlike way, we have not faith and we have not Christ. It is easily evident that faith is now everywhere prostrate and there are no Christians. Every corner is filled with masses and divine services—sheer idolatry.

77. But you will say: "By your doctrine you will suppress all the cloisters and other institutions, and give occasion for all occupants to leave them speedily, and to forsake their positions." I reply: These are not my words, nor

my doctrine. You can see that. Go to Paul, Christ, God, about the matter. Ask them why they denounce these institutions, these practices. Among the children of Israel was likewise a singular people, called people of Baal and of Moloch. All the country and the towns were filled with their self-devised and peculiar worship. Jeremiah (ch. 2, 28) and Hosea (ch. 10, 1) testify that their altars and gods equaled the number of the towns. All men desired to serve God in that way. Therefore God permitted the country to be destroyed.

The holy King Josiah, in his dissatisfaction with these idolators, cut off and destroyed all their forms of worship. 2 Kings 23, 5. He did not fear the Pope's ban; he was not afraid of having it said that he had destroyed the worship of God, as Rabshakeh charged the holy King Hezekiah with doing on a similar occasion. 2 Kings 18, 22. This doctrine, however, destroys no cloisters or institutions, but teaches their right and Christian use.

78. Mark how Paul guards either alternative, purposing to keep us squarely in the middle track. He says, "There can be neither Jew nor Greek," etc. Should a Jew, with reference to this subject, say, "If being a Jew avails nothing before God, I will let that go and take the opposite course; I will become a Greek"—should he think thus, he finds Paul meeting him on the other side. "No," Paul says, "to be a Greek avails nothing either." Should the Greek conclude. "I will no longer be a Greek, I will become a Jew," Paul says, "No, it avails nothing to be a Jew." Does the woman say, "Would I were a man since it avails not to be a woman," and does the bound say, "Would I were free since bondage avails not," Paul meets them with," To be male or female, bond or free, serves not." What, then, does avail? Just to turn not to either side, but to pass over, pass above, Jew and Greek, bond and free, male and female, into faith and Christ. The way of the Jew, the Greek, are earthly ways; the way of faith is the heavenly way.

Paul says also (I Cor 7, 18): "Was any man called being circumcised? Let him not become uncircumcised. Hath any been called in uncircumcision? Let him not be circumcised." What is this but teaching that on one hand a Jew should not say, "Circumcision profiting nothing, uncircumcision must avail, and I will now obtain righteousness thereby," and on the other hand the Gentile must not declare, "Uncircumcision profiting nothing, if I would be saved I must be circumcised." "No," Paul says, "neither proceeding is right"; and then he concludes (verse 19): "Circumcision is nothing, and uncircumcision is nothing; but the keeping of the commandments of God." In other words, First believe in Christ. Believing, the commandments of God will be honored. First be righteous and saved; then, be circumcised or uncircumcised, Jew or Greek, male or female, bond or free, do what you will, the efficacy is the same.

79. In like manner, a nun, priest or monk should not say: "My state avails nothing, I will leave it and become a layman." No, Paul says, to be a layman also avails nothing. On the other hand, if the layman says: "O, that I were a priest, monk or nun, for my state as a layman is a secular, unsaved one," Paul says, no, the state of a monk, nun or priest likewise avails nothing. It is as secular and unsaved as that of a layman. What, then, does avail? To ascend above yourself, above layman, above monk and nun, above the spiritual and the secular states. To believe in Christ and do to your neighbor as you believe Christ did to you, is the only true way to godliness and salvation. There is none other.

80. By way of a crude illustration: Suppose a lad learning the trade of shoemaking were to engage with a master foolish and knavish enough to teach him that such trade is the medium for obtaining righteousness and salvation; and suppose the boy were to believe him and to prosecute his trade under the impression that he will surely be saved threby, and only so can he be saved, and were to forsake faith, love and all other means of salvation—how would you look at the case? Would you not pity the boy? Would not the master incur your displeasure? Now, how would you help the boy? Would you say: "My dear son, the

trade of shoemaking does not render you righteous. It avails nothing in heaven. You must become a tailor"? That would be but to lead him from one hell to another. You would be just about as godly as that master. Just so do they do who advise a priest to become a monk, or a monk to enter some more difficult order. They thus cast souls and consciences from one frying-pan into another. The way to help the boy is to say to him: "My dear son, neither shoemaking nor tailoring counts in this matter. You must believe in Christ and then treat your neighbor as you believe Christ has treated you. Then you may be a shoemaker, a tailor, as you please."

Now you have liberated his soul. Now his conscience will have joy and peace. He will thank God and you. He will not need to abandon his trade; no, he may follow it with more pleasure and freedom than before. Christ does not release our hands from labor, our persons from office, our bodies from position or rank. He redeems the soul from a false experience and the conscience from a false faith. He is a redeemer of consciences; a bishop of souls, as Peter says (1 Pet 2, 25). Yet he permits our hands to continue their labors; he allows us to retain our offices and positions.

81. So, too, do thou, O priest, monk or nun. Believe not those who teach you that your position, your rank, is a means whereby to become righteous and be saved. They are but blind leaders of the blind; messengers of the devil and murderers of souls. Learn first that the true way is to believe in Christ and to serve your neighbor. Then remain stedfast where you are.

82. You will say, "But I took clerical orders because I wanted to be righteous and to be saved thereby. Otherwise I would not have taken the step. I believe not one in a thousand entered this station with any other intention. If people knew your teaching to be true, certainly no one would enter the clerical ranks, and in thirty years' time every cloister and similar institution would pass of itself, needing not to be destroyed." I answer: Think you, then, that Christ spoke irresponsibly or foolishly when he said

the false Christs would deceive many, even the elect if it were possible (Mt 24, 24)? Peter also prophesies (2 Pet 2, 2) that many shall follow these damnable sects. Is it astonishing that Christ spoke the truth? Will you believe the inventions of your own mind rather than the words of Christ?

83. Mark you, then, where the clerical state is not made use of to further faith and love in the way mentioned, I would, not only that my doctrines should be the means of destroying the cloisters and other institutions, but I would they already lay in ashes. If you can, through the doctrine of faith, liberate your conscience and your soul and at the same time make use of your clerical state, not as a supposed means of obtaining righteousness and eternal life, but as a medium for exercising your faith over your body, and for serving your neighbor—if you can do thus, then remain in your order; you need not to flee from it. But if you cannot do this, if your conscience remains captive, it were better you tore your caps and pates, forsook your masses and prayers forever and became a swineherd—if you could not do better. For nothing in heaven or on earth should keep us from liberating our souls, from freeing our consciences.

84. Should one reproach you as an apostate, a turn-coat, a vagabond monk, endure it, thinking of Christ's words (Mt 7, 3) about one with a beam in his eye rebuking another with a mote in his. You are an apostate from men, they from God; you forsook men for God, they forsook God for themselves and for men.

85. Be careful, however, not to deceive yourself and forsake your position from wrong motives. Your old Adam nature is very ready to adorn itself, and will take a yard if you allow it a finger-breadth. You may deceive men, but you cannot God. If you leave your station merely for the purpose of a free life, and to be liberated from your order, and not solely because you seek to liberate your conscience, you have not followed my teaching. I have not thus advised you. This I desire you to understand. According to our doctrine you can remain in your orders and maintain

a liberated conscience. Recall the illustration of the boy shoemaker I gave you. But, if you are so weak that you cannot maintain a free conscience, it is better to be far from your order.

86. In short, one of two things is offered: you must either cast aside your theory or you must get out of the order altogether. Faith will not tolerate the idea of your obtaining righteousness and salvation by the religious life of your order or position. But since faith tolerates the order, it is better to forsake the idea than the order. Otherwise, later the remorse of conscience, because of the forsaken order (if the idea is not dead) might equal a desire of having remained in the order. Aim must be directed solely at the head of the serpent—the false idea. With that disposed of, with men divested of the idea of righteousness and eternal life attainable through works and orders, all danger and dread would be dissipated.

87. The serpent protects her head with extreme care. Christ teaches us to be likewise careful of our heads where he says (Mt 10, 16), "Be ye wise as serpents, and harmless as doves." The serpent will expose all the rest of her anatomy, will risk all, to preserve her head, wherein is her life. We should likewise be careful of our head—faith—and risk all for it, whatever the consequences, for in that is our life. The evil spirit seeks to destroy faith by its showy orders and stations. Further, when we bruise the head of the serpent, when we destroy our own ideas, which are our false faith resting upon works, all else is harmless to us. Christ called the Pharisees a generation of vipers (Mt 12, 13) because of their tenacious adherence to their works and their opinions. Were we to secure our heads as do serpents, and were we as wise in our ways as are the children of the world in theirs, the simplicity of the dove would naturally follow; we would embrace no external works, positions or orders.

88. The greatest fault, however, is not that of Pilate, but of Caiaphas who delivered Christ into Pilate's hands. Caiaphas represents the Pope, the bishops, and the doctors of

the high schools, whose duty as shepherds is to prevent destruction, yet who, like wolves, themselves devour the sheep. While they should preserve the faith, they exterminate it. Not only do they permit the rise of orders and stations, but they institute these things. They establish and exalt them. They repose the head of the serpent upon silken pillows and feed her to fullness. They have introduced into the world two principles and inculcated them into men's hearts to the extent of making it impossible for the Christian faith to live. One is, "The clerical state represents perfection." By this claim they have effected such disparity between themselves and ordinary Christians that almost exclusively they have been regarded the Christians, and the common people unworthy, even reprobate, domestics Thus they have commanded everybody's gaze and attention. All men have come flocking into the order, desiring to be perfect and scorning as unprofitable the common walks of life; until they have come to think that no one can become righteous and be saved unless he embraces a clerical order.

89. Thus faith has been neglected for works and orders, as if on these depend not only our righteousness and salvation, but the perfection of our character. The fact is, however, all depends on faith. By faith alone do we attain righteousness and perfection. What a banner the infernal Satan hoisted at this point! With the introduction and establishment of the doctrine of works he unquestionably scaled the citadel of Christianity. Blindly the frantic multitude ever goes on about perfection, knowing nothing whatever of piety even, not to mention perfection, and thinking to become perfect by works and orders.

90. Further, they have left an ample loophole for themselves by saying: "Actual perfection and a state of perfection are different things. Man may be in a state of perfection and yet not be perfect. That is. he may be a clergyman and still not be holy. They of the clerical order generally, are in a state of perfection, yet none of them have become perfect." The clergy also quote St. Thomas of Aquin, who teaches that perfection is not necessary; that it is sufficient

to be in a state of perfection and looking toward that end.

Therefore the multitude today accepts the principle that one may occupy a perfect state and not be perfect; and that perfection is not necessary—only the striving for it. Blind, frantic, foolish and mad, emphatically so, are the people. Do we not all know that a monk may wear a cap and pate and at the same time be a rogue at heart? In a state of perfection, he is yet not perfect. A "state of perfection" now means monk, cap and pate. But let these erring teachers lead the blind. Christ says they are blind leaders of the blind. If St. Thomas Aquinas was holy—which I doubt—he surely attained his holiness in an extraordinary way, judging from his pernicious and poisonous doctrines.

91. The other principle of the Papists is: "The Gospel consists of two things, "consilia et præcepta," counsels and commandments. In the entire Gospel Christ has presented but one counsel—chastity; and this may be observed as well in the laical state by any individual having sufficient grace. But the clerical order has instituted twelve counsels in the Gospel, proceeding according to their own pleasure with reference to the Gospel. They have made a division of the world into two classes, their own lives to be directed by the counsels and the lives of the laity by the commandments. They have assumed to live superior to the commandments of God. Consequently, the life of the ordinary Christian, the life of faith, has become repulsive. All men gaze after the clerical ranks, despise the commandments and run after the counsels.

92. In the end they find the counsels to be human laws relating to clothing and pates, to meats, to singing and reading, and so on. Thereupon neglect of the commandments of God follows neglect of faith; both are exterminated and forgotten. Today to be perfect and to live according to the counsels is to put on black or white or gray or marked caps; to bawl in the churches; to shave the head; to eat no eggs, meat or butter, but at the same time to fare sumptuously and to live an idle, extravagant life.

93. Such a result, mark you, Satan has desired to ac-

complish through the two principles mentioned. The first exterminates faith and the whole New Testament, Christ included. The second destroys the commandments and the entire Old Testament, with Moses. The people who teach these principles are they concerning whom all Scripture testifies that in the end of the world they shall reign under Antichrist. Two principles more pernicious and virulent were never advanced on earth—principles that so speedily and forcibly expel from the knowledge of the world the entire Scriptures of God, until none know what commandment or Gospel is. The Gospel does not present commandments; it shows the impossibility of fulfilling them, and teaches faith in Christ, through which they are fulfilled.

I would that all the cloisters were supplied with ministers who preach the true doctrine of faith, or else that the cloisters were laid in ashes. For there is no medium condition, as there is with the laity; the layman does not regard the works of his station as productive of righteousness and salvation. The clergy, however, cannot sustain themselves without that false doctrine. There is no alternative; right or wrong they must put their trust in their works.

Now, let this suffice here in the matter of the sects. Alas, that their corruption warrants so much comment. I hardly know if it will be of use that we understand again the plain words of Paul:

> "And if ye are Christ's, then are ye Abraham's seed, heirs according to the promise."

94. How is it that all who put on Christ, who are his, are in consequence the seed and the heirs of Abraham when perhaps they are not of Jewish descent? It is clear enough from the explanation of the preceding verses that all who, through baptism and faith, put on Christ are his and he is theirs. Now, being all one in Christ and one with him—spiritually, not bodily—they must be all that Christ is and possess all he possesses. Christ being Abraham's seed, they must through him also be Abraham's spiritual seed. In the same manner in which they possess Christ are they Abraham's seed. They possess Christ not bodily, in flesh and

blood; but spiritually, in faith. Hence they are not bodily, but spiritually, his seed.

95. Note here, the apostle ascribes to Abraham three kinds of seed. First, there are those only physically his children, having in him a flesh-and-blood origin, merely by the law of nature. With them God has no more dealing than with the heathen, as illustrated in the case of Ishmael. Although of Abraham's flesh and blood, even his first-born son, Ishmael nevertheless was not in the Scriptures reckoned among Abraham's children. Again, Esau was Isaac's natural son, and Abraham's flesh and blood. Later many of Israel, all of them Abraham's flesh-and-blood children, were destroyed in the wilderness. And subsequently many others have been condemned. The Jews are for the most part still under condemnation.

Believers the True Seed of Abraham.

96. Second, there are those both physically and spiritually Abraham's children, having not only the flesh and blood but the spirit and faith of Abraham—Isaac, Jacob, the patriarchs, the prophets and all the blessed of the people of Israel. These are the true seed, with whom God deals. This seed he delivered from Egypt, led into the land of Canaan and favored with blessings innumerable, as the Scriptures testify. For the sake of this class he tolerated among them the seed merely physical, permitting the latter to enjoy similar temporal blessings. They to whom Abraham was a spiritual father through the faith of Christ, were his spiritual children, irrespective of their natural relationship.

Of this class of seed, Christ is the head. In him Abraham himself, as well as all his seed, his brethren and joint-heirs, is blessed. Now, this text refers to the seed spoken of in Genesis 12, 3 and Genesis 22, 18, "In thy seed shall all the nations of the earth be blessed." The prophecy is fulfilled in Christ. This class are wholly with Christ and in Christ, and Christ is with them and in them—one seed. Christ is blessed of God. Joint seed with Christ are blessed through him. The heathen are blessed through the apostles, and the Jews through Christ, which Jews are joint-seed with Christ.

97. Third, there are those who have not a flesh-and-blood origin in Abraham, but possess his spiritual character—his faith in Christ his seed. This class is represented by ourselves and all gentiles who are Christians in the true faith. While unbelief is powerful enough to separate even natural flesh-and-blood children from Abraham's relationship, until the Scriptures do not recognize them as Abraham's seed and the children of God; on the other hand, faith is more powerful, even unto constituting them true seed of Abraham who are not of his flesh and blood but who merely have the faith of Abraham, partaking of his spiritual character. Concerning this matter St. Paul speaks in Romans 4, 13, Romans 9, 8 and Galatians 3. This class of seed is indicated in the promise God makes to Abraham, "In thy seed shall all the families of the earth be blessed."

98. If the nations are to receive this blessing they must become like the seed of Abraham. Abraham and his seed have naught but the blessing. If the inheritance, the chief good, the blessing, is possessed alike by Abraham's seed and by all the nations of earth, all must alike be reckoned heirs, seed and children of Abraham, whether deriving physical existence from him or not. Therefore, the conclusion is that Abraham's seed are only the believers. In the Scriptures believers are reckoned as his seed. To this inference are we forced by God's promise that Abraham's seed shall be blessed and shall be a blessing to others. According to the words of the promise, the blessing must be to all who are seed and heirs of Abraham.

Now, no one is blessed unless he believes. The unbeliever remains under the curse. Well may Paul, then, call the spiritual seed of Abraham the seed of the promise (Rom 4, 13 and 9, 8). That is, they are not the seed of the flesh, but of faith. They are so designated in the promise. He says (Rom 9, 8): "It is not the children of the flesh that are children of God; but the children of the promise are reckoned for a seed." With this statement accords John

1, 13: "Who were born, not of blood, nor of the will of the flesh, nor of the will of man, but of God."

99. Now you understand the apostle's meaning here when he says, "If ye are Christ's, then are ye Abraham's seed, heirs according to promise." In other words: "Ye are not the natural seed of Abraham. That would profit you nothing; it profits no one. But ye are his promised seed. Upon that all efficacy depends." Abraham has no seed other than the promised blessed seed—God grant these—whether or no of flesh-and-blood origin in him. We must understand Abraham's seed in a scriptural, not in a natural, sense. The Scriptures regard not natural origin. They recognize alike all who are blessed and who believe, whether natural seed or not. Yet God foresaw there would undoubtedly be children of the blessing among the natural seed; not children in consequence of their nature, but for the sake of election through grace.

100. You must properly comprehend the phrase "Abraham's seed and heirs" in the light of the preceding epistle, as opposed to self-righteousness, recognizing that righteousness is not obtained by works, but must precede and induce them. The heir does not work to obtain the inheritance. He does not seek the inheritance as a reward. He already possesses it, and appropriates it with his works. Likewise the believer is already righteous and just, and saved besides, without works—through the grace conferred by faith. The works performed subsequent to believing are but the exercise of his inheritance.

101. Further, in believing, you must feel yourself an heir. You must confidently regard yourself a child of God. If you doubt on this point, you are not a child; you are not an heir; you do not rightly believe. You must not doubt your heirship, whether in life or death. What is the Christian life but the beginning of eternal life? However, at your least intimation that you are a child of God, your acknowledgement of your faith, Caiaphas, as if doing God great service, will rend his garments and exclaim over you "He blasphemeth God!" And all will say with him: "He

is worthy of death. We have a law, and according to this law he shall die. He has made himself a child of God. Crucify him! Crucify him! He is a heretic and a deceiver." (See Jn 19: 7, 15.) Look for this to be said of you; prepare for it. For so it must be.

Epiphany

Epistle Text: Isaiah 60, 1-6.

1. Arise, shine; for thy light is come, and the glory of Jehovah is risen upon thee. 2 For, behold, darkness shall cover the earth, and gross darkness the peoples; but Jehovah will arise upon thee, and his glory shall be seen upon thee. 3 And nations shall come to thy light, and kings to the brightness of thy rising.

4. Lift up thine eyes round about, and see; they all gather themselves together, they come to thee; thy sons shall come from far, and thy daughters shall be carried in the arms. 5 Then thou shalt see and be radiant, and thy heart shall thrill and be enlarged; because the abundance of the sea shall be turned unto thee, the wealth of the nations shall come unto thee. 6 The multitude of camels shall cover thee, the dromedaries of Midian and Ephah; all they from Sheba shall come; they shall bring gold and frankincense, and shall proclaim the praises of Jehovah.

THE CONVERSION OF THE HEATHEN.

1. This epistle lesson is an exhortation to faith. It also proclaims the future world-wide preaching of the Gospel and the gathering of Christians from all nations. The prophecy is clearly intelligible and requires but little explanation.

2. The reference to the Gospel as a light, a brightness, a glory of the risen Jehovah, implies a distinction between the light of the Gospel and that of the Law. This distinction should be carefully marked, to avoid confounding the Gospel and the Law and terming "Gospel" what is Law and "Law" what is Gospel. In the Advent and the pre-

ceding epistle lessons we found the Gospel to be a proclamation of life, a doctrine of grace, a joy-giving light, promising and presenting Christ with all his blessings. But the Law is a proclamation of death, a doctrine of wrath, a sorrow-yielding light, for it reveals our sins, demanding a righteousness we cannot produce. The conscience, recognizing that it deserves death and eternal wrath, is filled with sorrow and unrest. But this prophecy of Isaiah touches the wretched conscience in a cheering way. It reanimates it, fills it with joy and liberates it from the Law and from sin.

3. So we may designate the two lights as the light of the Lord and the light of the servant. 2 Cor 3, 13. The light of the Lord arose in Christ, and the light of the servant in Moses. Aaron and the children of Israel could not endure the light—the brightness—of Moses' face. He was obliged to cover it with a veil. But on Mount Tabor the face of the transfigured Christ was not intolerable. Rather, so delightful and pleasing was it that Peter in a transport of joy exclaimed: "Lord, it is good for us to be here: if thou wilt, I will make here three tabernacles; one for thee, and one for Moses, and one for Elijah." Mt 17, 4. There the light of Moses' face was not intolerable, but pleasing. The Gospel renders agreeable the Law, the tutor, which before was repugnant and intolerable to human nature. This we have already heard. So Isaiah says:

"Arise, shine; for thy light is come."

4. Plainly the injunction is addressed to one not risen, one who lies sleeping or is dead. I think Paul refers to this passage when he says (Eph 5, 14): "Wherefore he saith, Awake, thou that sleepest, and arise from the dead, and Christ shall shine upon thee." Undoubtedly, Christ is the light of which Isaiah here speaks, and which, through the Gospel, shines in all the world, enlightening those who rise—who desire him. That Jerusalem is mentioned here and not by Paul is of no significance: In the text of Isaiah "Jerusalem" is not found. Some one added it in the epistle,

because Jerusalem, or the people of Israel were addressed by the prophets.

5. Now, who are the sleepers and the dead? Unquestionably, all who are under the Law. They are dead because of sin. Particularly are they dead who disregard the Law and live independently of restraint. The self-righteous, who recognize not their wants and defects, are the sleepers. Both classes have little regard for the Gospel. They remain sleeping and continually die. The Spirit must awake them to recognition and acknowledge the light. But the third class, they who feel the power of the Law and the torments of the conscience, thirst after grace and sigh for the Gospel. They rest not until it comes and is given them. Then they proclaim it. Isaiah is one of these. In such manner do the sleepers and the dead awake and receive the Gospel light.

6. So Isaiah says, in effect: "Permit yourself to be enlightened; or, Let there be light. Allow the light to fall upon you. Thou dead one, crawl not into the grave of thy filthy life—that is, cease to love and to follow thine evil course of conduct—that the light of the Gospel may fall upon thee and abide in thee. And thou sleeper, awake! Seek not the bed of careless and lethargic security, and of presumptuous reliance upon thine own self-righteousness. Let the true light have some claim upon thee." It is necessary frequently to admonish both classes. The great hindrance of the class represented by the dead is an unrestrained life; and a secure self-righteousness will scarcely allow the sleeping class to recognize and accept the blissful light of the Gospel.

7. "Thy light is come." Why does Isaiah say "thy light" when God's light is meant, as will later appear? I answer, it is at the same time God's light and Jerusalem's light and the light of us all. It is God's in that he gives it; ours in that we are enlightened by it and enjoy its rays. Similarly, Christ speaks of the sun as the Father's (Mt 5, 45), "He maketh his sun to rise on the evil and the good." Again, he says (Jn 11, 9), "If a man walk in the day, he stumbleth

not, because he seeth the light of this world." That is, God's sun enlightens the world. Again, referring to himself, he declares (Jn 8, 12), "I am the light of the world." Further, the light Isaiah refers to is particularly the light of Jerusalem and the children of Israel, because of the promise. He was promised only to Abraham and his seed. So Mary sings in her Song of Praise (Lk 1, 55), "As he spake to our fathers, to Abraham, and to his seed for ever." In this sense, it is not the light of the heathen, unto whom no promise was made. Yet it is said they are to receive it. So the words of the promise imply, and so Isaiah here teaches.

8. Undoubtedly the prophecies of Isaiah, and of the other prophets, concerning Christ almost universally have origin in the promise God made to Abraham (Gen 22, 18), "In thy seed shall all the nations of the earth be blessed." These words clearly indicate that Christ, the seed of Abraham, is to be made known in all the world. For Christ to accomplish this in person was impossible; it must be done through the instrumentality of preaching. Not only was it necessary to proclaim the Gospel, but also to explain the character of the preaching—to show it a proclamation of blessings and of grace, intended for the blessing of the whole world.

There is evident, too, the conclusion that the seed of Abraham is true man as well as God; that he must be born of a virgin; that his kingdom cannot be temporal or of this world; and that he must die and shortly rise from the dead to Lordship over all creatures.

All this apparently is briefly but explicitly concluded in this divine promise. Did time admit, it were easy to trace, in a way comprehensible to any man, the source of the prophecies to this fountain-head promise. Hence, Abraham laughed in his heart when the promise was made to him (Gen 17, 17), for he understood it. Christ indicates as much where he says concerning the patriarch's feeling (Jn 8, 56,) "Your father Abraham rejoiced to see my day; and he saw it, and was glad."

"And the glory of Jehovah is risen upon thee."

9. We have frequently spoken of the little word "glory." It means honor, brightness, splendor. The Gospel is simply a grand report, a noble cry, having origin in a glorious reality; it is not a mere empty proclamation. A glorious being is to be compared to a sun or a light. The sun is a fountain of light, so to speak, and its luster is the glory, the diffusion, the distinction of that light. The luster may be called the natural expression of the sun, the sole medium whereby the sun is recognized in the world—through which it is diffused. Similarly, the glory of an individual is the fountain, the sun, the foundation, of his glorious reputation. His reputation is the luster of his glory. It is the medium whereby he is proclaimed, extolled, recognized as glorious. This much, you will perceive, is implied in the word "glory"—honor, renown, brilliancy.

10. Thus the Gospel is God's glory and our light. It is our light in that it reveals to us God, ourselves and all else. It is God's glory in that it is the medium whereby his work—all his glorious doings—are proclaimed, extolled, recognized and honored in the whole world.

11. But, carrying the analogy to a finer point, it might be necessary to say that the Gospel is not the actual brightness of the light, nor is it the light itself. It is the rising of the brightness, the approach of the light. It is simply a manifestation of the light and brightness which existed from eternity. As said in John 1, 4, "In him was life; and the life was the light of men." The light did not arise, nor was it openly manifested, except through the Gospel. Therefore, the Gospel is an expression, a cry, of divine brightness and glory. The Scriptures, in Psalm 29, 3, in 68, 33 and often elsewhere, call it the voice of God.

It is called "Gospel"—good message—because it reveals and proclaims divine blessings, divine glory and divine honor or brightness. "The heavens declare the glory of God; and the firmament showeth his handiwork." Ps 19, 1. And what do we understand by proclaiming and revealing, except the proclaiming of the Gospel through the heavens—the preaching of it by the apostles? What is the brightness, the work, of God but the great and glorious riches of his goodness and grace poured out upon us?

Paul says (Tit 2, 11), "The grace of God hath appeared, bringing salvation to all men." How has it appeared? Through the preaching of the Gospel. Such seems to be the import of the words of Isaiah, "Thy light is come, and the glory of Jehovah is risen upon thee." That is, the light and glory of God are revealed—are preached—to you. Christ is the light and the glory, according to the words, "And the glory of Jehovah is risen upon thee," or is revealed. Again, verse 20 of this chapter, "Jehovah will be thine everlasting light."

12. Now, the light and the glory are God himself. For Christ says (Jn 8, 12), "I am the light." We heard before, in the epistle for Christmas, that Christ is the effulgence of divine glory. Plainly, then, Isaiah is not here speaking of the rising of Christ in the sense of his coming birth. He refers to the rising of the Gospel after Christ's ascension. Through the Gospel Christ is spiritually risen and glorified in the hearts of all believers, bringing them salvation. The Scriptures make more frequent reference to his rising in this sense than they do to the birth of Christ. The Gospel is the important feature. On account of it was Christ born. Upon it Paul bases his teaching. He says that God beforetime promised the Gospel concerning his Son, through his prophets, in the holy Scriptures.

13. We learn from our text here what the Gospel is and what is its message. It is the coming of light, the rising of divine glory. It speaks only of divine glory, divine honor and fame. It exalts only the work of God—his goodness and grace toward us. It teaches the necessity of our receiving God's work for us, his grace and goodness, even God himself, if we would secure salvation.

The Gospel produces in us a twofold effect. First, it rejects our natural reason, our human light. It conclusively shows them to be mere darkness. Had we within ourselves light instead of darkness, it would not be necessary for God to send the light to rise upon us. Light enlightens, not light, but darkness. This epistle lesson forcibly expels and severely condemns all natural wisdom, all human reason, heathen arts and the doctrines and laws of man. Conclusively, these are absolute darkness, since it is necessary for the light to come. So we should guard against all human doctrines and the conceits of reason as darkness rejected and condemned by God, and should wake and arise to behold only this light, to follow it alone.

14. Second, the Gospel casts down all the glory of and pride in our own works, our efforts, our free will. We cannot draw comfort nor derive honor from these. On the contrary, they but contribute to our shame in the sight of God. If there were in ourselves anything worthy of honor and glory, vainly would the divine honor and glory rise upon us. Since the latter are called for, clearly there is in us nothing but what is productive of our shame. Paul says on this point (Rom 3, 23), "All have sinned, and fall short of the glory of God." In other words, "Men may, it is true, have their own nature and their self-righteousness, and from these derive temporal honor, praise and glory before their fellows, as if not sinners. But before God they are sinful, destitute of divine glory and unable to boast possession of him and his blessings."

15. Now, no one can be saved unless he have within himself the glory of God and be able to comfort himself solely with God and his blessings, and to glory in these. "He that glorieth, let him glory in the Lord." Jer 9, 24, and 2 Cor 10, 17. Such is the rising of divine glory. So the Gospel condemns all our efforts and exalts only the goodness and the grace of God—in other words, God himself. It permits us to console ourselves only with him and to glory in no other. As Psalm 144, 15 has it, "Happy is the people whose God is Jehovah." No one else is called happy. Accordingly it follows here in Isaiah:

> "For, behold, darkness shall cover the earth, and gross darkness the peoples; but Jehovah will arise upon thee, and his glory shall be seen upon thee."

16. Here the prophet clearly implies that wherever Christ

is not, there darkness exists, whatever the appearance of brilliance. Nor does he allow the medium devised by the high schools, which say that between darkness and Christ exists the light of nature and of human reason. They ascribe darkness only to the grossly wicked and the weak-minded. They highly value this mediatory light, claiming it is a sufficient preparation for the light of Christ, and that although it is darkness in comparison to the light of Christ, yet it is in itself light. They do not perceive how far they err in imagining themselves enlightened. Usually the most erroneous of the schools are the most rational. "The sons of this world are for their own generation wiser than the sons of the light," as Christ says in Luke 16, 8. Yet they of the schools are not nearer the true light than are others. Rather they are farther from it. This could not be if the light of reason were helpful in obtaining the true light. Devils are wiser, more artful and crafty, than men; yet they are not therefore better. No, that kind of light is always at enmity with the true light. As Paul tells us (Rom 8, 7): "The mind of the flesh is enmity against God; for it is not subject to the law of God, neither indeed can it be."

17. Therefore, God knew of no better way to deal with the pernicious light of reason than utterly to condemn and obscure it. Paul says (1 Cor 1, 19-20): "For it is written, I will destroy the wisdom of the wise, and will bring to nothing the understanding of the prudent . . . Hath not God made foolish the wisdom of this world?"

In this same chapter of Isaiah, verse 19, we have: "The sun shall be no more thy light by day; neither for brightness shall the moon give light unto thee: but Jehovah will be unto thee an everlasting light, and thy God thy glory." What is this but a rejection of all temporal wisdom? Away with babbling about natural light. Give close heed to the words of Isaiah and to other Scriptures which teach us to flee from the light of reason as from darkness and from an enemy of the true light. Human reason is the light which teaches the Jews, and all tyrants, to persecute and torture Christ and his saints, and which cannot, even to this day, endure the true light. Human reason always claims to be in the right and to be light, when really it is darkness and condemned by the true light. Being condemned, in its rage it instigates all forms of evil.

18. But the weak-minded may ask: "How can it be that all natural reason teaches is darkness? Plainly, three and two are five, are they not? Again, if a man make a coat, is he not wise to make it of cloth, or foolish to make it of paper? Is he not wise who marries a godly woman, and he foolish who marries a godless one? And are there not similar instances innumerable in human affairs? Never can you persuade me that all natural reason is darkness. Even Christ implies that it is light, when he says (Mt 7, 24 and 26): 'Every one therefore that heareth these words of mine, and doeth them, shall be likened unto a wise man, who built his house upon the rock . . . And every one that heareth these words of mine, and doeth them not, shall be likened unto a foolish man, who built his house upon the sand.' Now, if the builder upon the rock is in darkness, who builds wisely? Again, Christ says of the unjust steward who had wasted his lord's goods that he acted wisely in taking the course he did in regard to his master's debtors. Lk 16, 8. And Paul reminds the Corinthians (1 Cor 11: 5, 14-15) that nature teaches us a woman should not, in the church, pray with uncovered head."

19. I answer: This is all true, but it is necessary to make a distinction between God and men, between spiritual and temporal things. In earthly, human affairs man's judgment suffices. For these things, he needs no light but that of reason. Hence God does not in the Scriptures teach us how to build houses, to make clothing, to marry, to wage war, to sail the seas, and so on. For these, our natural light is sufficient. But in divine things, the things concerning God, and in which we must conduct ourselves acceptably with him and must secure happiness for ourselves, human nature is absolutely blind, staring stone-blind, unable to recognize in the slightest degree what these things are. Natural reason presumptuously plunges into them like a blind

horse. But all its conclusions are, as certainly as God lives, false and erroneous. In this capacity it proceeds like a man who builds on sand, or one who would use cobwebs for garments. Is 59, 6. It employs sand for meal in making bread. It sows wind and reaps the whirlwind, as Hosea 8, 7 has it. It measures the atmosphere with a spoon, carries light into the cellar upon a tray, weighs flames in a balance, performing all manner of perverted nonsense ever known or possible to be devised. For all its efforts are designed as service to God and they must utterly fail.

20. Ask nature what is necessary to please God and to be saved, and it replies: "Truly, you must build churches, cast bells, institute masses, observe vigils, make chalices, pyxes, images and ornaments; must burn candles, pray so long a time, fast in honor of St. Catharine, become a priest or a monk, go to Rome and to St. Jacob, wear hair-shirts, torture yourself, and so on. Such are good works and true ways to salvation." But if you ask for proof that these things are acceptable with God, reason is unable to give any other reply than that it thinks them acceptable. This doctrine is sheer imagination; more, it is gloom, it is darkness. It is what Isaiah refers to as "darkness" and "gross darkness." Into it must fall all who do not accept the divine light. It is impossible for them to do anything that shall be right in the sight of God.

21. Nothing is more offensive to God than the presumption that gross darkness is light, and the protest that it is darkness. It persecutes or puts to death all who defend the truth at this vital point. It cannot tolerate the true light. From that error arises all idolatry. The Jews had their Baal, their Moloch, Ashtaroth, Camon Peor and numberless idols of the sort. Jeremiah tells them (ch 2, 28), "According to the number of thy cities are thy gods"; and Hosea says (ch 10, 1), "According to the abundance of his fruit he hath multiplied his altars"; and again Isaiah (ch 2, 8), "Their land also is full of idols."

22. All this the Jews meant only for divine service. They presumed thereby to serve the true God. Consequently the

prophets who denounced their conduct were slain by them as destroyers of the divine service and blasphemers against God. But their services of God were instituted according to the dictates of human nature and not according to God's commands. In the true service of God, he himself will be the light and accepts only the worship he has instituted and commanded. We read (Lev 10, 2) how Nabad and Abihu, sons of Aaron, were consumed by fire at the altar even though they were God-ordained priests and had transgressed no farther than to put strange, or unconsecrated, fire into their censers; a thing, however, not in accordance with the commandment of God. And just as little will God tolerate us when we style as divine service what he has not so appointed, and when we recognize it as such. What else does he who presumes so to do, but make of God an idol? He imagines him to be of his opinion, and forms in his mind his own God, presuming that God must be delighted with anything he devises.

Such a proceeding is but changing God's will and perverting his design to accord with our will and our design. It is mocking God and regarding him as man of straw, a spectre or wooden image, to be changed and fashioned at our pleasure. This is a thing God will by no means allow. He will not permit us to make of him an image—an idol; the first commandment makes that plain. Nor will he allow us to misuse his name, as the second commandment clearly shows. And both comandments are just and right. Hence it is impossible for us to please God thus, according to the dictates of nature. Indeed, such conduct is in the highest degree presumptuous, and of all things the most offensive to God.

The True Light.

23. Recognizing this distinction concerning the things of God and man, there can be no difficulty in discerning between the true light and the false. Whatever is not commanded of God is to be most carefully avoided, though ordained of angels or saints. For the most part, the laws of the Pope and the orders of the ecclesiasts must be false. For in the main they are but human devices relating to out-

ward works not commanded of God. Idolatry is more prevalent in the world today than it was in the Jews' time. Men presume to serve God in this humanly-appointed way, notwithstanding it is wholly wrong.

24. Divine light teaches us to trust in God, to believe in him, to leave all to him, to submit readily to his workings, to accept whatever in his providence may present, bearing all and performing every duty, and to serve our neighbor throughout life. With such faith there is no difference in works; all works are alike. Having faith, well may we serve God in erecting buildings, in planting and threshing, in performing any sort of external works. These things are the proper expression of faith, of divine light. God regards them as service to him, as devotional conduct.

So little, however, does human nature, man's reason, know of the truth, that it proceeds to condemn this faith as error and heresy. It accepts the works it beholds in the beloved saints and the orders, but is unable and unwilling to recognize those works as wrought under the influence of the divine light—the faith—they condemn. Thus they make of the examples of the saints idols for themselves, and irrevocably persist in their blindness and idolatry. Hence Solomon gives the wholesome instruction (Prov 3, 5), "Lean not upon thine own understanding"; again (Prov 3, 7), "Be not wise in thine own eyes," which thought Paul expresses (Rom 12, 16) as, "Be not wise in your own conceits."

25. The introduction to the Pope's laws teaches this principle of relying not upon one's own understanding. But his object is, by these Scripture warnings to intimidate the world from rejecting his foolish laws, the right and essential thing to do, however. His object is to lead captive the minds of men, and to have them regard him alone as wise and to follow him in disregard of the wisdom of God. His laws are mere human devices and directly opposed to the doctrine of Solomon and of Paul. He forbids everyone to think for himself, and yet abominably enforces his own opinions in all the world. Solomon means that we are to be taught neither of ourselves nor of any human reasoning

or device, but only of God our Lord. Whatsoever is not taught of God we are to avoid as darkness. He cannot tolerate an assistant in teaching and doing divine things. He intends to be himself the teacher, the light, that our faith may be pure, our understanding of divine matters clear.

26. In temporal affairs, however, one may do differently. You may learn from the carpenter, or teach yourself, how to construct a building; from a painter you may learn to paint; from a shoemaker, to make shoes; from a scribe, to write. But how to serve God, how all works become good—this you must learn, not from man, but from God. God teaches you to believe in him and to love your neighbor, in all your works. Men teach you to work without faith and to love only yourself, forgetting God and your neighbor.

27. Such, you perceive, is the meaning of Isaiah where he says, "Behold, darkness shall cover the earth, and gross darkness the peoples." He cannot be understood as speaking of literal darkness; the sun has continued to give its light. He has reference to a darkness opposed to that light whereof he says, "Thy light is come," and, "Jehovah will arise upon thee." Now, they upon whom Jehovah has not risen, upon whom he has not shone, are in darkness. The darkness here meant is simply unbelief, the darkness of human reason; just as the light represents Christ, or faith in Christ whereby Christ dwells in the heart, as Paul says. Eph 3, 17. Similarly, the reference here to the earth does not mean the material earth; the material earth was not darkened through Christ. The meaning is, earthly or worldly men; men who do not believe, do not accept Christ through the Gospel; men who remain in their earthly conceptions, in the natural light of reason, as Isaiah himself explains when he says:

"Gross darkness shall cover the peoples."

28. But what is implied? Were not men in darkness previous to the advent of Christ? If he, through the Gospel, brought the light, how is it that darkness made its first appearance at that time? We must remember that Isaiah is speaking only of the Jewish people. He divides them into

two classes. One class enjoys the light and the other is overwhelmed in darkness. This was really the case. So he speaks of "the earth" and "the peoples." David, too, says concerning them (Ps 2, 1-2), "Why do the nations meditate a vain thing against Jehovah and against his anointed?" The entire people of Israel awaited Christ. In the shadows of the Law, through Christ, they enjoyed light. But with his coming their condition apparently was reversed. The majority of them fell, entering but deeper darkness.

Previous to Christ's advent was the light of the Law, in which Christ was promised to the Jews. But when he came in fulfilment thereof, they continued to cling to that Law, to still look for his coming. In this way they seem to have lost what they once recognized, the meaning of the Law. And so it befell them as befalls one who leaves far behind him the light properly going before, or the light that once preceded him, and now goes deeper into darkness, without that light. He who has his eyes fixed on a light before him, however far away, may see where he is going. But he who leaves the light behind, who turns his back upon it, walks toward the darkness, not seeing his objective point.

29. Such is the conduct of the Jews, who have behind them the Law shining upon Christ now come. They reject its Christ-revealing light, expecting it to shine for them upon another Christ yet to come. Thus they are without light. Their expectation will come to naught. The Law points to no other Christ.

So Isaiah declares the earth covered with "darkness" and even with "gross darkness." He indicates that the wretched Jews are not only blind, but covered with gross darkness; the light rises not upon them. The Gospel is not preached to the Jews; they are unwilling to hear it. Christ the light does not, through the Gospel, rise upon them. They remain covered in their unbelief—without preaching and instruction. God says on this point (Is 5,6), "I will also command the clouds that they rain no rain upon it." In other words, no preacher shall speak to them concerning Christ. This condition, you see, is not merely experiencing the darkness of unbelief; it is being covered with that darkness, hearing no preaching whereby the light might rise. O terrible prophecy, awful example, for all rejecters of the Gospel!

30. Yet Isaiah says, "Jehovah will arise upon thee." Not the entire nation was blinded. From it is derived the better and greater portion of the Christian Church—the apostles, the evangelists and numerous saints. These are not in darkness, nor covered with darkness. To them Jehovah was preached, and with the result that his glory is manifest in them. Isaiah does not say merely, The glory of Jehovah is risen upon thee, but, It "shall be seen upon thee." Not only was the glory of Jehovah revealed to the Church—a revelation embracing even the unbelieving Jews—but it appeared to them, and they knew him and his glory. They held these fast. Therefore the rising of the light—the Gospel—was not taken from them.

31. Apparently we are to understand Isaiah as referring in the latter part of the text to the fruits of the preached Gospel, and in the first part to the preaching of the Gospel. The Gospel arose, admonishing men to arise. After its advent some became so hardened, so overwhelmed in darkness, that the light did not again arise upon them; it was no more preached to them. But others were enlightened and continued in that illumination. Such has ever been the case unto this day with reference to the preaching of Christ and the Gospel. Some accept it and are enlightened. Others—the majority of them—condemn it as error and turn from it. Consequently they are overwhelmed in their unbelief. The Gospel is no longer proclaimed to them and they are not disposed to hear it. Truly, then, they must be concealed from the rising illumination of this light.

32. Let no one regard this as new or strange. The Scripture is unchangeable—"Darkness shall cover the earth, and gross darkness the peoples." If this was true of the chosen people, the Jews, the natural seed of Abraham, to how much greater degree may it be true of us heathen, descendants from one of different blood and nature! We see

today that the people will permit no one to preach to them what the Pope and his followers have condemned; they will not tolerate it. Therefore they remain covered in their darkness. They have their own preaching wherewith they foster and conceal their blindness. And it befalls them as they desire, as it befell the Jews.

"And nations shall come to thy light, and kings to the brightness of thy rising."

33. When the majority of the Jews refused to cultivate the fruits of the Gospel—and fruit essentially accompanies the Gospel—and continued in their blindness, the Gospel expanded into all the world, gathering the gentiles in place of the blinded and fallen Jews. So says Isaiah in this verse, the accomplished fulfilment of which renders it clear. The heathen nations embraced Christianity and by genuine faith walked in Christ the true light. Such was the increase of the Gospel fruit that even kings, the most exalted of earth, humbled themselves under the faith. The revelation of these future conditions was made that preachers might not be unduly elated over their conversion of kings, or any other, as if they had accomplished it of themselves. God foresaw it all and caused it to be revealed. Besides, he promised the Gospel.

34. This prophecy of Isaiah had strong fulfilment in former times. Many of the nobility and of high standing among the gentiles embraced Christianity. Today, however, so perverted are these nations by the Turks and the Pope, the prophecy seems to have little bearing. And it is a remarkable fact that even other heathen nations have been led astray by the converted gentiles. But it is revealed that Antichrist shall mislead the entire Christ-restored world.

35. What is the import of the phrase, "to the brightness of thy rising"? The prophet styles Christ the glory, or brightness, of the rising; that is, of the Gospel. For the Gospel will be continually advanced and preached; it will ever rise to oppose human doctrines, doctrines formerly in the highest degree dangerous to kings and holders of lofty positions. Upon these individuals first the evil spirit seizes

with his perversions and human doctrines. Having them in his power, he can easily drag along with them the common, illiterate people. Thus the Pope first grasped kings and princes and then the masses. He could not have accomplished it had the Gospel continued to rise. No such thing was wrought when the Gospel first arose. But now it has set, and human doctrines have come up. None today walk in God's light.

> "Lift up thine eyes round about, and see: they all gather themselves together, they come to thee; thy sons shall come from far, and thy daughters shall be carried in the arms."

36. Now, the prophet is about to enumerate the countries where gentiles are converted to the faith. From the fact of his calling upon Jerusalem to lift up her eyes round about and see, it is easily evident he refers to spiritual sons and daughters, men and women who believe in Christ. Likewise the assembling of these must be understood in a spiritual sense. They did not bodily come to Jerusalem, but they believed with heart and spirit in the light risen upon her and round about her. No man can come to the light upon his material feet. Otherwise all the inhabitants of Jerusalem would have been enlightened; but the fact is, as before stated, they for the most part remained in blindness and darkness.

The light being spiritual, we are forced to conclude that the children, the gathering and the future, must also be understood in a spiritual sense. Were we not to regard the light spiritual, we would have to accept the reference to the gathering of the children in a physical rather than a spiritual sense, as the words imply. But with the light spiritualized, the gathering and the coming are spiritualized, and so, too, must the children be regarded. The seed of Abraham, his natural children, did not come to the light from the mere fact of their flesh-and-blood descent; they came because they were his spiritual children, as stated in our last sermon.

37. The clause "Thy sons shall come from far" implies

spiritual children from among the heathen. The apostles Peter and Paul allude to the heathen as far away, and to the Jews as near. "Ye that once were far off are made nigh in the blood of Christ." Eph 2, 13. Again (verse 17), "He came and preached peace to you that were far off, and peace to them that were nigh." The reason for this distinction seems to be that the Jews had the Law and the promises of God concerning Christ, and the heathen had not. Now, it being impossible for the heathen to be the natural children of Abraham, or of Jerusalem, Isaiah's allusion to them here must certainly be in a spiritual sense.

38. Similarly, when he admonishes Jerusalem to lift up her eyes round about and see, he does not address the material city of Jerusalem. The city of Jerusalem is not the mother of these spiritual children. She is a murderess of mother, father and children. Isaiah refers to the spiritual mother—the assembly of the apostles and of all holy Christian Jews. This assembly is the Christian Church. It is spoken of as "Jerusalem" because it originated in that city, assembling there first and thence extending throughout the world. A definite place of origin was necessary to Christianity and the spread of the Gospel. The Gospel began in Jerusalem, in the midst of its worst enemies.

39. Isaiah's meaning seems to be: "Look round about thee, unto the four quarters of the world. I will expand thee into all the earth, and thy children shall dwell everywhere." The words of the text were designed to comfort the first Christians at Jerusalem in view of the fact that they were few in number, despised and in the midst of those who, when they should have been their best friends, were their enemies, as appears later on this same chapter. It was seemingly absurd for so small a band to attempt an undertaking so vast and unusual and to defy the overwhelming masses.

40. The Jews thought soon to check the efforts of the Christians, even to exterminate them. They began everywhere the work of persecution, expulsion and slaughter, presuming it easy to root out these poor and powerless people.

Foolishly, they failed to see how they but fanned the fire already kindled, and scattered it world-wide. Their violence only helped to fulfil this God-directed prophecy of Isaiah against themselves. Their persecution drove Christians into all the world and extended the Gospel until everywhere the sons and daughters of Jerusalem were gathered to the light.

41. To accomplish an object with eminent success through the instrumentality of an enemy is characteristic of the divine hand. By the very fact of their furious attempts to exterminate the Word and the people of God, men but destroy themselves and only further God's Word and his people. Therefore, it is good and profitable, to have enemies and persecutors for the sake of the faith and the Word of God. Incalculable comfort and benefit result. Psalm 2, 1 is in point here: "Why do the nations rage, and the peoples meditate a vain thing" against Christ? The thought is, they violently strive to exterminate Christ, and fail to see that in so doing they but strengthen him.

42. Isaiah's message here to his beloved Jerusalem is, practically: "Fear not, grieve not. Cast not down your eyes, but joyfully raise them and look about. Be not misled by the fact that your nearest relatives are your worst enemies, seeking to exterminate you and regarding you too mean to dwell among them. Let them go on in their rage. Where they kill one among you, a thousand shall rise in his place. Where they drive one away, he shall return with many thousands. If they extinguish the Gospel at one point, it will spring up in ten others. At length, without their consent and with no thanks to them, you shall everywhere have sons and daughters to fill the places of those others now become enemies. Thus ultimately you shall be strengthened and multiplied, and your enemies shall be diminished even to extermination. Their evil designs for you shall fall upon themselves and you shall enjoy what they begrudge you. We see plainly the complete fulfilment of this prophecy.

"Then thou shalt see and be radiant, and thy heart

shall thrill and be enlarged; because the abundance of the sea shall be turned unto thee, the wealth of the nations shall come unto thee."

43. By "the abundance of the sea," we must understand, not the water of the sea itself, but the inhabitants of the country bordering on the sea. As, for instance, we might say that the whole Rhine is risen up, when we mean the people of the country adjacent to the Rhine. Scripture usage, notwithstanding there are many seas in the world, terms the Mediterranean Sea simply "the sea," while it designates the Red Sea by its particular and full name.

Geographers give the Mediterranean that name because of its position. It lies midway between the continents, west of Asia. On the left, or the north, are Spain, France, Italy, Greece and Asia Minor, as far as Cilicia. On the right, or the south, are Africa and Egypt, as far as Palestine. The sea is touched on both sides by great countries, powerful kingdoms. It has numerous islands—Candia, Rhodes, Cyprus, now for the most part in control of the Turks. The Mediterranean is, as we said, in the Scriptures called "the sea." It is west of the Jewish country; for Palestine is at the end of the sea in the east.

44. The people of the territory bordering this sea, particularly those on the north, are scripturally given the general term "gentiles." To those on the south and to the east the Scriptures give particular names. To the gentiles we belong, as do all on the north, or left side, of the sea. Paul, in Second Timothy 1, 11 and elsewhere, calls himself a preacher and apostle to the gentiles. To this section of the country on the north side of the sea, he preached. To it he addressed all his epistles. He did not go south of the sea.

Isaiah refers to these gentiles or nations when he says, "The abundance of the sea shall be turned unto thee, the wealth of the nations shall come unto thee." "The abundance of the sea" is synonymous with "the wealth of the nations." Thus he shows we are not to understand by the former expression "water" but "peoples."

45. Again, "wealth of the nations" does not signify their strength, or power. Of what advantage would that be to the Church? The reference is to great multitudes. We are wont to call a large quantity of coin "a power of money"; that is, a great pile of money. Likewise here "wealth" of the nations means a great mass or multitude of them. Again, we speak of the lord of a great country, one who rules over vast territory and many peoples, as a "mighty" lord.

This prophecy of Isaiah was largely fulfilled through the instrumentality of Paul our apostle. Through his preaching "the abundance of the sea" was converted and "the wealth of the nations" came into the faith. The latter part of this verse is designed to explain who are the sons and daughters that come from afar; namely, the abundance of the gentiles on the great Mediterranean, whom Paul converted.

Thus we have further evidence that the coming to Jerusalem is not to be literally understood. How could such a multitude, such an "abundance," such a "wealth," gather within the limits of that single city, to say nothing of dwelling there permanently? Isaiah says the abundance of the sea shall be "converted," or turned about. The thought is of a facing about. The word itself is opposed to the idea of a literal gathering of the gentiles at Jerusalem. The "turning about" is the assembling. Before, they were turned to the world; now they are changed, turned to the Church.

46. Again, Isaiah uses the Hebrew term "Hamon" when he speaks of the abundance of the sea. The word implies mass, or abundance. Undoubtedly there is a connection here with the promise God made to Abraham that he should be the father of many nations, or gentiles. For God said (Gen 17, 5): "Neither shall thy name any more be called Abram, but thy name shall be Abraham: for the father of a multitude of nations have I made thee." God adds the first letter of the word "Hamon" to "Abram," making it "Abraham," and gives us a reason for the change that Abraham should be the father "Hamon"; that is, the

father of a multitude of nations. He says with Isaiah, in effect: He shall be the father, "Hamon," of the sea—a father of a multitude of nations. Accordingly, Paul in his epistles urges the statement that through faith the gentiles are the children, the seed of Abraham, according to the promise of God. Isaiah has reference to this promise and describes its fulfilment. At first the patriarch was called "Abram," a father of the high, or exalted father. Afterward he was named "Abraham," a father of the abundance, or multitude, of the gentiles. In the gentiles was completed his exaltation.

47. But why does the prophet here multiply words: "Then thou shalt see and be radiant, and thy heart shall thrill and be enlarged"? What is implied by "see," "being radiant," and "the heart thrilling and being enlarged"? These are terms of comforting promise. Hebrew usage makes the word "see" expressive of satisfaction of mind over accomplished desire. For instance (Ps 54, 7), "And mine eye hath seen my desire upon mine enemies." That is, "I see what I have long desired for my enemies, namely, their suppression and the perpetuation of the truth." Again (Ps 37, 34): "When the wicked are cut off, thou shalt see it"—"then thou shalt see what thou didst desire." And again (Ps 35, 21): "Yea, they opened their mouth wide against me; they said, Aha, aha, our eye hath seen it." In other words, "Indeed, what pleasure! We have long desired to see it." So here we interpret "Then thou shalt see," etc., to mean: "You are now a poor, weak little band. Your enemies see what they desire for you. You desire to see yourselves great and numerous, but you may not yet. You must behold for a little time what you do not desire to behold. Afterward you shall see and they shall not. When the multitude of the sea shall be turned to you, then you will see what you have long desired to behold, and your enemies shall not witness what they have so ardently desired concerning you. You must have patience for a time, seeing not. You must endure apparent insignificance and bear the cross."

48. The expression is a natural one. Our eyes are prone to turn away from what we do not wish to see; but toward the things we desire they pleasantly and readily turn, to admire and enjoy. Hence the proverb, "Where the heart is, the eyes turn." We may aptly say, "He does not see," when we mean, "It does not please him." Of all our members, the eyes are the best index of the heart's pleasure or displeasure.

49. The word "radiant" here also implies pleasure and comfort. For it is said of one who is successful and delighted, his countenance is radiant. Whatever is soft is pliable and yielding; but that which is dry, hard and rough is inflexible and suggestive of trouble and displeasure. Isaiah's thought is, then: "You shall see what is pleasing to your heart, and consequently be filled with delight. Your pleasure will make you radiant to perform your duty and to endure all things joyfully, cheerfully and promptly, without trouble or unpleasantness." This is the fruit of the Spirit, the outcome of the comfort the divine promise yields. Thereby all men are rendered mild, happy and radiant, and always content with their circumstances.

50. In the third place, how does the statement, "Thy heart shall thrill," or be amazed, accord with the thought of pleasure? Real pleasures, those so great as to exceed our thoughts and desires, induce a thrill of amazement in their very transcendance of our expectations. When at Peter's preaching the Holy Spirit fell on the gentiles—on Cornelius and his company—according to Luke (Acts 10, 45) they "were amazed, as many as came with Peter, because that on the Gentiles also was poured out the gift of the Holy Spirit." The gift was something they did not in the least expect. Similarly, Isaiah says that Jerusalem in her great joy shall be thrilled with amazement in heart, because of the vast multitude of gentiles joining themselves unto such a poor little persecuted flock.

51. Fourth: "Thy heart . . . shall be enlarged." Plainly, this phrase suggests true greatness, security and freedom. These things are the result of the comfort of the

Spirit and the joy of heart experienced when God does for us in excess of our expectations and desires. Such is God's way of doing, as Isaiah here teaches. And similarly Paul says (Eph 3, 20) that God always does "exceeding abundantly above all that we ask or think." And thus did God deal with this his little flock. He permitted the small band to be persecuted and decreased until apparently it was destitute of life and influence. But almost before one might face about, Christianity had spread throughout the world and surpassed in strength and influence all its enemies. This is amazing in our eyes.

> "The multitude of camels shall cover thee, the dromedaries of Midian and Ephah; and they from Sheba shall come: they shall bring gold and frankincense, and shall proclaim the praises of Jehovah."

52. Having mentioned the nations coming from the "abundance of the sea," west of Jerusalem, Isaiah now refers to the nations that are to come from the east. Midian, Ephah, Sheba, the countries where men travel with camels, lie east of Jerusalem. We read (Gen 25, 2-4) that Abraham had six sons by his third wife, Keturah: Zimran, Jokshan, Medam, Midian, Ishbak and Shuah. The fourth son, Midian, begat Ephah and Epher. There we have two, Midian and Ephah, of whom Isaiah here speaks. Also we read there that the second son, Jokshan, begat Sheba and Dedan. Again, we read (Gen 10: 1, 6-7) that Noah begat Shem, Ham and Japheth; that Ham begat Cush and his brethren, and Cush begat Raamah; and that Raamah begat Sheba and Dedan. These last two names are the same as those of Abraham's sons.

Now, it is doubtful, and must ever be, whether Isaiah here refers to the Sheba who sprang from Abraham, or to Ham's descendant. That, however, is of little importance. It comes to pass on earth that nation routs nation, and one occupies the other's territory, as private property in cities changes hands, is bought and sold, or passes from one landlord to another. As said before, the countries east of Jerusalem are variously named; not designated by the general name "gentiles" as are the Mediterranean countries. They are called Chedar, Nabajoth, Midian, Ephah, Ishmael, Ammon, Edom, Moab, Sheba, according to their primary lords. Moses says (Gen 25, 2-6) that Abraham separated from Isaac the sons of his wife Keturah and sent them toward the east. Hence undoubtedly they occupied many of the countries mentioned, Midian, Ephah and Sheba becoming the most important.

53. In the Latin and Greek geographies these people are called Arabs. They divide all Arabia into three parts: Arabia Deserta, Arabia Petrea and Arabia Felix; or, desert Arabia, stony Arabia and fertile Arabia. Desert Arabia lies between Egypt and Judea, east of the sea. It was through this section Moses led the children of Israel. In the Hebrew it alone is called Arabia, for the word means "desert." Stony Arabia lies east of and touching the Jordan. It includes a large territory. But Isaiah does not here refer to either of these countries.

Fertile and greater Arabia, far distant from Judea and beyond desert and stony Arabia, is called in the Hebrew "Sheba." Whether it derives its name from the son of Abraham or from the son of Ham is immaterial. Ephah is a portion of fertile Arabia. From this Arabia, or from Sheba, came the Turk Mohammed. His sepulcher is there in the city of Mecca. The country is called fertile, or rich, from its abundance of precious gold, fine fruits and particularly frankincense, something produced nowhere else in the world. The Queen of Sheba brought frankincense with many other costly spices, to King Solomon. 1 Kings 10, 2. The Sultan is today its absolute ruler, though he is not such in the eyes of all the Turks. This is the Sheba and this the Ephah to which Isaiah here refers. Their inhabitants used camels and dromedaries. Midian, however, was a neighboring country, bordering like them on the Red Sea, and lying between Egypt and fertile Arabia.

54. The thought of Isaiah is that camels and dromedaries shall come out of Sheba and Midian, spreading in multitudes over the country, as a vast army covers the land, moving

or encamped. And the idea is not of riderless droves. Caravans are indicated by the explanatory sentences: "All they from Sheba shall come: they shall bring gold and incense; and they shall show forth the praises of the Lord." In other words: "In such vast numbers shall the inhabitants of Midian and Ephah come, the multitude of their camels and dromedaries shall cover thy country. And why speak only of Midian and Ephah, portions of Arabia? For all, every part, of fertile Arabia shall come."

55. It may be asked: Is the reference to actual camels and dromedaries? Did they bring material gold and incense? Did the entire inhabitants of fertile Arabia really come to Jerusalem? We must admit that we do not read of any of these things literally coming to pass. Many explain the passage as referring to the wise men who came to Jerusalem from that country after the birth of Christ, as the Gospel relates. But it cannot be said of these few that their camels covered the country in great multitude. Nor were they the entire population of Sheba; they were but a small fraction of the people.

We must not interpret spiritually unless necessary. But since these events have never transpired literally, nor may we reasonably expect that they ever will; since it is a thing inconsistent with natural law that the whole population of Sheba shall actually come to Jerusalem—a mighty nation assembling in one city; since the foregoing portion of the chapter has reference merely to the spiritual light of the Gospel and of faith, and to a spiritual assembling and coming, and since the gathering to the Church is not by any means to be understood to refer to Christ's physical person—considering all this, we shall maintain the same method of the interpretation, feeling satisfied that the facts force us to spiritualize this latter part of the chapter. We understand, then, the Christian Church shall see and be radiant, her heart shall thrill and be enlarged, when not only the abundance of the sea on the west shall be gathered to Jerusalem, but also the greatest and richest people of Arabia from the east.

Further, many other things in the chapter inconsistent with a literal coming force the spiritual conclusion upon us. For instance, verse 7: "All the flocks of Kedar shall be gathered together unto thee, the rams of Nebaioth shall minister unto thee; they shall come up with acceptance on mine altar." Again, verse 10: "And foreigners shall build up thy walls, and their kings shall minister unto thee." These things have never occurred in a literal sense, nor will they ever occur.

56. Therefore, Isaiah's meaning must be: "The people of the great country Arabia shall come in vast numbers to the faith of the Gospel, offering up themselves and all they possess—their camels and dromedaries, their gold, incense and other things." For true Christians will always give up themselves and all they have to serve Christ and his followers. Note, among ourselves, the generous donations made to the Church, and how all freely and willingly surrender self and property to Christ and his. Paul mentions the same practice among the Philippians and the Corinthians. 2 Cor 8, 1 ff.

57. The passage includes the greatest, richest nations, the most numerous and powerful people, on earth—the abundance of the sea and the wealth of the nations. In respect to numbers and power, these represent the heart of the earth's inhabitants. Arabia is regarded the richest and grandest nation of the world. The thought is, the whole world will be converted to the faith. Even were we to regard the gold, the incense and the camels in a strictly literal sense, we must still understand the "coming" and the "bringing" as suggesting the spiritual Jerusalem. As to what the spiritual interpretation is, we leave that for the Gospel to teach us.

The phrase "All they from Sheba" does not imply that individually they will all become believers, but that the country as a whole will accept Christianity. There must remain, of course, some unbelieving individuals. Similarly we may say of Germany, which has abandoned its old heathen customs, that the country is now Christian. Though only the minority are true Christians, yet for the sake of these we call the German nation Christian. Again, the Jewish people as a whole were called the people of God (Num 25) when many of them worshiped idols.

58. Finally, Isaiah says, "They shall proclaim the praises of Jehovah." The true, the special, work of a Christian is to confess his sins and his shame, and to proclaim God's grace and work in himself. No man who fails to behold God's grace and this light of the Gospel, can show forth God's honor and praise. No man who clings to his own light, his own human nature, who values his own works, his own efforts, can perceive the grace of God. He continues in his old, blind dead Adam nature. He does not rise to behold the light; he prefers to sound his own praises. Isaiah exalts the people of wealthy Arabia because they are true Christians who proclaim only the praises of Jehovah, taught to do so undoubtedly by the light of grace and the Gospel.

Date Due

APR 29 '50			
MAY 23 '50			
APR 16 '54			
MAY 25 1954			
NOV 22 '54			
MAR 2 '59			
[illegible]			
APR 13 '60			
APR 5 '61			

Library Bureau Cat. No. 1137

Zeitfracht Medien GmbH
Ferdinand-Jühlke-Straße 7
99095 Erfurt, Deutschland
produktsicherheit@kolibri360.de